Rethinking the Roots of Terrorism

Rethinking Peace and Conflict Studies

Series Editor: **Oliver Richmond**, Reader, School of International Relations, University of St. Andrews

Titles include:

Jason Franks
RETHINKING THE ROOTS OF TERRORISM

James Ker-Lindsay
EU ACCESSION AND UN PEACEMAKING IN CYPRUS

Carol McQueen
HUMANITARIAN INTERVENTION AND SAFETY ZONES
Iraq, Bosnia and Rwanda

Oliver P. Richmond
THE TRANSFORMATION OF PEACE

Rethinking Peace and Conflict Studies
Series Standing Order ISBN 1–4039–9575–3 (hardback) & 1–4039–9575–1 (paperback)

You can receive future titles in this series as they are published by placing a standing order. Please contact your bookseller or, in case of difficulty, write to us at the address below with your name and address, the title of the series and the ISBNs quoted above.

Customer Services Department, Macmillan Distribution Ltd, Houndmills, Basingstoke, Hampshire RG21 6XS, England.

Rethinking the Roots of Terrorism

Jason Franks
Research Fellow, School of International Relations
University of St Andrews, UK

First published 2006 by
PALGRAVE MACMILLAN
Houndmills, Basingstoke, Hampshire RG21 6XS and
175 Fifth Avenue, New York, N.Y. 10010
Companies and representatives throughout the world

PALGRAVE MACMILLAN is the global academic imprint of the Palgrave Macmillan division of St. Martin's Press, LLC and of Palgrave Macmillan Ltd. Macmillan® is a registered trademark in the United States, United Kingdom and other countries. Palgrave is a registered trademark in the European Union and other countries.

ISBN 13: 978–1–4039–8718–1   hardback
ISBN 10: 1–4039–8718–1   hardback

This book is printed on paper suitable for recycling and made from fully managed and sustained forest sources.

A catalogue record for this book is available from the British Library.

Library of Congress Cataloging-in-Publication Data
Franks, Jason, 1969–
    Rethinking the roots of terrorism / Jason Franks.
       p. cm.
    Includes bibliographical references and index.
    ISBN 1–4039–8718–1
    1. Terrorism. I. Title.
HV6431.F722 2006
363.325–dc22

                                                              2005056377

10   9   8   7   6   5   4   3   2   1
15   14   13   12   11   10   09   08   07   06

Printed and bound in Great Britain by
Antony Rowe Ltd, Chippenham and Eastbourne

Contents

Preface

This study examines the new terrorism debate and is intended to rethink the root causes of terrorism by examining alternative approaches, in part provided by conflict theory, to the predominant understanding of terrorism provided by what it identifies as orthodox terrorism theory. It presents a critical and discourse analysis approach to explaining and understanding the roots of terrorism and focuses initially on a description and explanation of the existence of orthodox terrorism discourse, clarifying how and why it is constructed, what it is used for and the associated implications it has for understanding terrorism. The study also aims to explore the range of alternative perspectives of terrorism created in terrorism and conflict studies by using different levels of analysis. The purpose is to develop a multi-level and multi-dimensional framework for rethinking the roots of terrorism based upon the most sophisticated theoretical approaches provided by terrorism and conflict studies. This framework, which also provides a reflexive critique of orthodox terrorism theory, is not intended as a new theory of terrorism but represents an attempt to provide a broader, more comprehensive and holistic approach to the problem of terrorism.

In order to test this comprehensive framework for the analysis of terrorism, this study examines the Palestinian-Israeli conflict and discusses how orthodox terrorism theory is employed by Israel. It also demonstrates how Palestinian terrorism can be re-examined through the application of the alternative framework to reveal a considerably more comprehensive, multi-dimensional and multi-level understanding of the root causes of terrorism. The conclusion of this study suggests that rethinking terrorism will provide an increasingly sophisticated understanding of political violence and equip the study of terrorism with more robust analytical tools with which to create a number of potential channels to facilitate resolution of the deep underlying problems that cause terrorism.

Acknowledgements

The writing of this book began with an initial interest in the study of terrorism and then inspired by deeper questions relating to how it is understood and ultimately why it occurs. The navigation points for these questions were provided by the study of the roots of conflict. So this book is a product or hybrid of conflict and terrorism studies. I would like to thank all at St Andrews University who helped me with this project, and in particular Oliver Richmond for his guidance, diligence and interest in my work. My thanks also to Vivienne Jabri and Magnus Ranstorp for their valuable comments and recommendations for the project. I would also like to express my appreciation to the Carnegie Trust and St Andrews University who generously provided the funding for my fieldwork. My gratitude also goes out to all those in the Palestinian Territories and Israel who took the time to speak to me during my research, some of whom have already become victims of the brutal conflict. In particular my thanks go to Gershon Baskin at IPCRI, Fathi Tobail and Sami Abu Salem at the Palestinian State Information Service, and Tahur and Najwa al Assar for their hospitality in Gaza. I am also grateful to Agnes Spink for meticulously proof reading this work. Finally, thanks to my family and friends for their support during this period. All errors are of course my own responsibility.

Glossary of Terms and Abbreviations

ALF   Arab Liberation Front
BCE   Before Common Era
CE   Common Era
DFLP   Democratic Front for the Liberation of Palestine
ETA   Basque Homeland and Liberty
EOKA   National Organisation of Cypriot Fighters
EU   European Union
FARC   Revolutionary Armed Forces of Colombia
Fateh   Palestinian National Liberation Movement
FBI   Federal Bureau of Investigations
Fedayeen   Irregular Arab Fighter
FLNC   National Front for the Liberation of Corsica
FLN   National Liberation Front (Algeria)
Hamas   The Islamic Resistance Movement
ICT   International Policy Institute for Counter Terrorism
ICs   International Corporations
IDF   Israeli Defence Force
IJ   Islamic Jihad
IPCRI   Israeli/Palestinian Centre for Research and Information
IRA   Irish Republican Army
JRA   Japanese Red Army
MNC   Multi-National Corporations
MPLA   Marxist Party for the Liberation of Angola
NATO   North Atlantic Treaty Organisation
NGOs   Non governmental organisations
NIS   New Israeli Sheckle
PA   Palestinian Authority
PASSIA   Palestinian Academic Society for the Study of International
            Affairs
PDFLP   Popular Democratic Front for the Liberation of Palestine
PFLP   Popular Front for the Liberation of Palestine
PFLP-GC   Popular Front for the Liberation of Palestine-General
            Command
PIOOM   The Interdisciplinary Research Programme on Causes of
            Human Rights Violations

PIRA	Provisional Irish Republican Army
PNC	Palestinian National Council
PLA	Palestinian Liberation Army
PLO	Palestinian Liberation Organisation
PSC	Protracted Social Conflict
RAF	Red Army Faction
RB	Red Brigade
RCs	Regional Organisations
UN	United Nations
UNC	Unified National Council
UNEF	United Nations Emergency Force
UNLU	Unified National Leadership of the Uprising
UNRWA	United Nations Relief and Works Agency for Palestinian Refugees
UNSC	United Nations Security Council
US	United States
WMDs	Weapons of Mass Destruction

Freeing the great human conflicts from the naïve interpretation of a battle between good and evil, and understanding them in the light of tragedy is an enormous feat of mind; it brings forward the unavoidable relativism of human truths.

Milan Kundera

Introduction

'Terrorism' has become the plague of the twenty first century: it is a concept that has seemingly penetrated all quarters of international society, especially in the wake of the September 11th attacks in New York and the subsequent 'war on terrorism'. Few places on the globe are now unaffected by the hysteria caused by 'terrorism'. It has given new meaning to ongoing 'domestic conflicts' and redefined wars in all continents of the planet. Previously considered indigenous 'terrorist' groups involved in local conflicts are now often perceived to be linked to the worldwide nebulous bin Laden organisation that has truly globalised 'terrorism'. From Europe and Russia, through the Middle East to the Philippines, Indonesia, Nepal, South America and Africa multifarious new 'terrorist' situations are continuously being identified.[1] However, despite having its international profile raised immeasurably, 'terrorism' is far from a new phenomenon, as the consensus of academic opinion dates it to the French revolution and the Nihilists of nineteenth century Russia,[2] suggesting that it has been a continuous part of modern world history.

Nevertheless, despite the historic existence and the apparent global omnipresence of 'terrorism' in wars, politics, the media and society in general, there is no commonly accepted understanding of what actually constitutes 'terrorism', as no clear and universally acknowledged definition actually exists. 'Terrorism' is essentially a contested concept. This assumption, which is also disputed, forms the basis for this study, which is designed to rethink and re-examine how terrorism can be explained and understood. Terrorism can be seen as a concept that is defined and understood relative to the legitimacy of state governance (as an illegal and illegitimate act),[3] or as specific methods of political violence, such as hijack or bombing[4] or as acts of violence against a specific target group, particularly civilians.[5] As a result of the apparent confusion surrounding the understanding and definition of terrorism, the study of terrorism has become preoccupied with the constant debate that revolves around explaining *what* actually constitutes terrorism and *how* to counter it. Instead of perhaps concentrating on *why* it actually occurs. This has become increasingly more difficult in the shifting sands of the 'post-modern' contemporary world where the definitions and understanding of war and conflict, relatively uncontested concepts in the Cold War, are now increasingly uncertain.

These new war/new conflict and new terrorism debates challenge the traditional understanding of conflict as inter-state war or symmetric conflict. The crux of the debates suggest that conflict is no longer conducted in a highly organised and ritualised manner between designated armies with established codes of conduct and comprising of particular and stylised violence, all of which is intended for the specific purpose of achieving perceived gains such as political advantage or territory. The debates argue that this old type of warfare existed and was propagated by the perceived existence of the realist state-centric Westphalian international state system. A system that is based on the governmental and territorial legitimacy of the state, one in which the sovereign state is the principal actor and the standing state army its policy tool. This was particularly prevalent during the Cold War when conflict was related to the state-centric and ideologically polarised bipolar world. However, in the confusion of the post-Cold War world, the propensity for inter-state conflict has been replaced by intra-state conflict. These so called 'new wars' take the form of asymmetric warfare between groups, movements and organisations often against the state but predominantly within it. These conflicts are often described as ethnic identity conflicts, characterised by irredentist and secessionist movements and multi-party civil war. They are often underwritten by religious or ethno-nationalist ideas and characterised by hatred, fear and genocide and have no declarations of war, few battles and are typified by attrition, terror and violence against civilians.[6]

The new war debates suggest that recognition of these new forms of conflict have occurred in the disorder and uncertainty caused by the end of the Cold War and the realignment of the international system following the collapse of the Soviet Union. However, the degradation of an established structure of governance by ethnicity and identity could have been occurring chronically in recent history, but may have been obscured by the ideological monochromatic veil of the Cold War. These new conflicts could also be due to the failure of the state as an institution and the unsuitability of the Westphalian system as an international order. The fracturing of the institution of the state and the growing doubt as to its compatibility with the trends of the contemporary world is also personified by the globalisation debate in which the established borders, populations and governance of the state are increasingly undermined by social interconnectedness and trans-state and suprastate forms of global governance.[7] This coincides with the rise of identity and importance of the individual in terms of ethnicity and security and is typified by the growing value attached to individual human rights. This argument suggests that in order to recognise these contemporary trends and understand this new type of conflict. Conflict that relates to nations, communities, groups and individuals, often within states or irrespective of established state boundaries. It is necessary to move beyond the state into the late or post-Westphalian system.[8] By departing from the rigid state-centric Westphalian system it will be possible to recognise the roots of contemporary conflict as existing in areas such as identity, representation and participation.[9] Arguably, conflict studies is making this transition into recognising and dealing with conflict outside of the traditional state-based understanding and is moving into employing more sophisticated, and comprehensive approaches for resolving it. This is apparent in third and fourth generation multi-dimensional approaches to conflict, found in conflict resolution and conflict transformation and peace building techniques.[10]

The understanding of terrorism or terrorism theory is at a similar point of crisis, as it is affected by the same post-Cold War and globalisation trends and is also in the international spotlight following September 11th and the war on terrorism. However, the study of terrorism it seems has not yet embraced the changes pioneered by conflict studies and made the transition to a more holistic understanding of the roots of political violence. This is largely because attempts at understanding 'new terrorism' are still located in the Cold War state-centric, realist and positivist perception. This is primarily because the understanding and definition of terrorism is contained within a state discourse. Terrorism is defined primarily in terms of state legitimacy and is largely understood to represent a challenge and threat to state authority by an illegitimate body. This is the conventional or the 'orthodox theory' of terrorism and is based on the legitimacy/illegitimacy dualism that constructs non-state violence as terrorist while state violence is deemed to be legitimate. As a result it does not engage in a roots debate about the causes of terrorism, as this would legitimise non-state violence. This is a problem not just for approaching and dealing with terrorism by the symptomatic management of the violence, but also for enacting long-term solutions that attempt to solve the root causes. More importantly it is also becoming a problem for understanding the manifestation of 'new terrorism', which like new war does not necessarily fit the state-centric parameters employed in the past. In contrast to the rational political actions of orthodox terrorism, 'new terrorism' according to Walter Laqueur is deadly violence perpetrated by unidentified amorphous non-state groups, who often bear no relation to their

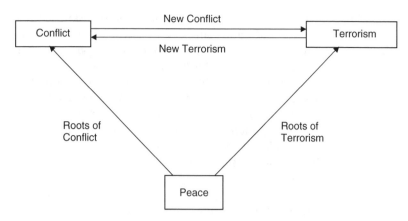

Figure 1.1   The 'new war'/'new terrorism' nexus

country of origin and who claim no responsibility for their actions. They intend to kill as many people as possible, predominantly non-combatants and their blind lethal violence is typified by hate, aggression and anger.[11]

The new war/new terrorism debates suggest that those involved in these types of violence are becoming increasingly hard to separate, especially as those involved in terrorism often perceive themselves to be in conflict. This conceivably accounts for the high lethality against non-combatants and the similarities in the type of violence used in both new war and new terrorism. This implies that if the symptoms of these types of violence are becoming increasingly similar then perhaps the root causes might also share a common ground (see Figure 1.1).

The problem is that whilst the study of conflict has moved on and engaged with alternative methods of understanding war and conflict, the orthodox terrorism understanding is still constrained by the relative moral legitimacy debate,[12] out of which it is presently unable to break. This definitional situation therefore significantly hinders any engagement in a 'roots of terrorism' debate using alternative multidimensional analytical tools.

The intention of this study is to engage with this problem of explaining terrorism and argue that just as a rethinking has been successfully applied to conflict, what needs to happen now is a rethinking of terrorism in order to provide alternative approaches that can deal with the root causes. The aim of this is to resolve and end the endemic forms of atrocious violence currently being experienced worldwide.

Defining the book

This study is an attempt to rethink the roots of terrorism by relocating the study of terrorism into a conceptual space in which it can gain access to the tools provided by conflict studies. As a result it addresses a significant gap in the field of terrorism studies. I argue that the study of terrorism has not progressed beyond the realist positivist state-centric approach because it is a discourse created and employed with the express purpose of providing the state with an understanding of terrorism that is based upon a relative legitimacy. This allows the state to deal with terrorism without engaging in a roots debate, as it perceives terrorism as a threat to its security. It can therefore employ whatever means it chooses against whomever it wishes. This is the 'orthodox terrorism discourse' and is based on the legitimacy/illegitimacy dualism that constructs non-state violence as terrorist while state violence is deemed to be legitimate. It is an understanding supported by an extensive body of literature based on a 'conventional' definition aligned to the authority and legitimacy of the state. It also forms the basis of counter terrorism and anti-terrorism policy construction.

This study focuses on:

1. An explanation and clarification of the existence of orthodox terrorism discourse. How and why it is constructed, what it is used for, and the associated problems.
2. The creation of an alternative theoretical framework for rethinking the roots of terrorism based upon the best theoretical approaches provided by terrorism and conflict studies.
3. A demonstration of how different approaches to terrorism can reveal different root causes when applied to the case study of the Palestinian-Israeli conflict.
4. A working example of how the application of the alternative framework can provide a comprehensive multi-dimensional understanding of the roots of terrorism.

This book employs a critical approach to orthodox terrorism discourse and the normative use of the conventional understanding of terrorism. It seeks to rethink the roots of terrorism by employing two methodological approaches; critical theory[13] and discourse analysis.[14] Critical theory is used to question all theories and assumptions, where no theory is the *right* one and the facts are not independent and objective but the product of specific theoretical frameworks.[15] This method of examination is adopted throughout this study in order to rethink terrorism and principally question how, why and for what purpose terrorism is understood, ultimately questioning if it can be understood in an alternative way to the orthodox approach. Critical theory attempts to find the source of understanding by stepping outside the confines of existing relationships. It 'asks how the order came about and calls into question the nature of the existing structures'.[16] Centrally, the critical method seeks to ask, why is the theory employed? What tasks is it designed to perform? And, what is the purpose of the particular interpretation of the facts?[17] Thus 'critical theories problematise existing power relations and try to understand how they have emerged'.[18] They also help to examine boundaries, particularly within the political community, and question the reason for their existence and nature of their role.[19]

Discourse analysis complements this and questions the 'category of reality'.[20] Discourse, according to Jim George, is a 'matrix of social practice that gives meaning to the way people understand themselves and their behaviour'.[21] By engaging in discourse analysis, George built upon the Foucaultian power-knowledge relationship[22] by arguing that, contrary to the positivist debate,[23] knowledge *is* linked to power and thus only through power (within a particular discourse) can 'truth' be established.[24] Although this is a subjective 'truth' or 'regime of truth' the critical process can help to identify the root of power, which it can be argued, is the key to understanding issues, institutions, structures and relationships. 'Discourses are a most viable conceptual tool, they facilitate an exploration of the close linkages that exist between theory and practice'.[25] Thus theory and practice 'do not exist in some separate way but are mutually constituted'.[26] This implies that discourse and practice cannot be separated, and is an argument that I apply throughout this study. As Foucault suggests, 'Theory does not express, translate or serve to apply practice: it is practice'.[27] This emphasises recognition of the link between discourse and practice. Hence, 'empirical theory or policy analysis should not be isolated arbitrarily from meta-theoretical and philosophical assumptions that are often drowned out by appeals to objectivity or reality'.[28]

Critical theory and discourse analysis attempt to question the nature of the theory used to interpret 'facts' which are seen, not as independent and objective occurrences, but as a product of the specific social and historical frameworks.[29] This approach is in direct contrast to the ideas of an established and scientific order to the international world as provided by positivism. The implications for reassessing the roots of terrorism using these methods is particularly useful in respect to the well established and institutionalised normative understanding of terrorism provided by orthodox terrorism theory. As a result this theory can be viewed as a specific discourse or 'just a theory' instead of the accepted 'truth' to explain the manifestation of lethal political violence. However, it is important to stress that by employing this approach any proposed theory for understanding terrorism is subject to the same critical analysis, thus no single theory for the roots of terrorism is possible as each is subject to a relative understanding.

The principle aim of this study is to critically examine the different discourses that relate to how terrorism is understood. These discourses are provided by international relations theories, which produce their own specific perspective. In the first two chapters of this study, terrorism and conflict are critically examined relative to how they are understood at different levels of analysis. The levels of analysis adopted in this study are the state level, the non-state level, the structural level and the individual level. These levels are employed because they correspond to the perspectives provided by mainstream international relations theory. These theories or lenses create different perspectives, and thus provide alternative approaches to explaining and understanding,[30] and thus form the basis for an ontological and epistemological examination of the root causes of terrorism.

The purpose of this project is to provide a wide-ranging and broad theoretical framework containing as many different perspectives of terrorism as possible. This is achieved on a multi-level basis by highlighting and filling the gaps that exist in the existing literature on the roots of terrorism and drawing heavily on the debates provided by conflict studies. It is important to stress however that this is a theoretical study (a fact that might vex proponents of orthodox terrorism), which intends to combine different perceptions of terrorism, which by definition[31] are mutually exclusive. The aim of this study therefore is not to establish a new theory of terrorism but to attempt to provide a broader and more comprehensive and holistic framework with which to understand the problem. This may provide an increasingly sophisticated approach to terrorism and equip the study of the problem with more robust analytical tools. Which can be employed to create a number of potential channels to facilitate resolution of the violence.

Chapter 1 is a comprehensive multi-level literature review of terrorism studies and explains the current state of research on terrorism including the definitional debate and seeks to encompass the principal methods, lens, frameworks and ideas through which terrorism can be defined and understood. It will also reveal the existence of orthodox terrorism discourse and clearly explain how and why it is employed.

Chapter 2 is an extensive literature review of conflict studies encompassing the main theories, paradigms, frameworks and ideas through which the roots of conflict can be defined and understood. This is also an interdisciplinary and multi-level investigation.

Chapter 3 is a comparative chapter and contains the construction of an alternative comprehensive framework for rethinking the roots of terrorism. It provides a comparative analysis of both terrorism and conflict literature in order to critically compare and contrast what tools the two approaches can offer as a way of comprehensively understanding terrorism and its root causes. It identifies the apparent gaps in the terrorism theories used to explain the root causes of terrorism and shows how conflict studies can provide approaches to violence with which to successfully fill these spaces. It consists of the composition of a theoretical multi-level and multi-dimensional framework that essentially combines the various perspectives of terrorism into a single framework. It also discusses what issues arise from this comparison and what implications they have for understanding terrorism.

Chapter 4 deals with the historical roots and the evolution of the Palestinian-Israeli conflict as the chosen case study for this book. It contains an historical evaluation of the Palestinian-Israeli conflict to date via a comprehensive review of the literature to establish how the events and facts of the Palestinian-Israeli conflict are understood in reference to the two central conflict discourses, Palestinianism and Zionism. It also shows how the roots of the conflict and of terrorism are understood relative to these discourses and how they help to sustain the conflict via the construction of historical narratives.

Chapter 5 is a defence of the central claim of this study, questioning if it is possible to profitably rethink the root causes of terrorism by employing an alternative and comprehensive framework. The theoretical framework constructed in Chapter 3 is applied to the Palestinian-Israeli conflict in this chapter. The application of fieldwork data to this framework demonstrates the two central claims of this study. First, the existence of the orthodox terrorism discourse its uses and its limitations. Second, how an alternative understanding that combines the various perspectives of the roots of terrorism can be revealed and how useful this is for viewing the existence of multifarious political, social, economic and psychological causes of violence.

The conclusion is a summary of the study and deals with the implications for the use or employment of the alternative terrorism discourse and what future applications it may or may not have. It suggests the disadvantages and the central problems of employing this approach in a project to investigate the roots of terrorism and it discusses how this discourse might be employed alongside more normative counter and anti-terrorism policies that are employed by states dealing with terrorism.

Research method and design

This is book is based on a theory-then-research strategy that is intended to construct a multi-level and multi-dimensional theoretical framework for rethinking the roots of terrorism. It forms a hybrid, created from theories drawn from the literature in terrorism and conflict studies, and then tested by data collection from fieldwork in the Palestinian-Israeli conflict. The primary intention is to deconstruct the accepted orthodox theory of terrorism and challenge its understanding of the roots of terrorism with an alternative theoretical framework.

The research design selected for the collection of data and application of the central thesis is the Palestinian-Israeli conflict. This is a study of the contemporary events of the Palestinian-Israeli conflict up to and including the first two years of the second Intifada and includes the period January–April 2003 for fieldwork. The Palestinian-Israeli conflict provides an interesting and suitable example of a contemporary conflict in which the orthodox understanding of terrorism is a central feature and a roots debate is contested. Whilst it is accepted that the Palestinian-Israeli conflict is unique, it does demonstrate extensive similarities with other types of contemporary ethno-nationalist and identity conflicts. This suggests that this selected case study can produce credible generalisations to support this study of terrorism.

Data collection concentrates on fieldwork in Israel and the Palestinian territories of the Gaza Strip and the West Bank. It focuses on representatives of the Israeli State, such as the government, military, police and intelligence services. The principal Palestinian political groups, namely Fateh, PFLP, Islamic Jihad and Hamas, and their respective armed wings: Tansim, Abu Ali Mustapha Brigade, al Quds Brigade and al-Qassim as well as the al-Aqsa martyrs brigade. Also interviewed are the individuals in the conflict both Palestinian and Israeli, these include, Israeli Soldiers, settlers, and civilians as well as Palestinian fighters, refugees and civilians. Also included is a broad representation of Palestinian and Israeli academics and non-governmental organisations. Attention is focused primarily on those directly in the conflict such as Israeli soldiers and Palestinian fighters and the leaders and politicians on both sides. However, 'ordinary' Israeli and Palestinian people are also observed and questioned in the belief that even though they are not perhaps directly involved with violence, they are, as Israeli or Palestinian people, automatically part of conflict at some level.

Research was conducted in the main cities of Israel, particularly, 'new' Jerusalem, Tel Aviv and Haifa, as well as numerous smaller towns and villages. The Palestinian research was conducted in the Gaza Strip and the West Bank, specifically in Gaza city and the refugee camps of Nuseirat, Khan Younis and Jabalia and in East Jerusalem. Also the Old City of Jerusalem, Ramallah, Jericho and Nablus.

1
The Root Causes of Terrorism: Orthodox Terrorism Theory

Introduction

Terrorism has been the subject of a vast amount of research especially during the last thirty years.[1] The production of which has notably increased since the end of the Cold War and more recently in the shadow of the events of September 11th 2001, and the 'War on Terrorism'. The reason for this growth is two fold; first is the apparent omnipresence of terrorism, especially in the ambiguous post-Cold War world or Grey Area Phenomenon.[2] Second, is the actual study of terrorism, which has become locked in an endless definitional debate, based around the question of legitimacy. Consequently, no clear and universally acknowledged definition exists. As a result terrorism studies has become the source of a constant debate as to what actually constitutes terrorism. Due to this lack of any universally recognised and accepted understanding of what the problem is and the preoccupation within terrorism studies of trying to define and establish what constitutes Terrorism. It is naturally proving difficult to establish a firm basis of research with which to investigate why it actually occurs. As Walter Laqueur has pointed out 'disputes about a detailed, comprehensive definition of terrorism will continue for a long time and will make no noticeable contribution towards the understanding of terrorism'.[3]

The lack of investigation into the reasons for terrorism is further compounded by the obsessive interest generated within terrorism studies for the methodology of violence. Although the orthodox study of terrorism has engaged in a limited roots debate concerning *why* terrorism occurs,[4] the majority of research has been largely preoccupied with *how* it occurs. Orthodox approaches to understanding terrorism tend to focus on the type of violence employed; this is clearly illustrated by the

11

United Nations (UN) Conventions on terrorism. These conventions focus not on why the violence might be occurring but instead seek to establish what type of violence is it and how can it be countered.[5] This has located the study of terrorism into the study of methods of violence. As a result, terrorism has become an academic analysis of the mechanics of the actual violence, dealing with research ranging from the formation, construction and operation of terrorist groups, to the type of weapons, tactics and operational methods employed.[6] This has become the central basis for the existence of terrorism studies: how to respond and deal with terrorism. It represents the core of terrorism literature[7] and relates directly to the formation of governmental policy on intelligence and security and feeds the construction and implementation of anti-terrorist and counter-terrorism policies.

The effects of the intuitional development of the study of terrorism have been to further proliferate the ongoing comparative definitional debate. This is not helped by growing political pressure to establish an accepted single definition of terrorism that can be used to institute a general scientific theory of terrorism, enshrined in law. The purpose of which is to institute a common governmental and international basis with which to approach, and deal with terrorism.[8] The institutional study of terrorism has also firmly established within its remit the production of in-depth methodological studies of the techniques and tactics of varying types of terrorist groups. Although these are useful for understanding and countering terrorist groups in relation to methods of response and policy formation, they are often of little help in understanding why the groups are engaging in violence.

In this chapter I intend to review how terrorism studies understands the roots of terrorism. This will involve a critical theory based interdisciplinary and multi-level approach to terrorism literature. It will take the form an examination of the ways terrorism is perceived and understood through the various lenses provided by mainstream international relations theory. These perspectives will be represented as levels of analysis and correspond to the state actor, the non-state actor, the structural and the individual level; this will comprise Part 2 of this chapter. However, preceding this, in Part 1 will be a brief examination of orthodox terrorism theory.

Part 1: Orthodox Terrorism Theory

Legitimacy: the problem with the orthodox definition of terrorism

In a review of current research, Andrew Silke points out the development of the study of terrorism is constrained by the supposed emotive nature of the subject and the confusion surrounding the conception and definition of the phenomenon.[9] It is not my intention here to add to the definitional debate but it is an important step in analysing orthodox terrorism theory to consider why it exists. The debate exists because the orthodox definition of terrorism is based on legitimacy, which can be defined as the acceptance and recognition of the authority of the established government by the population. Terrorism can be viewed as violence generated by the conflict over the contention for political legitimacy. States believe they have legitimacy and brand any challenge to their authority as illegitimate. Terrorist groups, by the orthodox definition, challenge the political authority of the state and deem themselves and their cause legitimate and view the state as illegitimate.

Due to the dominance of state power, the 'relative legitimacy' explanation has become the widely accepted understanding of terrorism. As a result, terrorism has become a pejorative term adopted by actors to make a moral justification of their claim to legitimacy and moral condemnation of their opponents. States call groups terrorist, not necessarily because they use lethal violence to attempt to attain political goals but because they view their challenge as illegitimate. Equally groups label states terrorist not because they use lethal state violence to maintain their political position, but because they see it as illegitimate. Hence, the constant referral in the definition of terrorism debate to the expression, 'one man's freedom fighter is another man's terrorist'. Consider therefore the United States Department of Defence definition of terrorism; 'unlawful use of force or violence against individuals or property to coerce and intimidate governments to accept political, religious or ideological objectives'[10] and Sheikh Fadlallah, spiritual leader of Hizballah who suggests terrorism is 'fighting with special means against aggressor nations in religious and lawful warfare against world imperial powers'.[11]

The roots of this legal and moral legitimacy debate can be seen to originate in the western understanding of liberal democracy. Connor Cruise O'Brien suggests that the terrorist label has been used to describe and politically condemn groups who use terrorist methods in a liberal democracy, where the opportunity exists to articulate grievances through the non-violent political and legal process.[12] Thus as Paul Wilkinson points out, '[I]n a liberal democracy aggrieved man enjoys full protection and rights of participation...violence for political ends cannot be morally justified'.[13] However, for a group to resort to violence they must have already rejected the legitimacy of the ruling regime, and so have created their own relative understanding. The existence of democracy whilst it promotes the state's claim to the moral argument does not necessarily change the relative understanding of legitimacy held by the actors. This argument implies that the orthodox definition of terrorism is based on the assumption that the employer of the definition is liberal and democratic and therefore has legitimate grounds to judge and morally condemn the user of political violence. However since many instances of terrorism exist outside the liberal democratic framework and are even reasons for it, a universal moral definition is perhaps unhelpful. Furthermore, a minority within a liberal democratic framework, whose representation is so small that it is denied all participation except voting, and is consequently outvoted, will loose the ability for peaceful representation and participation.[14]

Legitimacy however, is enshrined in the power of the state and exists in the orthodox definition of terrorism. This produces a relative understanding of terrorism that is locked into an endlessly cyclical moral debate between relative perceptions of right and wrong. However, the state as the more powerful actor can enforce its legitimacy with state violence. The orthodox definition of terrorism is employed in this agenda to legitimise violence. For example, when terrorism is defined as, 'the systematic use of coercive intimidation for political ends and is used to create and exploit a climate of fear among a wider target group than the victims to publicise a cause and to coerce a target to acceding to the terrorists' aims'.[15] States can employ orthodox terrorist theory and suggest a terrorist attack is a provocative, symbolic act to intimidate and terrorise, intended to undermine the established and legitimate political rule. Using this, the state is able to legitimately respond with the forces of state control, namely the legal and military machinery. However, groups can similarly use terrorism theory to suggest the state is attempting to intimidate them by using state violence against their symbolic targets, such as group leaders and training camps. This allows the group to respond with whatever means of violence is available, causing a cycle of violence that can be characterised by a protracted and intractable conflict over legitimacy. The cycle of terrorist violence and recrimination is a common characteristic in so-called terrorist conflicts and is clearly illustrated in the Palestinian-Israeli conflict. The Israelis view Palestinian attacks as terrorism and respond with military violence, the Palestinians view this as terrorism and respond with violence. Both claim legitimacy of action, both view the other as terrorists.

Connected to the problem of legitimacy is the relative understanding of force and violence. Wilkinson suggests violence is the opposite of legitimate force, and is defined as 'the illegitimate use or threatened use of coercion resulting in death, injury, restraint, and intimidation of persons or destruction of property'.[16] This argument suggests that illegitimate violence is used in terrorism and legitimate violence is force, (which is used against it). This serves to obscure the causes of terrorism because it perpetuates the relative understandings in which both sides claim moral legitimacy. It also increasingly polarises the actors within their own comprehensions and further exacerbates and in some cases can justify the underlying problems that initially generated the political violence in the first instance.

The inherent contradictions and ambiguity of legitimacy also exist in the 'process of legitimisation'. This is a practice whereby the orthodox definition of terrorism is manipulated to serve political ends. In this process, a number of groups and individuals are labelled, relative to state legitimacy, as terrorist. As a result they are outlawed and tackled with state measures, such as the rule of law and military force. However, in reaction to changing political situations, some individuals and groups will begin to become legitimised. Group members will be released from prison or return from exile into accepted society, and in some cases become recognised politicians.[17] This is reflective of the historical events of the French Revolution and the historic precedent of reversing accepted legitimacy by violence. However, it makes a mockery not only of the moral legitimacy inherent in the definition and understanding of terrorism but more importantly of the rule of law and the principle of justice.

The problems and inherent relative contradictions of the concept of legitimate violence that are built into the orthodox definition and understanding of terrorism, can also be found in two other important concepts that are associated with the causes of terrorism. These are tyrannicide and just war theory, and both clearly illustrate the confusion and disarray that accompanies the legitimacy debate. Tyrannicide is the legitimate use of violence by non-state actors against a 'tyrannical' regime and is often cited as *the* justification for terrorism. However, the obvious problem with this is how to establish what exactly constitutes a 'tyrannical regime', and when to decide that terrorism, as 'legitimate violence', is permitted. Actors engaged in terrorism believe they are acting legitimately; this is the contradiction of the definition of terrorism and the basis of the morally relative argument. Thus by the subjective definition of a cruel dictatorship any group could morally justify terrorism against the incumbent regime if disaffected by it. Laqueur suggests tyrannicide is legitimate if it is the only feasible means of overthrowing a cruel dictatorship, as 'the last resort of free men and women facing intolerable persecution'. However, he is then forced to question if terrorism is always morally wrong.[18]

Just war theory is similarly problematic, associated with the work of Aquinas and Grotius, it offers actors a similar justification for terrorism and is also open to relative interpretations. According to Aquinas in *Summa Theologica,* just war requires jus ad bellum (justice of war). This is war for a just cause with no other alternative, which incorporates the correct authority and right intentions.[19] Kennedy suggests that modern just war theory also incorporates jus in bello (justice in war), which is proportionality and discrimination.[20] The problem, which is also inherent in the definition of terrorism, is that the claim to a just cause can be made as a legitimate claim relative from almost any perspective and authorised by any source of perceived political grievance. In addition, the just war theory implies that only one of the belligerents is waging a just war, which immediately invites subjective interpretations.

The concept of just war theory can also be undermined and manipulated by relative interpretations of the justice *of* war and also the concept of justice *in* war. Both have little normative orientation as different actors view proportionality and discrimination differently. Whilst the method of terrorism can be considered by some as not satisfying justice in war and so violating the modern embodiment of just war theory (embodied in the Geneva Convention of 1929 and 1949). Terrorist actors can cite the 'end justifies the means' to validate whatever means employed as acceptable in war to achieve the just cause.

Terrorism is also often associated with violence against non-combatants as a violation of the most basic human right, the right to life.[21] However the relative comparison is often made between the considered illegality of groups detonating improvised explosive devices (IEDs) against innocent civilians and the perceived legality of military bombardment of non-combatants by the armies of the state. This perhaps implies that in conflict and war there are no innocents. Omar Malik deals with this issue by pointing out the relative nature of the concept of innocent. He suggests, '[A]t any time the boundary between guilty and innocent is set primarily by the killers' current view on their own necessity, capability, and the victims accessibility, they kill whom they can kill'.[22]

Contested legitimacy also questions the nature of war in relation to terrorism because uniformed soldiers, armies and war relate solely to states for whom the declaration and conduct of war is considered their preserve. The reason for medieval just war theories and latter day conventions on the 'rules of war' is an attempt by states to control and restrict the use of warfare. Non-state actors without the military strength of the state, use whatever means of violence they have available in order to conduct what they perceive as a war or conflict.

However, by virtue of the terrorist method of violence they employ, which maybe the only one available, they are outlawed and deemed illegal. Not only by the legitimacy of the state definition of terrorism but also under international law. This is illustrated by the international conventions on terrorism and the law of armed conflict. Once again this implies that the term terrorist exists, as a label for 'illegal' war or conflict conducted by a non-state actor from the relative perception of the state.

Towards a working definition

The understanding of Terrorism needs to be deconstructed and decoupled from the imposed relative legitimacy debate and recognised as neither legitimate nor illegal but simply as conflict. As Stohl argues, 'force is warfare and war is the power to inflict hurt and damage'.[23] Terrorism in my understanding has two main definitional components, lethal violence and a political agenda. Many researchers agree that terrorism can be seen as the expression of a particular type of lethal violence and can be defined methodologically as a 'special method' of armed struggle or as a 'weapons-system'.[24] That incorporates recognised techniques such as assassinations and bombing,[25] and is characteristically directed against people or property. These acts are differentiated from similar forms of violence by the existence of a political motive. This Hoffman argues is the key characteristic of terrorism. He suggests, 'in the most widely accepted contemporary usage of the term [of terrorism] it is fundamentally and inherently political'.[26] A political motive implies an agenda that involves some violent interaction by, with or against the established power centres in order to affect the nature of the power centre. So in its most basic manifestation terrorism can be seen as *lethal violence for a political agenda*. I would argue that this basic definition of terrorism provides a useful point of departure from which to begin an examination of the roots of terrorism as it is a value neutral expression and focuses on an approach to terrorism based on the simplicity of the act of violence for a political purpose. It also provides a level of clarity in which it will be possible to investigate the reason or root cause for terrorism unencumbered by the problems of the moral legitimacy debate found in the orthodox definition.

Orthodox terrorism theory: a discourse for understanding terrorism

Normative or orthodox terrorism definitions should be viewed as part of the wider orthodox terrorism discourse. This is the principal paradigm that is used to explain, understand and deal with terrorism.

'[T]errorism is a doctrine about the efficacy of unexpected and life-threatening violence for political change and a strategy of political action which embodies that doctrine'.[27] Orthodox terrorism theory is a discourse built upon the act of terrorism in order to understand its logic. Although this is intended to explain the act from the perspective of both the instigator and recipient, be it a terrorist group against a state or indeed vice versa. Orthodox terrorism theory concentrates mainly on acts of terrorism as violence against the established authority or state, not necessarily by it. Whilst it does expound state terrorism, orthodox terrorism theory is essentially a western model of understanding rooted in western freedoms, the rule of law and the liberal democratic state.[28] This is due to the necessity for a requirement to deal with acts of terrorism, which according to orthodox terrorism theory, are seen as threats to the state.

Orthodox terrorism theory is based on a number of common themes that reoccur throughout terrorism literature. These can be grouped into three areas, *functional, symbolic*[29] *and tactical*.[30] By using each of these types as a guide it is possible to expound the orthodox theory of terrorism. *Functional* relates to the orthodox belief that terrorism is intended to 'provoke a response to further the cause by strategic manipulation'.[31] This is a central concept and suggests that the aim of the act of terrorism is to force a reaction, hopefully an over-reaction by the established power centre, governing authority or state against the instigators, their supporters and even the population in general. Rubenstein calls this 'heroic terrorism' and suggests that the aim is to 'provoke intense indiscriminate state repression in order to deprive the government of legitimacy and radicalise the masses'.[32] Laqueur calls this 'the terrorist theory of provocation' and suggests that it is intended to produce (state) repression, draconian measures and thus ultimately undermine the 'liberal' façade.[33] Alongside this attempt to demonstrate the unsuitability of the incumbent authority to govern and by exposing its 'true' nature, orthodox terrorism theory suggests that the terrorists endeavour to wrest legitimacy from the state and bestow it upon their own cause. The intention of terrorists is to undermine the security of the population by demonstrating that the state is unable to provide adequate protection and therefore force them to turn to alternative sources such as the instigators of the terrorist violence to negotiate a settlement or provide alternative governance. This is illustrated in the post-World War Two anti-colonial conflicts in Cyprus and Algeria, in Northern Ireland and Spain and present day situations in Chechnya, Nepal and Iraq.

A second theme is *symbolic*. This is arguably the basis of orthodox terrorism theory, which according to Hoffman has its origins in the earliest forms of nineteenth century terrorism and is encapsulated in Carlo Pisacane's 'theory of propaganda by deed'.[34] Orthodox terrorism theory uses this concept of symbolism to explain an act of terrorist violence as being highly symbolic and an attempt to terrorise, intimidate and strike fear into the those against whom the violence is directed, (even if they are not the actual physical recipients of the violence). Obviously the actual targets of the act and the wider audience who witness it are directly affected by it. The orthodox explanation of the symbolic value of terrorism is as 'coercive intimidation' or 'pure terrorism' which is 'the systematic use of murder and destruction or the threat of, to terrorise individuals, groups, communities and governments into conceding to terrorists demands'.[35] Classically, the conventional philosophy of terrorism is as a symbolic act, intended to affect more than just the target of the violence. In the writing of Sun Tzu, orthodox terrorism theory suggests the aim of terrorist violence is to 'kill one and frighten ten thousand'.[36]

Whilst much of the literature on orthodox terrorism theory supports these psychological implications it also emphasises the communications value aspect of symbolic violence. The orthodox discourse suggests that acts of terrorism are committed in order to publicise and internationalise the political aim, thereby demonstrating the high propaganda and publicity value that can be gained from acts of terrorist violence. Jenkins encapsulates this concept by describing 'terrorism as theatre'.[37] This understanding of terrorism applies equally to the state. Which is known to generate the symbolic terrorism of fear and intimidation against its own domestic population in order to ensure political loyalty and compliance to authority.[38] Moreover, some terrorism theorists argue that the symbolic nature of terrorism theory allows an act of terrorism to be categorised into domestic or international depending where it occurred.[39] Both the psychology of fear and the role of publicity contained in the symbolic nature of orthodox terrorism theory demonstrate quite graphically the significance of the role of media in propagating the psychological implications of the terrorist message to an even wider audience.[40] This understanding for example, is used by the Israeli State to explain the reason for a Hamas suicide attack on a school bus.

The third component of orthodox terrorism theory is *tactical*. This can be understood in two ways, first as a limited means to achieve short-term gain, such as the exchange of hijack hostages for prisoners or a bank robbery to fund arms procurement. This was a common understanding during the hijacks in the 1970s by Palestinian groups. The second is as a tactical part of a wider strategic initiative; this has its roots in the theories of revolution and guerrilla warfare[41] by proponents such as Mao Tse-Tung[42] and Carlos Marighela.[43] They suggested that acts of terrorism should be part of the wider struggle for revolution or an initial stage preceding popular revolt. Schmid and Jongman define this phenomenon as 'the insurgency context of terrorism'.[44] This understanding is applied to the current situation in Nepal, where the incumbent government have labelled the Maoist insurgents as terrorists.

Orthodox terrorism theory is employed to understand acts of terrorist violence and is based upon the assumptions I have discussed above. It is interesting to note however that by adopting this terrorism theory, assumptions are made about the nature of the terrorist actor. Crenshaw investigates this and develops 'strategic choice theory' which she argues is a representation of the perpetrator of the act of violence as a rational actor, who has calculated the implications and made a rational choice among alternatives as part of strategic reasoning.[45] This suggests that acts of terrorist violence whilst appearing to be indiscriminate and random, and the behaviour of mad and crazed individuals, are in fact tactical parts of a carefully planned and calculated strategy to influence decision-making and effect political change.

Orthodox terrorism theory is based on normative definitions that incorporate the above components and thus help to provide an understanding, especially for governments and agencies involved in dealing with terrorism. The US Department of Defence defines terrorism as, 'the unlawful use of – or threatened use of – force or violence against individuals or property in order to coerce or intimidate governments or societies, often to achieve political, religious, or ideological objectives'.[46] Schmid and Jongman suggest terrorism is 'a method of combat in which random or symbolic victims serve as instrumental targets of violence. These instrumental victims share group or class characteristics, which form the basis for the victimisation. Other members of that group or class are put in a chronic state of fear (terror).... the purpose of which is to change attitudes or behaviour favouring the interests of the user of method of combat'.[47] This particular definition of terrorism was produced after an exhaustive survey of academics and practitioners in the field, and has consequently had a profound influence on the general understanding of terrorism.

Orthodox terrorism theory however is a discourse; it does not necessarily represent the 'truth' about terrorism but exists to provide *an* explanation of the violence. Unsurprisingly not all actors accept the orthodox understanding of terrorism. This is due primarily to the moral problems inherent in the relative legitimacy definition, which allows terrorism discourse to be employed (a purpose for which it is perhaps designed) to legitimise state violence whilst simultaneously delegitimising the use of political violence by opposition movements.

The definitions and the theory of orthodox terrorism discourse whilst comprehensively explaining *how* terrorism works and *what* it is intended to achieve, does little to explain *why* it occurs. Once again, this is perhaps the designed purpose of terrorism discourse. It provides an explanation of political violence that can be employed against it without any recourse to a roots debate. As any form of roots debate might affect the political legitimacy of the dominant power centre. This is because investigation into why terrorism occurs could potentially result in the legitimisation of the terrorist group and the delegitimisation of the state. Orthodox terrorism theory has a particular and important purpose. It is a discourse employed by the state to tackle terrorism without undermining its legitimacy. Terrorism however is an endemic problem worldwide and despite the continued use of orthodox terrorism theory terrorism remains so. Is orthodox terrorism theory therefore really the best approach?

Terrorism theory in crisis

Orthodox terrorism theory it seems appears to be in a state of crisis. Although the theory I have expounded above is still very relevant and instrumental in the understanding of terrorism, a number of new trends identified by terrorism theorists are becoming increasingly apparent and bring into question its very foundations. Hoffman identifies what he terms as 'new terrorism' which he suggests is characterised by less comprehensible motives and an unwillingness to claim or credit responsibility. He also highlights the increased lethality of acts of terrorism.[48] Wilkinson calls this trend 'mass terror' and links it to the large number of people killed in ethnic conflict.[49] This obviously problematises the orthodox understanding of terrorism as symbolic – which suggests the intention is low lethality and high publicity.

Walter Lacquer in *The New Terrorism* reiterates these themes and adds that new terrorism is motivated by hate, blind violence and aggression and therefore questions the role of ideology in terrorism.[50]

This argument causes difficulty in supporting the functional understanding of terrorism, which is further compounded by the actions of millennial groups, or extremist sects whose sole purpose is to kill and therefore lack any obvious political objective.[51] This brings into question whether they actually constitute a terrorist organisation. These themes are increasingly apparent in the contemporary literature on terrorism theory, especially in the aftermath of the destruction of the World Trade Centre and the implications of the high death toll. It is also particularly relevant in the debate over the terrorist use of weapons of mass destruction (WMDs).[52] The understanding of 'new terrorism' may therefore require new theories as it certainly brings into question the psychological foundations of traditional terrorism theory, as Jenkins makes clear when he stated that 'killing a lot of people has seldom been the terrorist objective'.[53]

Part 2: Theories of terrorism

The roots of terrorism at the state level

By applying a critical approach to examining the relationship between the state and terrorism, it is possible to investigate from the literature in terrorism studies, if the roots of terrorism can be located at the state level. The state is defined in international law as a permanent population within a distinct territory under the authority of an established government.[54] This implies the existence of legitimacy[55] and sovereignty.[56] These two concepts are instrumental in the state-based understanding of the root causes of terrorism because they imply that the state is the embodiment of centralised power over a population and that a relationship exists between other states. The 'state system' according to realism in international relations theory is maintained by the existence of a political relationship between the governing machinery and the governed population of the state, and the recognition and acceptance of these concepts in other sovereign states. These are mutual relationships and terrorism can be located in the conflict generated between the actors in these political interactions. These can be found internally between the state (governing authority) and governed population as conflict over legitimacy, and externally between states as conflict over sovereignty.

Internal state terrorism

Internal state terrorism can be seen as acts of terrorism by the state within its own borders. This is a common theme in terrorism literature[57] and is often associated with the reign of terror, perpetrated by the Jacobins during the French revolution. Calvert in his '*Theory of Revolution*' suggests that terror is 'the consolidation of revolution' and argues that the reign of terror of the Jacobins was directed as much at the established aristocracy as it was against other revolutionaries, as it was used to maintain, consolidate and stabilise revolution. He also cites War Communism in Russia in 1917 as a further example of this theory.[58] Eugene Walter in *Terror and Resistance* understands all acts of terrorism to signify violence designed for political control. This is 'regime terror theory', and is state rule by violence and fear.[59] Hannah Arendt points to the Russian Revolution and suggests that this heralded the use of 'terror as an institutional device'.[60] Terrorism can be employed as a potent instrument of the state or established authority to subjugate a population and enforce political compliance. As the state, according to Leon Trotsky, is much richer in the means of physical destruction and mechanical repression than terrorist groups are.[61]

It seems to be part of the natural condition of the state to generate and employ terrorism in order to create and maintain political power. This is illustrated by the existence of the social contract, which Rousseau identified as the implied relationship between the government and the citizen. He suggested this contract allows for the monopoly on the use of violence by the state, in return for the protection of the rights of the individual citizen.[62] Alexis de Tocqueville identified this concept and termed it 'containment' and concluded that terror is a consequence of maintaining social peace and personal safety.[63] States have a category of assets, which include armies, money and police in which to protect power, repress rebellion, impose order and reinforce legitimacy.[64] Hoffman points to extreme examples of this theory, such as Nazi Germany and Soviet Russia, which he calls the 'abuse of power by governments'.[65] However with the legitimacy bestowed on established states this could equally be called the legitimate exercise of political power.

This concept has been termed the 'discipline of terrorology' or 'the science of terrorism'. This theory suggests the ability of the state to employ terrorism. Not only directly against its own population to keep them in-line, but also indirectly, as a means to develop, by propaganda, a fear of terrorism as a threat to the state within the population. The maintenance of a type of public paranoia effectively sanctions the legitimate use of state terrorism against a perceived threat.[66] This is demonstrated in Israel, where despite the human losses and questions about its effectiveness, the majority of the Israeli public maintain support for the use of state violence against the Palestinians.[67]

However, the use or indeed misuse of terrorism has been recognised and scepticism has been voiced. Miller suggests, '[T]he agencies of government to which we entrust our security and who devote themselves to the eradication of terrorism, maybe more a part of the problem itself than we wish to acknowledge'.[68] Moreover, Chomsky identifies the existence of 'image' and 'reality' concepts of terrorism. 'Reality' he argues, is 'literal terrorism', which is an identifiable and real threat to the state. 'Image' however, is 'propagandist terrorism', which he sees as the 'construction of the concept as a weapon to be exploited in the service of systems of power'.[69] These ideas relating to internal state terrorism can also be seen as counter or anti-terrorism, as both advantages and disadvantages. Thus 'the domestic or internal threat of terrorism can strengthen the modern state to the detriment however of the rule of law and security of civil liberties'.[70] This argument is particularly relevant in the approach of many post-September 11 states that have introduced national emergency anti-terrorism laws that blatantly contravene individual human rights.

Internally, terrorism can be regarded as endemic to the existence of the modern state as whenever political power is in contention it is a method that can be used to establish and then maintain political power or purely to strengthen an existing position. This implies that the relationship between political power and governance makes terrorism practically synonymous with the institution of the state.

External state terrorism

External state terrorism is also a common theme in terrorism literature and can be defined as an act of terrorism sanctioned by states outside of its own borders. It is also referred to as state-sponsored, surrogate, state directed, or proxy terrorism. By employing this approach the state can be regarded as *the* primary source of terrorism since the Second World War. As it has been employed by the state as an instrument of propaganda and control in order to preserve the international status quo by maintaining the respective position of power of the state by the domination of others.[71] For this reason state terrorism can be regarded as immeasurably more destructive and indiscriminate than small-group violence.[72] Thus the state can be regarded as a root cause of terrorism due to the perceived utility of terrorism when employed as a tool of foreign policy for assisting the maintenance of state security or the projection of power and influence abroad.

The concept of state-sponsored terrorism permeates virtually every aspect of the study of terrorism. For this reason Stohl divides state terrorist behaviour into three types; coercive diplomacy, covert behaviour and surrogate terrorism.[73] This typology can be enhanced by adding direct military action. States can perpetrate acts of terrorism outside of their borders to enact what can be termed low-cost, low-risk, high yield foreign policy. This can take the form of acts of overt violence by one state carried out in another state, or as covert violence by agents of the perpetrator state (or 'third party' 'proxy' state) in the form of direct military action or secret financial, technical or logistical and support. Covert state terrorism is also often practiced because it avoids direct military confrontation between states and considerably reduces the danger of inter-state war, especially if the states concerned have nuclear weapons. This type of confrontation was prevalent during the Cold War, as indigenous terrorist groups would often be supported by the superpowers in 'proxy conflicts', depending upon their ideological perspective. During this period, Clare Sterling produced a thesis entitled *'the network theory'*, in which she argued that the cause of world terrorism was state-sponsorship of terrorism by the Soviet Union.[74] Whilst this serves to highlight the importance of state sponsored terrorism, it overlooks the role of other states, especially western, in state terrorism and can also obscure other reasons for the manifestation of terrorism. This 'network' thesis whilst largely discredited now appears to be re-emerging as an Islamisist terrorist network theory.[75]

Seemingly, from the perspective of a neutral understanding of terrorism as lethal political violence, I suggest that the most contentious acts of terrorism are overt acts by states, such as retaliatory and pre-emptive strikes.[76] State terrorism is a method by which states can project military and political power and can be brought into action whenever a state wishes to project its power without accepting responsibility.[77] State sponsored terrorism however, is not just the preserve of the powerful states as all states fear for their security and employ a proactive foreign policy to attain their goals. Other factors that might cause state sponsored terrorism include, the weakness of some states to field comparative military strength, religious or ideological causes and endemic socio-economic problems.[78]

Examination of the causes of terrorism at the state level produce a perspective of terrorism inextricably rooted within the modern state and realist state system. The manifestation of terrorism therefore can be attributed directly to the existence of the state, which is 'as an instrument of internal repression and control and a weapon of external aggression and subjugation'.[79] This perspective is linked closely to orthodox terrorism theory and employs a positivist approach to understanding acts of terrorism as illegal and illegitimate violence against the state. From this respect it is an invaluable level of analysis for the examination of the roots of terrorism.

However because of the state-centric orientation produced by the state level perspective, a serious flaw exists for a holistic understanding terrorism. The state level approach only sees terrorism as originating from established states and therefore does not recognise the importance of the non-state actor. Acts of terrorism against states are perceived as instigated only from other states. For example, the Palestinian-Israeli conflict is understood at the state level as a conflict between the established Arab states in the region. The Palestinians as a non-state group are viewed as either the proxy agents of the Arab states or as an Israeli internal security issue. They are certainly not seen as politically and socio-economically marginalised or oppressed actors in their own right. Furthermore, the cause of the September 11th attacks in New York were seen as state sponsored terrorism emanating from the Taliban in Afghanistan. This is an obvious gap in the understanding of terrorism, one that needs to be addressed by employing other, alternative levels of analysis.

The non-state actor and the roots of terrorism

To compensate for the shortcomings of the state approach to terrorism it is useful to examine how terrorism is understood, within the existing literature, at the non-state level. Examination of the perceptions provided at this level enable the roots of terrorism to be investigated by focusing attention on the role of the non-state actors as a cause of terrorism. This can be achieved by examining the nature of the terrorist challenge to the state and why it occurs. Bowyer Bell calls this concept 'the dream', and suggests that it is apparent in all actors seeking political change. The opposition and resistance that the institution of the established state produces to this dream is a major determinant of the nature of the armed struggle and of terrorism.[80]

Opposition to the state as the accepted source of political power can be recognised in two principal forms. *Reactionary,* which is violence, intended to instigate change and reform of the existing system. And *revolutionary* which is violence that seeks the complete destruction of the state and the established authority. Terrorism therefore exists 'in the state and non-state contest between the forces of order and change, power holders and challengers and forces of social control and dissent'.[81] Before examining these two catalysts for terrorism, it is important to investigate why the state as an institution is such a lightning rod for political violence.

Terrorism against the state

Terrorism against the state is arguably the most commonly accepted and widely understood cause of terrorism within terrorism literature. This is primarily because the state is considered to be the accepted and established source of political power, in the form of a national and internationally recognised ruling authority. The institution of the state is therefore the obvious and natural target for those seeking political influence. Consequently, the state and its legal, security and defence machinery is orientated to oppose any form of political change, especially violent, that attempts to affect the state monopoly of political and socio-economic control. The roots of terrorism exist in this dynamic. This is clearly illustrated by movements for national liberation or socio-economic reform that harbour a political claim to some or all of the power of the state.

To explain the roots of terrorism it is crucial to investigate the root causes of terrorist challenges by various groups against the established authority of the state. This is particularly important when some states employ a form of parliamentary democracy or at least provide the facility to potentially obtain political power through peaceful means.[82] Aside from the obvious violent opposition that can be generated by an illiberal state, it can be argued that the Liberal state is in fact a major cause of terrorism. This relates to the ideological inception of the modern state in the French Revolution.[83] Paradoxically, whilst the French Revolution is held in the highest traditions of western thought as *the* example of gaining freedom and liberty, it was actually achieved and consolidated by the use of terrorism. For this reason terrorism is located in modern western political thought originating from the French Revolution. As '[I]t led men to believe that it was within their power to remake society from top to bottom'.[84]

This implies that a revolution of thought occurred, triggered by the example of the French Revolution. Thus it was demonstratively no longer necessary to accept without question the ruling elite or established political and indeed socio-economic situation. Liberal political change could be facilitated by violence. Chaliand suggests that the ideas of the enlightenment also helped generate the concepts behind rights and freedoms and supports his argument with quotes from the work of Rousseau and Burke.[85] Individuals and nations, he continues, developed an understanding and belief in 'natural rights' especially for the creation of a representative state. These beliefs, enshrined in the concept of the state, have been instrumental in the cause of terrorism since the French Revolution. They reoccur in the concepts of European nationalism, ethno-nationalism, self-determination and de-colonisation.[86] These types of asymmetric power challenges from non-state actors are widely regarded as some of the main causes of terrorism, especially in orthodox terrorism theory. The irony is however, that these expressions of violence are enshrined in the western value systems of freedom and liberty that helped establish the state in the first instance.

A further cause of terrorism is the arbitrary nature of the state itself. States, especially liberal democratic ones, are arguably created as representative, yet it is very unlikely that they will represent the entire population. Political grievances are therefore very likely to materialise. Laqueur argues that because of this, terrorism is endemic to the state and he is doubtful if a peaceful settlement to all the demands of all terrorists could ever be met.[87] States are also territorially arbitrary. Their borders do not necessarily reflect social, ethnic or religious divisions. States are a 'model' and often reflect the will of the majority therefore marginalising minorities into terrorism.[88] States are also artificially created political 'products', characterised by a population who may be socially, economically, ethnically and religiously diverse but who are forced together into a bounded territory and governed by an established authority under an enforced political system. Whilst this may be acceptable to some, especially the ethnic majority or the ruling elite, the nature of the relationship of violence between the governing and the governed and the diversity of people in a state might suggest otherwise. An interesting argument to complement this is by Cassese. He suggests that terrorism exists in the fragmentation of state, not its forcible creation. Terrorism, he argues, should be seen as occurring in the 'framework of the progressive decline of the nation-state and the disintegration of communities into smaller groups, sub-groups and minorities'.[89]

A further cause of terrorism by non-state groups is the reaction and response of the state itself. The ability of the state to employ violence to maintain its security is well documented. The roots of terrorism can therefore be attributed to the repressive nature of the state. In detailed studies of ideological terrorist groups Donatella della Porta argues that the strategy chosen by the state is often instrumental in the development of anti-state terrorism. She suggests the existence of the 'radicalisation of protest'. This happens to political demonstrations that start peacefully and culminate in violence, and result in the creation of potential terrorist groups that are driven underground by harsh state oppression.[90] Rubenstein suggests that it is the violence perpetrated by the state that causes acts of terrorism, he argues that terrorists gain respect for violence from the state.[91] Moreover, Carlos Marighela in his *'mini-manual of terrorism'* stated that, 'the tactic of revolutionary terrorism must be used to combat the terrorism used by the dictatorship against the people of Brazil'.[92] An example of the socialisation of violence or the inheritance of violence from the state by non-state groups is provided by Sayyid Fedlallah, the spiritual leader of Hizballah. He was quoted as saying, 'the extraordinary and unconventional methods of waging war are necessary to redress the imbalance of power and as an obligation for self-defence'.[93]

The state can exist for many as a passive faceless and oppressive monolith that obstructs and frustrates the political and social goals of weaker opponents. It exists as the symbol against which the violence created by frustration and anger is often vented. It is also an insensitive and hostile leviathan that dispenses its own brand of arbitrary violence. It is interesting to note however, that groups often perpetrate terrorism against the state with the intention of forming their own version of a state, in which they hope to realise their own political power and accomplish their own particular goals. This Orwellian nightmare continually propagates terrorism, as the 'new incumbent state' dispenses its own violence whilst being the recipient of violence from new opposition groups. Prior to the formation of the State of Israel in 1948 Menachem Begin, representing the Irgun, (a terrorist group opposing British rule in Palestine) proclaimed that 'a fighting underground is a veritable state in miniature: a state at war'.[94] This statement could now equally apply to the Palestinians. The state is an institution built on violence and the majority of states were formed through it. Terrorism is therefore synonymous with the state.

Revolutionary terrorism

Revolutionary terrorism is terrorism conducted by a sub-state group in order to overthrow the state, completely destroy the existing political system and replace it with a new political framework. Ironically a primary cause of terrorism is the desire for state formation located in liberal ideas, which support the rights of individuals and the attainment of freedoms. Terrorism employed by groups engaged in anti-colonial conflict is triggered by the perceived need to achieve some form of legitimacy and sovereignty through self-government and political autonomy. These concepts are enshrined in the political institution of the state and form the basis upon which individuals, communities and nations gain, exercise and more importantly protect their individual rights and freedoms. These liberal principles however, especially the concept of the right to self-determination and independent state rule, are instrumental in causing terrorism. UN Resolution 1514 states, 'All peoples have the right to self-determination'.[95] It is controversial argument to suggest that a UN resolution approves the use of terrorism to achieve statehood, but it certainly exists as a justification for seeking an independent state through violence. Yasser Arafat in his address to the United Nations General Assembly in 1974 argued, 'A revolutionary is one who stands by a just cause and fights for the freedom and liberation of his land'.[96]

The existence of the institution of the state, the power it holds, the access it permits to the international society and the protection under international law it provides, is a clear incentive for groups to seek their own state. 'The state is the tool-box containing the instruments for access to the West's power and superiority' and that access to this is a 'natural right'.[97] Groups and communities that exist as minorities in states due to race, ethnicity, religion or culture actively seek this goal and often resort to terrorism to achieve it. This is supported by the typologies of terrorism widely adopted in the terrorism literature; such as anti-colonial, irredentist, separatist, nationalist, ethno-nationalist, insurgent and revolutionary. Hence, the struggle for a state by the 'submerged nation' is a very serious problem for modern societies.[98]

Terrorism literature and the orthodox theory of terrorism suggest that it is possible to achieve revolutionary change and the formation of an independent state through the use of terrorism. This is due to the constant reference to the 'success' of the terrorist campaigns mounted in the 'anti-colonial conflicts', such as Algeria, Palestine, Cyprus and Aden. All of which culminated in political autonomy and state formation. This graphically illustrates the apparent benefits of terrorism. Although this argument suggests that terrorism causes terrorism, it does appear nevertheless to be a successful way or method of achieving statehood to all potential terrorist groups who desire political change and state formation. Whilst the central purpose of orthodox terrorism literature is to condemn terrorism, it is forced to concede that anti-colonial terrorism was 'successful' albeit due to a number of 'special conditions', and the apparent success of terrorist tactics employed during the anti-colonial period were very influential in facilitating the emergence of modern terrorism.[99]

Reactionary terrorism

Reactionary terrorism is terrorism employed by non-state groups attempting to reform the political system within the existing state structure. The objective of this violence is not to overthrow the state, but to reform it, in order to redress for example, perceived political grievances or socio-economic inequality. It is important to stress that this classification is adopted for ease of examination and does not necessarily suggest a formal demarcation between groups who seek state formation and those who do not. Reactionary intentions may lead inadvertently to revolution and conversely revolutionary groups may only succeed in reactionary reform. Furthermore, although I have argued that the desire for state formation is the cause of revolutionary terrorism, it is possible to suggest that some of the causes of reactionary terrorism may also be secondary underlying causes of revolutionary terrorism. For example, government repression, economic deprivation, political opposition, ethnic persecution and class cleavage could all trigger more fundamental political change.[100] Also non-state groups do not necessarily follow state borders and therefore can and do exist inside, outside and across the borders of established states.

Reform of the existing political system by terrorism is a common theme in terrorism literature. The causes of terrorism are commonly seen as political or socio-economic grievances expressed by groups or communities. In 1972 the United Nations Secretariat produced a document on the causes of international terrorism, it suggested that the roots of terrorism were in 'genuine frustration and despair with national and international policy in the political, economic and social situations'.[101] The concept of grievance is also a reoccurring theme as a 'real grievance', such as 'hunger, misery, disease and humiliation'.[102] Or more ethereal concept such as 'hope and desperation (hope for profound political change and desperation in political defeat and economic decline)'.[103] This has been termed 'anomie violence', and is an expression of social and cultural dislocation.[104] It also draws attention to social conflict and suggests that terrorism is located in decaying and unstable social systems. These are structures that trigger the disadvantaged in 'blocked societies' to seek to reassert their rights.[105]

Terrorism caused by the need for reform was also an argument articulated by the former US president, Bill Clinton, who suggested 'terrorism is the last desperate pitch of the humiliated and hungry and is a raw message of those neither heard nor understood'.[106] Crenshaw argues that causes of terrorism can be divided into 'preconditions and precipitants'. Preconditions are factors that set the stage such as modernisation, urbanisation and the development of social habits and historical traditions. Precipitants are specific events that trigger a violent reaction.[107] Donatella della Porta explains this build-up to violence as 'a protest cycle' in which claims or demands gather momentum within specific social groups and can radicalise into violence unless addressed by the government.[108] This has also been referred to as 'a crisis of confidence' and suggests that protest movements begin, not necessarily because of fundamental faults in the system but because of rulers misleading behaviour and misguided policies.[109]

The outcome of these frequently occurring causational arguments in terrorism literature is to conclude that the roots of terrorism are in social conflict. Groups and communities engaged in terrorism often refer to concepts such as order and justice. They demand the redress of the perceived social imbalance due to social inequality, injustice, discrimination, marginalisation and the lack of political representation. Two important theories of terrorism emerge from this line of argument; the first is relative deprivation. This theory expounded by Ted Gurr in *Why Men Rebel*, suggests that the perceived discrepancy between what the group expect to have and what they actually have is a source of violence.[110] The second is functionalism or utility theory; this has its roots in the work of Coser on social conflict theory,[111] but is developed and applied to explaining terrorism by Crenshaw. She suggests that terrorism has a positive social function to ease social tension by creating and maintaining necessary social change.[112] Further to this is change theory, which sees terrorism as a purposeful safety valve for dangerous social pressures and serves to raise awareness and help governments make timely reforms in order to avoid a potentially violent situation from worsening. This ultimately implies that terrorism has a purpose, and the means of violence, no matter how abhorrent, leads to an important end, which justifies it. 'Armed struggle is a means to change history and not an end in itself'.[113] This theme is also explored by Albert Camus in *The Rebel*. He suggests that revolt is a spontaneous response to injustice and a chance to achieve change without giving up personal and collective freedom. Rebellion, he argues, 'is the basis for human progression and freedom'.[114]

The existence in society of ideas of grievances, demands and problems that can act as potential and indeed actual causes of terrorism, are identified as 'corrigible terrorism'. This is terrorism in which the causes, such as desires and grievances can be addressed.[115] Reform of grievances is not however a panacea for terrorism despite Lacquer's optimism that, 'rarely do happy and contented people throw bombs'.[116] It occurs not only for many other reasons but also grievances and especially the concept of relative deprivation can by definition prove to be both endemic and unsolvable.

Structural causes of terrorism

An examination of the causes of terrorism at the structural level of analysis is essentially an investigation into the actions of the actors in relation to each other and the perceived structure that causes this or is
created by it. Crenshaw believes that 'terrorism cannot be adequately
explained without situating it in its particular social, political and
economic situation'.[117] Structural causes of terrorism can manifest themselves in many forms. These range from material concepts such as global
economic disparity, territorial disputes and colonialism,[118] to wider ethereal concepts such as subjugation and oppression. Terrorists, according
Rubenstein, are normal people driven to extremes by situations.[119] In the
following section I have chosen to examine the structural causes of
terrorism by exploring ideology, culture and socialisation.

Ideology

Classic examples of terrorism ideology are provided by Mao, Guevara,
and Marighella and were directed primarily at conducting revolutionary and guerrilla warfare. As the basis of a theory used to justify actions
these ideas were widely adopted by terrorist groups. However, perhaps
the most influential ideology for terrorism is Marxism, this relates to
employing violence to break the structural constraints of political,
social and or economic oppression. *The Manifesto of the Communist
Party* states, 'Their ends can be attained only by the forcible overthrow
of all existing social conditions...the proletariat have nothing to lose
but their chains. They have the world to win'.[120]

Marxism is a common feature in the ideology of many terrorist
groups as it justifies the use of violence to achieve political goals.
Examples include, PIRA and ETA in Northern Ireland and Spain, the
PFLP in the Middle East, FARC in Columbia and the MPLA in Africa.
Also, the Palestinian *Intifada* or 'shaking off' can be seen a reaction to
the structural oppression of Israeli occupation. Marxism is an antidote
to the illegitimacy of violence of orthodox terrorism theory. It serves to
legitimise violence against oppression. George Sorel in *Reflections on
Violence*[121] suggested that the function of violence was as 'the weapon
of the proletariat... to be used as the supreme act of resistance'.[122]
Resistance, struggle, oppression and freedom are words in the common
lexicon for both Marxism and terrorism.

Franz Fanon and Jean-Paul Sartre also developed powerful ideas of
violence and resistance as a response to structural oppression and
made significant and influential contributions to the development of

terrorist thought.[123] Fanon and Sartre constructed their ideas in response to anti-colonial conflicts and suggested the existence of structural violence, which in itself had become a cause of terrorism. Fanon in *The Wretched of the Earth* saw violence as an omnipresent structural force. He advocated an even greater violent response to the violence of colonial oppression, and implied that only through violence could true individual and group expression be found. Violence he believed was a unifying force and a way to gain self-respect and vent frustration. He argued, 'Violence alone, violence committed by people, organised and educated by its leaders makes it possible for the masses to understand social truths and gives the key to them'.[124] Sartre developed a similar understanding of violence in *Critique de la raison dialectique*. Like Fanon he saw violence as the cohesion to all social and political relationships and advocated violence as self-expression and ultimately an end in itself. 'Violence, like Achilles' lance, can heal the wounds that it has inflicted'.[125]

Culture

Culture can be defined as a structural influence on the actions of society developed through history, behavioural habits and institutions. Culture is an 'arena or ecosystem in which the armed struggle is generated and comprises of a combination of history, culture, vulnerability and possibility'.[126] Terrorism can be created and propagated by the structural characteristics inherent in culture. Violence, according to Carlos the Jackal, is the only language the Western democracies can understand.[127]

Violence can be enshrined in the history and culture of society and is apparent from the level of occurrence or propensity for violence in a society, community or region in both historical and contemporary events. A culture of violence can be propagated and prolonged by the continuity provided by historical and cultural memory.[128] Societies can be sensitised to accept different levels of violence depending on their history and experience. Some environments are therefore more conducive than others in generating terrorism. This is as apparent in the Basque region and Northern Ireland, as it is in the Middle East, Africa and South America where 'a culture of violence has developed that tends to perpetuate itself'.[129]

Della Porta argues however that the expression of terrorism is not necessarily representative of society as a whole and suggests the existence of a 'sub-culture of violence'. This is terrorism instigated by different social groups who by definition and action consider themselves outside accepted society.[130] This can be regarded as 'the underground' and is a subjective reality created by history, habits, customs, institutions and assumptions and is not understood by those outside it.[131] This implies that terrorism is caused by the structural effect of culture and suggests that in order to understand the origins of terrorism an investigation of history and cultural institutions of a society is required if the root causes are to be understood. The problem however is that this is based on the assumption that the acts of terrorism are perpetrated within a single society, suggesting that the entire society is representative of the violence.

Socialisation

Socialisation is an attempt to investigate the structural causes of terrorism from a socio-economic perspective. It is an approach that is intended to understand the structural nature of the relationship between the individual, group and socio-economic environment. A relationship that is responsible for causing people to behave in a certain way. Reoccurring socialisation themes in the causes of terrorism are poverty, low standards of living and limited socio-economic opportunity. Terrorism is often seen as a product of social dislocation and a symptom of political instability, class struggle and economic disparity.[132] Social and political trends are also seen ahead of religious reasons to explain the root causes of violence. Walter Laqueur cites a tradition and culture of violence coupled with poverty, unemployment and unfulfilled political promises.[133] However, it is important to point out that the socio-economic structure is not always seen as a cause of terrorism. A study entitled *'Does poverty cause terrorism?'* concluded that any direct connection between poverty and terrorism is probably weak and a more accurate cause is in response to political conditions and long-standing feelings of indignity and frustration.[134]

Socialisation issues exist as a structure that is not initially apparent and are significantly more deep-rooted and underlying in society. As a result the problems produced by it are not necessarily solvable by quick-fix solutions that deal only with the symptoms. Crenshaw cites issues such as divided societies, long-standing protracted conflict and instutionalised discrimination and inequality as the structural context. She links these to specific events that provoke despair, rage and vengeance.[135] This implies that terrorism can be generated by a self-perpetuating dynamic created by the socialisation between the long-term structural issues, such as economic inequality, political marginalisation and social discrimination and immediate trigger events such as election results, price rises or racial violence. These structural problems can be identified in the relationship between environment and sub-culture and suggest regional and global factors such as the international system, colonialism and revolution, coupled with urbanisation and modernisation as structural causes of terrorism within socialisation.[136]

A further socialisation theory that examines psychological issues in the causes of terrorism is the 'social construction of reality'. This is the idea that terrorism cannot be understood unless the interaction between the structural conditions and the objective or subjective reality is acknowledged.[137] This implies terrorism can be caused by the construction of a subjective reality that is unintelligible to those outside the group. Hence, the causes are situationally dependant upon the social construction of reality and are dependant upon the uniquely human involvement in the construction of social order.[138] This subjective reality is 'the rebel dream' and suggests that the structure or 'arena is in the mind of those involved'.[139] This implies that only by examining the psychological structure inherent in the mind of the terrorist will it be possible to understand the subjective reality and thus accurately comprehend the context in which the reasons for the violence exist.

Socialisation provides an insight into the construction of the political and socio-economic environment, as the interaction of this environment with the actors can generate acts of terrorism. It also stimulates a useful recognition of the subjective realities that exist within the mind of the terrorist actor and which comprise the mental structure through which they operate. However, it should be pointed out that this is a theoretical approach to understanding terrorism. Difficult socio-economic environments are not automatically synonymous with the generation of terrorism, nor is it possible to predict the construction of an actor's subjective reality. It is perhaps enough to appreciate that they exist as components in a potential structure that can cause terrorism.

The roots of terrorism at the individual level

The role of the individual in the root causes of terrorism should not be underestimated. Ultimately it is the individual who carries out a lethal act by detonating a bomb or pulling a trigger. This level of analysis focuses on an examination of the individual root causes of terrorism by considering the influence of ideology, religion, psychology and single issues.

Ideology

Ideology is examined in this section because of the importance of the ideas and belief systems that are employed by the individual in the generation of terrorism. Ideology provides the individual terrorist with the cognitive reasoning with which to justify the use of violence. From a definitional perspective a political cause or ideology is a pre-requisite for acts of terrorism. Ideology can therefore be regarded as fulfilling an instrumental role in generating; executing and sustaining acts of terrorism as any political ideology held by an individual can lead potentially to violence.

The ideological motivation of the individual terrorist has been compared to that of a 'dream'. The rebel 'dream' is both the source and determinant of the armed struggle and is pursued by the faithful who believe that the only way of transforming it into reality is through the use of violence.[140] The 'dream' is the ideology that provides the subjective reality to the terrorist. 'The rebel is driven by a vision only the faithful can see and this determines his world'.[141] This subjective vision is the source of the perceived legitimacy of the political claim of the individual and provides the justification for the use of violence in order to achieve it.

The roots of terrorism exist within the beliefs of the individual. This is a concept Dostoevsky explores in *Demons*. In this novel he suggested that terrorists are individuals who had become possessed by ideas.[142] Terrorism is seemingly a product of thinking people and is produced by a 'social and moral crisis in the intelligentsia'.[143] Individuals not the masses generate terrorism as Lenin suggested, 'terrorism is the violence of the intelligentsia not the proletariat'.[144] Rubenstein in *Alchemists of Revolution* argues that acts of terrorism are generated by the intelligentsia within a society. They are subject to the forces of political, socio-economic and structural change and are forced to resort to violence to create the impression of a mass movement in order to cope with this fundamental transformation.[145] Hence the terrorist is fundamentally a violent intellectual prepared to use force in the attainment of goals.[146]

It is also apparent from the literature on terrorism that ideology, when regarded as a specific political system, is seen as the cause of a certain type of terrorism. In a basic typology of terrorism, Wilkinson suggests the existence of 'ideological terrorists...who seek to change the entire political and social system either to an extreme left or extreme right model'.[147] Although I would argue that terrorists, by definition require some form of ideology. The typology of ideological terrorism is useful as it illuminates causes of terrorism that are left or right of the existing regime. Porta argues that the foundation of the term 'terrorism' originates from the nature of the challenge to the existing regime; she identifies the appearance of both right and left wing groups, who use terrorism in opposition or support of the existing regime depending on their respective ideological perspectives.[148]

Religion

Religion is arguably the most widely assumed cause of terrorism within orthodox literature and it is often portrayed as the major driving force behind international terrorism. Bruce Hoffman states that religious motivation accounted for half of all active international terrorist organisations in 1995. It also generated the most serious terrorist attacks of the decade.[149] Although the apparent influence of religion in terrorism is a well-established assumption, what really requires investigation is the actual role of religion as a cause of terrorism. Religion, using a critical approach can be seen as purely an ideology that provides the reality, legitimacy and justification for terrorist acts. This is the basis of the argument of Juergensmeyer, who suggests that violence by religious groups is an expression of political power mandated by God, an attempt to express the legitimacy of religious rule against the state. He suggests religious violence occurs because of the nature of religion, the nature of secular politics and the nature of violence itself.[150] Religion, using this argument can be regarded as just another political ideology, which is vying with other secular ideologies for political power.

Conversely, religion can be seen as more than just a political ideology. Arguably it is inextricably linked to the identity and culture of a socio-economic community and exists in the very roots of the terrorism. Wilkinson argues that religious terrorism has arisen out of the disillusionment with secular ideology and also points to the fact that some religious groups have moved beyond the political by establishing socio-economic community structures.[151] Furthermore, Berman argues that religious terrorism has developed within the understanding of liberalism, as a response to the freedom of action and thought provided by liberalism in society.[152]

Religious terrorism can also arise as a direct political challenge to the established political authority, in a similar way to secular terrorism. It can be a socio-economic and cultural counter reaction to perceived threats to the religious cultural fabric or it can exist simply as an expression of religious principles. The different meanings associated with the concept of 'Jihad' illustrate this diversity. 'Jihad' can represent the effort to lead a good religious life or to attempt to purify society. It can also mean the desire to spread Islam through preaching, teaching and or armed struggle.[153] Rapoport suggests that the roots of religious terrorism are cultural, and points out that compared to secular terrorism it has established precedents and determinants, enshrined in sacred texts, which are unalterable. Religious terrorists, he argues, take their example from history and culture.[154] Kramer calls this 'the incalculated sense of sacred mission' and suggests that far from restricting the actions of terrorists it allows them the justification to deviate from the fundamental teaching of their religion. This argument refers to acts of violence that take the lives of others as well as their own and applies particularly to suicide bombing.[155]

The ambiguity of the role of religion as a cause of terrorism centres on whether religion is a motivation for it own sake, as a purely theological inspiration, or if it is actually overtly a political discourse. This can be illustrated by examining the development of Islamic extremism,[156] which is widely recognised as a cause of terrorism. According to Esposito, the architect of radical Islam was Sayyid Qutb who through his writing, the most notable of which was the book *Signposts,* established the radicalisation of Islam. Qutb was a dedicated Muslim but the orientation of his understanding of religion was in relation to the politics of state. In *Signposts,* Qutb identified and literalised the basics of Islam from the Koran and ancient texts in relation to the secular (Egyptian) state. Although religious in principle these text gained fundamental political implications. The most important of which are, the division of the world into those for Islam and those against it and the theological clarification that state and society is controlled by God and not man. This concept implies that authority and sovereignty over man must come directly from God and puts the secular state in direct conflict with extremist Islam. He also presented a reinterpretation and development of the understanding of jihad. According to Qutb, Jihad is the coordinated, legitimised and authorised use of violence in order to overthrow the secular state and oppose any non-Islamic entity, including uncommitted Muslims.[157] This implies that religion whilst it has theological overtones can exist as a political ideology and belief system and therefore act as a discourse for justifying terrorism.

This does not just apply to established world religions, as the seemingly theological texts of some more marginal religions, which includes all manner of religious cults, sects and millenarian organisations, can suggest a moral and ethical justification for violence. These groups are unrestrained by the moral or political considerations often applicable to secular groups. 'Terrorist groups motivated by religion contemplate massive acts of death as a reflection of belief and as a sacramental act of divine duty'.[158] Thus Laqueur's *New Terrorism* is rooted not in individuals, demands or concessions but in the destruction of society and elimination of large sections of the population.[159] This returns the roots debate back to the nature of the religion itself and turns on its head the argument that religion may obscure the real socio-economic and political reasons for acts of terrorism. This is aptly summed up by a Hamas commander, who stated, 'We are not fighting so the enemy recognises us and offers us something. We are fighting to wipe out the enemy'.[160]

Identifying the roots of religious terrorism is very complicated and can at best be misleading. Principle arguments suggest a quick-fix solution implying that terrorism is synonymous with religion and is used to attempt to enforce the propagation of the religion. The justification of which can be found in increasingly militant and extreme interpretations of religious texts that are used to relate directly to ideology or a political belief system. However, others argue that it occurs for various other deeper underlying socio-economic, nationalistic or ethnic reasons, which are often obscured by the influence of religion and politics in a similar way to the effect of the Cold War on the understanding of the cause of regional conflict. Rubenstein argues that religious terrorists are fundamentally nationalist, he suggests, 'Religious fundamentalism expresses widely felt longings for national redemption, national power, self-purification and revenge'.[161] However, in millennial cults and extremist groups religious terrorism can also occur as violence for an end in itself, violence for no other purpose than to kill. This obviously makes a roots debate highly problematic and thus locates the causes of this form of terrorism deep in the psychology of violence.

Psychology

An examination of the psychological causes of terrorism is an investigation into the nature of the individual and involves exploring behaviour, attitudes and group dynamics. Arguably, the most important causes of terrorism are in the mind of the individual and the creation and existence of a subjective reality. Although acts of terrorism can be committed for any number of different reasons it is within the particular mindset and subjective reality of the individual that acts of terrorism occur. The cause of this thought matrix and subsequent reasoning to resort to violence can be seen as the psychological root cause of terrorism. This perceived reality is a vision created and reinforced by faith in the terrorist goal. It is a shared reality as all rebels assume their truth is universal and produces an arrogant intractable belief in the group and results in 'killing for a world others cannot see'.[162] Sprinzak calls this phenomena 'transformational delegitimation', he suggests it is the complete separation of a group from reality and is preceded by increasing radicalisation as the collective group identity takes over.[163]

Arguably the most important development for understanding the causes of terrorism are within group dynamics. In this area terrorism is generated by like-minded individuals who join together to create a subjective world, made by their own rules to support their own subjective feelings and reinforced by their own collective understanding. This ultimately serves to justify their actions. This underground or alternative society can become even more insular and self-perpetuating as the terrorist actions can increasingly cut the group off from exposure to alternative 'realties'. Whittaker believes that the mindset of terrorists in the underground is such that they see themselves as reluctant warriors driven by desperation and lack of alternatives. He suggests self-denial and an altruistic desire to serve a good cause are primary psychological characteristics of terrorists.[164] The separation of the group from wider society is also an important development. This 'splitting' produces polarisation and a Manichean black and white, them and us attitude which not only accounts for acts of terrorism but also triggers further psychological consequences such as stereotyping and dehumanisation. Ulrike Meinhof is reputed to have said in response to a challenge about killing policemen; 'the person wearing a uniform is a pig and not a human being'.[165]

Internal group dynamics can also produce an increasingly intractable situation where the only action is violence. Groups can become exclusively orientated towards violence, as it becomes their sole mode of communication. Crenshaw suggests that indoctrination of group members is such that they are forced to commit acts of violence. This is a prerequisite for acceptance into the group and also ensures group cohesion, as members can no longer return to wider orthodox society. Moreover it serves to accustom them to violence as a form of social conditioning.[166] In a further study she suggests that small group dynamics produced by conditions of isolation lead to galvanised feelings of self-righteousness, trust, identity and loyalty.[167] This can also be accompanied by 'organisational violence' within the group to ensure discipline and loyalty. Recognising this, Lustick suggests the existence of 'solipsistic violence'. This, he argues, is the expression of symbolic violence, which is violence directed *at* the 'enemy', but intended *for* the group, as a means to develop group psychology in order to strengthen group needs of identity and purpose.[168]

Other psychological causes of terrorism within group dynamics can be attributed to leadership. Strong dominant leaders or persuasive entrepreneurial types can generate group directed violence, such as the influence of Ulrike Meinhof in the Red Army Faction or Dighenis Grivas of EOKA in Cyprus. This was identified by Max Weber, who suggested three types of leadership authority that provided motivation for obedience. These are rational; based on legal standing. Traditional, relating to established authority and charismatic, indicative of the personal qualities of the leadership.[169] Group members can also commit violence *for* group leaders and therefore absolve themselves from the blame by transferring responsibility for it to the leaders. Stern calls this 'displacement of responsibility'.[170] Bandura also identifies 'diffusion of responsibility' in which acts of terrorism are committed by group decision, thus when everyone is responsible no one is responsible.[171] Miller suggests that individuals and groups commit act of violence against symbolic targets, such as political or religious leaders or emblematic buildings as a substitute for the more complicated actual cause of the social, political or economic distress.[172] This cathartic cause of terrorism can also be termed 'displacement violence'.

Group dynamics can also be maintained and given purpose by violence. This can cause a cult of violence, which can rule the group and establish their existence solely for the sake of violence. This justifies their existence and makes the recourse to acts of terrorism the natural choice. The Israeli terrorist group leader Menachem Begin famously stated 'we fight therefore we are!'[173] Post calls this phenomenon 'group think' and suggests it provides an illusion of invulnerability, builds confidence and risk taking. It also presumes group morality polarises the opposition and produces intolerance to challenges by group members to key beliefs.[174] An indicator of group dynamics as a cause of terrorism is the question: why do groups continue violence even after a form of political settlement has been reached or the position is no longer tenable? This could be due to the strength of the terrorist group dynamics and the belief that if members of the group died for the cause then it must be continued at all costs. This can also be seen as a form of survivor guilt.

The arguments discussed above have been correlated in paper on psychology and terrorism by Jacob Rabbie who suggests a behavioural interaction model that can provide a social-psychological framework for examining terrorist behaviour. He bases his model on the assumption that behaviour is a function of the interaction of the actor with the environment. For environment, he includes a social environment, which he sees as the behaviour of people within and outside the boundaries of the group. He combines this with psychological orientations distinguished as cognitive, emotional, motivational and normative. Rabbie suggests that the interaction of these psychological orientations with the environment provided by group dynamics can cause terrorist behaviour.[175]

Single-issue

Thus far I have considered causes of terrorism that are accountable to wider issues and have implications beyond the immediate terrorist group, suggesting that the causes of the violence are open to a roots debate. However, it can be argued that terrorism can be generated by causes that are not subject to a roots debate. This is primarily because they are related directly to single issues. These are specific and localised individual or small group problems, and are the direct cause of the violence. Single-issue terrorism can be defined as violence committed with the desire to change a specific policy or practice within a target society.[176] These might include employment or financial disputes, racial or homosexual hatred, socio-religious extremism or in fact any act of lethal violence with a localised political agenda. It also includes extremist factions of peaceful protest groups such as animal rights and ecological movements. Whilst it is possible to identify the cause of this type of terrorism, it is perhaps not so easy to solve it. Often their demands are so intractable, extreme and fanatical that it is totally unrealistic and virtually impossible to offer a workable solution. Wilkinson calls this type of terrorism 'incorrigible'.[177]

A further cause of single-issue terrorism identified within terrorism literature is initiated by organised crime and the drugs trade. This is a contentious area in the roots debate, as organised crime and the drugs trade is often perceived to be inextricably linked to terrorist groups, not only as justification for violence but also to mask criminal activity and narcotics trafficking. However, an important study by Miller and Damask decries the myth of narco-terrorism and argues that the term was established during the Cold War by the United States to suggest a Soviet sponsored conspiracy to undermine the west and therefore justify American foreign policy, especially in Latin America.[178] In addition, pioneering work by Wardlaw suggested that so-called 'narco-terrorism' served only to group together disparate terrorist and guerrilla groups with different motives, divergent agendas and diverse links into an association with the drugs trade. This had the effect of implying that the relationship between terrorism and the drugs trade is very simple, as the term narco-terrorism suggests.[179]

The link between political violence and crime and the dugs trade as a cause of terrorism, according to Miller and Damsak, is more to do with greed than political agendas. Although they do suggest linkages between groups over a common opposition to the government, they point out that the agendas of insurgents and narcotics traffickers are virtually incompatible as they are diametrically opposed over the nature of the governing power structure. Insurgents operate outside the political structure in an attempt to overthrow it, whilst the drugs trade profits from it and seek to maintain it.[180] Despite these arguments crime and drug trafficking are still seen as a serious cause of terrorism. Richard Clutterbuck suggests that the cultivation, processing and distribution of narcotics are probably the greatest single generator of political violence and crime.[181]

Examination of single issues as causes of terrorism within the individual can provide a useful understanding into why particular violence is occurring. Despite the belief that it negates a roots debate, as single-issue terrorism assumes that if the issue is solved then terrorism will stop. But if the issue is so radical it cannot be solved then the terrorism will continue indefinitely. This discourse causes problems for attempts at solving so-called issue terrorism, as actors cannot be placated except with recourse to remedying the particular issue, which might be a political impossibility.

The individual level of analysis is also vital in examining the place of the individual in the generation of acts of terrorism. However it is a framework that focuses on the individual and assumes that the individual terrorist is a rational actor who acts in accordance with an ideologically created psychological mindset that is constructed from a reasoned and cognitive understanding of the political situation. But as Joseph Conrad suggests in *The Secret Agent,* individuals who commit acts of terrorism can equally be the unwitting violent end product of a chain of events caused by complicated political relationships and socio-economic situations of which they are completely unaware.[182]

Perspectives of terrorism

I have constructed the above survey of the roots of terrorism, according to the literature in terrorism studies, from a multi-level perspective.

Although each level of analysis has its own strengths and weaknesses, it is important to note that the causes of terrorism are often viewed using only one of these perspectives. This is particularly relevant at the state level, where orthodox terrorism theory is the dominant discourse. My survey of terrorism literature implies that if a comprehensive and holistic understanding of terrorism is to be achieved then it is vital to apply a multi-level analytical approach to the causes of terrorism, incorporating all these perspectives. This will allow an explanation of terrorism at all the levels and will be far more useful in attempting to understand the root causes and conceivably resolve them.

Consider, for example, that an act of terrorism occurs. It is viewed at the state level, (through orthodox terrorism theory), as an illegitimate and unlawful attack against the legitimacy of the state. This represents a direct and illegal challenge to the established authority, and therefore warrants a legal and military response. The non-state level perspective however sees an actor requiring the formation of a state in order to satisfy the need for self-determination or the requirement for socio-political change. Yet, from a structural perspective the violence can be seen as a product of a culture of violence caused by systemic socio-economic and political problems. Whereas at the individual level the violence is explained as individual grievances enshrined in ideology or religion through the creation of a subjective reality. I am not suggesting that one or any of these approaches is the right one. Instead I am merely illustrating that by recognition of the existence of different ontological comprehensions, discourses, theories or perceptions, all of which relate to different levels of approach, it is possible, if all these perspectives are recognised, to combine them into one single holistic approach.

Nevertheless, orthodox terrorism theory is still the primary and normative discourse for explaining, understanding and dealing with terrorism. It dominates the literature and is recognised by the state-centric and positivist understanding of terrorism as illegitimate and unlawful violence. It is based on the assumption that the terrorist is a rational actor and suggests that terrorism is a carefully planned and calculated strategy directed against the state in order to influence decision-making and effect political change by the use of functional, symbolic and tactical violence. Its exists as a pejorative term adopted by actors, predominantly state actors, to create a moral justification for their claim to legitimacy.

However, orthodox terrorism theory is just *a* discourse. It does not necessarily represent the 'truth' about terrorism. It is created and employed as a paradigm by the state for the purpose of providing a theoretical interpretation of facts and events and providing an accepted explanation of the political violence, thus allowing the legitimisation of state violence through moral and legal justifications.

The obvious key result of this survey is the importance of a multilevel approach that examines the multitude of different causational factors depending on which model or perspective is employed. This suggests that for a comprehensive and holistic understanding of the roots of terrorism a combination of these different perceptions is required. Second, the survey of terrorism literature suggests a general differentiation between approaches to explaining the roots of terrorism.

These are,

1. Orthodox terrorism theory, this is the predominant explanation and understanding of terrorism. It does not engage in a roots debate as it favours the illegal and illegitimate approach to explaining terrorism that mirrors the realist, state-centric understanding. It is the basis for governmental anti-terror and counter terrorism policies. It is supported by a well-known school of terrorism academics particularly Wilkinson, Hoffman, Alexander, Schmid and Jongman.
2. Radical terrorism theory, this is occasionally apparent in the literature and explains and understands terrorism largely from the perspective of the terrorist. It is a justification for violence and a defence of the root causes that exist predominantly in the structure. It is expressed by writers such as Fanon, Sartre, Camus, Qutb and Marx.
3. Moderate terrorism theory, this is a limited approach in terrorism studies that deals with a roots debate. It is a trend that attempts to explain and understand the roots of terrorism in relation to socio-economic and structural as well as political causes. Examples of this are Gurr, Bowyer Bell, Crenshaw, Della Porta and Berman.

Although these different approaches suggest a wide understanding of the roots of terrorism, alternatives to orthodox terrorism theory are marginal. The discipline is dominated by orthodox terrorism discourse. In order to develop a more sophisticated and advanced understanding of the root causes of terrorism I have three recommendations. The first is to adopt a definition of terrorism that is outside of the moral legitimacy debate. One that will free the understanding of terrorism from pejorative, moral and legal judgements that continually obscure the reasons for the violence and are unhelpful in understanding the root causes. The simple definition I suggest is, terrorism as 'lethal political violence'. Although this definition is an attempt at neutrality it loses the understanding of terror. Which it can be argued, is integral to the understanding of terrorism. However, terror is linked with orthodox theory, which suggests that the perpetrators of the violence are attempting to illegally and illegitimately coerce and terrorise a political group into complying with their demands. Acts of violence, in both conventional war and unconventional conflict all serve to terrorise, which I would argue is the nature of political violence. A neutral definition of terrorism helps to move the understanding of terrorism closer to the realm of conflict. The second recommendation is draw upon thinkers outside of the terrorism studies. These I suggest could be found in the work of conflict theorists. This will be examined in the next chapter on root causes of conflict. The third is to apply a multi-level holistic approach.

Terrorism studies is a largely dormant academic discipline, it focuses on examining and justifying an already established discourse which only serves to promote the positivist understanding of terrorism. This is the design and purpose of a discourse, thereby reinforcing its own reality. The study of terrorism needs to break out of the mono-dimensional and pejorative moral legitimacy definition. It needs to move beyond the state-centric understanding of terrorism provided by the orthodox discourse and into a wider and more holistic approach to political violence. One that will provide access into the deep roots of the violence and facilitate movement towards a resolution of terrorism.

2
Approaches to Conflict: The Root Causes

Introduction

Conflict is an issue that is said to have occupied the thinking of humankind more than any other, save only god and love.[1] This is probably because conflict and violence have not only been a ubiquitous phenomenon in the progress of human history but have often been the reason for the creation of history itself. The events of the Trojan Wars, catalogued in *the Iliad* of Homer, exist as an example of the first written primary source record of the history of mankind and was inspired by conflict. This is also true of primary source histories of medieval warfare, modern accounts of the first and second world wars and also contemporary wars in the Arabian Gulf. Some would argue that this is to be expected, as in a Hobbsean world, war and conflict is a state of nature. Although this is debatable, few philosophers neglect the study of conflict when examining the composition of human kind. The study of conflict represents not only an effort to comprehend the nature of human kind, without which it would not exist, but also shows an attempt to understand why it occurs, and then produces measures to try and prevent it. This is no more apparent than in the periods immediately after the first and second world wars, when the shock of over 20 and 50 million deaths respectively[2] prompted the international community to actively seek the avoidance of conflict by creating institutions such as the League of Nations and the United Nations. Nevertheless, the prevention of conflict has always been a process fraught with difficulty. Despite the fact that the UN was created to end war (it claims in the preamble to the UN charter that it intends 'to save succeeding generations from the scourge of war'[3]), it actually fails to support an absolute ban and in fact, somewhat paradoxically, explicitly sanctions the use of force in defence of the Charter.[4]

Attempts at creating systems to prevent war are not new. The realist state-centric international system based on the governmental and territorial legitimacy of the state was created in the peace of Westphalia in 1648, in order to promote international stability and peace. However, although this so-called Westphalian system was created to establish order, its foundations are paradoxically in conflict. The Westphalian system creates a structure in which the use or threat of violence, as war, represents the accepted method by which sovereign states maintain their international and territorial integrity. This is the reason for the continual recourse to security and the reoccurring problems of the security dilemma. Moreover, it also represents the attainment of the international status of a state with all the associated benefits, by the use or threat of violence. This is clearly illustrated by the number of states in the international systems that are created through violence, and implies that the Westphalian system exists as the instigator and propagator of institutional violence. As a result there are a number of important implications for understanding conflict by employing the Westphalian system and the associated state-centric perspective. The first is the reliance on the highly stylised warfare of the state involving established armies and symmetric conflict. The second is the employment of an international system that is not only founded on conflict, but which also creates an inherent conflict based structure that recreates and propagates inter-state violence. However, the most important implication is the inability of this system to perceive intra-state conflict. This is identified by Richmond who suggests the central problem is 'the psychosis of Westphalian imagery and its inability to understand or address issues outside the rigid state-centric organisation'.[5]

The Westphalian system, nonetheless, has been the accepted way to understand conflict, especially during the state-centric and ideologically polarised bi-polar Cold War world. However, in the uncertainty after the fall of the Berlin wall, the focus on inter-state conflict has been replaced by intra state conflict. These 'new wars' are predominately in the form of ethnic identity conflict, characterised by irredentist and secessionist movements and civil war.[6] This shift suggests that in order to understand the new type of conflict, which relates to nations, communities, groups and individuals often within states and or irrespective of, established state boundaries. It is necessary to move beyond the Westphalian system and employ a discourse that deals with issues such as non-state identity, representation and participation. Conflict in the post-Cold War period, referred to from this point on as *contemporary conflict*,[7] is a complex and inconsistent phenomenon. As a result, the state-centric Westphalian system of understanding conflict can be seen to be in crisis. In order to explain and understand this 'new' phenomenon, alternative approaches need to be applied, if paths into dealing with the roots of contemporary conflict are to be established.

By employing different theories and discourses, understanding conflict becomes an ontological and epistemological problem. In this chapter I intend to consider the potential root causes of conflict by employing a critical approach to investigating and examining the main theoretical approaches provided by the conflict literature. To achieve this I intend, as I did in the first chapter on the causes of terrorism, to examine the roots of conflict at different levels of analysis. These levels of analysis correspond to different perspectives created by international relations theory. As with Chapter 1, they will be state, non-state, structural and individual levels of analysis. It is important to stress that the theoretical levels of analysis constructed in this chapter are an aid to examination and are not mutually exclusive. Prior to the theoretical survey of conflict literature I will discuss an overview of how conflict can be defined and understood with particular reference to typologies of conflict. This will comprise Part 1 of this chapter. Part 2 will then deal with a survey of conflict literature, comprising of an investigation of the roots of conflict viewed through levels of analysis.

Part 1: Conflict theories

Approaching and understanding conflict

Attempting to deal with conflict, which is the assumed aim of conflict studies, requires an understanding of conflict. This is in itself problematic, as no normative definition exists because definitions are enshrined in the theoretical frameworks used to understand them. Nevertheless, a broad working definition would be useful at this juncture in order to facilitate a point of departure for this study. An initial definition of conflict is 'a serious disagreement or argument; an incompatibility between opinions'.[8] This definition is useful in highlighting the incompatibility of goals, a central concept in the understanding of conflict. However it is very broad and fails to distinguish between violent and non-violent conflict. A lack of violence does not necessarily mean an absence of conflict; this concept is explored in the literature on peace research, which problematise the accepted understanding of peace and conflict by examining the concepts of 'positive' and 'negative' peace. Boulding suggests, 'Negative peace is to pacify, manage and appease the existence of conflict'.[9] Galtung calls this 'the absence of direct violence',[10] implying that conflict exists in peace. Boulding also argues in his pioneering study, '[P]ositive peace is resolution and is the absence of conflict'.[11] Galtung, who developed research on structural causes of conflict, complements this by suggesting positive peace, is the removal of the root causes of structural and cultural violence.[12] This argument suggests peace without conflict. Boulding succinctly illustrates the ambiguity of this argument by suggesting, 'all non-conflict is peace but conflict is war and peace'.[13]

Conflict as an incompatibility of goals that is represented by both sides using force is often termed *armed conflict.* Wallensteen and Sollenburg define 'armed conflict' as a 'contested incompatibility which concerns governments or territory where the use of armed force between two parties (of which at least one is a government state) results in at least twenty-five battle related deaths'.[14] Although this definition helps to orientate an understanding centred on the manifestation of violent conflict, it incorporates problematic terminology such as 'battle related' and 'government state', both of which suggest a specific type of conflict, which in the context of this study might prove too constraining. I intend to adopt a classification of conflict for the purpose of this study from the approach of Miall et al to 'actual or potential violent conflicts'. These they suggest range from 'domestic conflict situations that threaten to become militarised beyond the capacity of domestic civil police to control, through to full-scale interstate war'.[15] Although this provides the most useful focus for the study of conflict it does introduce the concept of war, which has traditionally been understood to signify symmetrical inter-state conflict, whereas conflict is an attempt to delineate non-state or intra-state violence. Nevertheless, current conflict researchers are widening the traditional criteria even further in line with the current trends in contemporary conflict. For example Jabri broadly defines war as 'a contest or conflict over valued resources and belief systems carried out through the use of violence by one group against another'.[16]

The reason for the adoption of this broad definition of conflict and indeed war is to incorporate the present thinking currently surrounding the understanding of contemporary conflict. This is because historically, conflict and war have had a narrow definition and specific application, due primarily to the understanding of war in the 'the modern period', (from 1648 and the Peace of Westphalia) as the preserve of sovereign states. This is illustrated by the highly stylised conduct of war and is represented in the writing of Machiavelli and latterly Von Clausewitz, who classically believed in war as the continuation of state politics by other means.[17] Holsti suggests that warfare during this period was a highly organised and ritual affair between designated armies with established codes of conduct and comprised of particular violence between armies in order to achieve perceived gains, such as political advantage or territory.[18] Hence the sovereign state was the principal actor in these situations and an established army was its policy tool, involved predominantly in inter-state conflict.

According to Kaldor this type of conflict reached an apex in the first part of the twentieth century, culminating in 1945.[19] During the subsequent Cold War, but more apparent after 1989, was the appearance of what has been termed a 'new type of conflict'. This is typically intrastate and classically involves asymmetric conflict between groups, movements and organisations against the state for succession, irredentism or self-determination. It can also exist between groups in multiparty civil wars, all of which are often underwritten by religious or ethno-nationalist ideas and characterised by hatred, fear and potential genocide. Holsti labels these conflicts 'wars of the third kind' and suggests, in direct contrast to traditional conflict, that they are typified by 'no declaration of war, few battles, attrition, terror, psychology and violence against civilians'.[20] This contemporary trend is empirically illustrated by Wallensteen and Sollenberg who show by statistics that 94 out of 110 armed conflicts between 1989–1999 were intrastate.[21]

The traits in this trend of contemporary conflict have been attributed to the role of the state, which, it can be argued, has been shifted from its central role in driving inter-state conflict and can now be seen as a cause of conflict. Kaldor argues that 'new wars' as she calls them, are attributed to the erosion and in some cases disintegration of the state.[22] Within this argument are questions relating to the state system and the suggestion that in order to understand and deal with contemporary conflict, such as those illustrated in new wars, it is necessary to move beyond the Westphalian system. Richmond calls this post- or late-Westphalia and suggests that traditional concepts such as sovereignty are losing primacy and that only by moving away from the rigid state-centric Westphalian system will it be possible to recognise the roots of contemporary conflict or new wars. He suggests the state-system is inadequate in dealing with certain forms of conflict such as insurgency, belligerency, secessionism, irredentism, revolt and other forms of political violence.[23] This argument is also identified by Jabri who suggests that 'our understanding of war cannot be limited to inter-state conflict or to the definition of world politics as external relations of states as behavioural entities'.[24]

The appearance of this contemporary type of conflict is the reason for the current difficulty experienced in explaining the roots of conflict. It is now necessary to try and discern differences between conflicts in order to establish routes into attempting to understand them. This is because the pre- and Cold War causes of war and conflict were easily understood in the mechanics of state. But now the realist tradition has problems explaining intractable conflicts over identity and representation as they are beyond the Westphalian system.[25] This crisis in trying to understand and locate contemporary conflict in conflict studies has produced extensive typologies of conflict that attempt to catalogue various forms and types of conflict. For example, the interdisciplinary Research Programme on Causes of Human Rights Violations (PIOOM) have established five stages of conflict:

(1) Peaceful stable situations.
(2) Political tension situations.
(3) Violent Political Conflict (not more that 100 killed in a year).
(4) Low Intensity Conflict, open hostility and armed conflict (100–999 people killed per year).
(5) High Intensity Conflict, open warfare, civilian displacement (1,000 or more killed each year).[26]

This new approach is also illustrated by Miall et al, who present a very useful working conflict typology formed by a synthesis of the typologies of conflict provided by Holsti and Singer. They suggest conflict can be divided into 4 types:

1. Interstate conflict.
2. Non-interstate: revolutionary/ideological (which is defined as conflict attempting to changing the nature of government).
3. Non-interstate: identity/secession (which is conflict generated by the relative status of communities within states).
4. Non-interstate: factional (which is conflict arising from attempts to control the state).[27]

These examples of typologies of conflict are by no means exhaustive and merely represent an example of how contemporary conflict can be approached. They are also useful primarily for highlighting different forms or types of conflict. However this can be problematic as non-interstate conflicts are particularly difficult to understand especially from a causational perspective and could conceivably exist as all the above types. Azar points this out in reference to protracted social conflict, he suggests, 'conflict is an inseparable part of social inter-actions and relates to multifarious mutually incompatible goals among parties'.[28] The existence of different typologies of conflict illustrates the need to comprehensively examine the root causes of conflict in a multi-dimensional and multi-level examination. This is the purpose of Part 2 of this study, which investigates the roots of conflict by embark-ing on a survey of conflict literature viewed through multi-levels and critiqued by critical theory and discourse analysis.

Part 2: The roots of conflict

Conflict at the state level

Conflict studies and indeed international relations theory have been dominated by state level approach or theory of realism for most of the latter part of the twentieth century. In fact some scholars point to as far back as the writing of Thucydides in the fifth century BC to argue that the politics of state is the way to understand international rela-tions and conflict.[29] The state-centric approach to conflict focuses on political elites within the state, as well as the established state authority that exists within an international state system.[30] This approach is based on a number of concepts or assumptions that are common themes in conflict studies and the understanding of the causes of conflict. By critically examining these assumptions it should be possi-ble to establish routes into explaining and understanding the reasons for conflict. In this section I aim to examine how the concepts of inherency, sovereignty, power, and security can be seen as the root causes of conflict according to literature contained in conflict studies.

Inherency

The principal assumption that endorses the state level approach to conflict is inherency theory. This is an ontological claim that attempts to explain the very nature of mankind and the existence of a common set of primordial and intrinsic characteristics. Not only is it the starting point for the majority of academic debate concerned with the epistemo-logical nature of human existence but it is also identified by Thucydides in one of the earliest text on war, *The History of the Peloponnesian War*, as a root cause of conflict. Thucydides central claim is that the endless struggle for power is firmly rooted in human nature.[31] Inherency theory is centred on the assumptions of human aggression especially selfishness, greed, malevolence, and immorality. Doyle calls this 'fundamentalism' and suggests, '[A]ll social interaction is rooted in mankind's psychological and material need for power'.[32]

The most important implication of the human inherency debate for understanding conflict is in relation to the state. The state is assumed to be a selfish, aggressive and a unitary rational actor that interacts cynically with other states based on the assumption that they are also power hungry, self-centred and self-interested actors. This is the basis of the Hobbesian world represented in *Leviathan*, and the understanding of international anarchy in which all actors relate to each other in a natural condition based on a constant state of war. Hobbes stated, 'Out of civil states, there is always war of every one against everyone'.[33] In testament to the strength of the inherency debate as a cause of conflict, three hundred years after Hobbes, it was reiterated by Kenneth Waltz in *Man the State and War,* who stated, '[W]ars would not exist were human nature not what it is'.[34]

The inherent conflictual nature of state relationships was also identified by Rousseau in *The State of War.* Although he did not necessarily believe aggression was in human nature, he saw instead the inherency of war in a number of areas relating to the state. The first was the construction of the state. He argued, 'It is only when man enters society that he decides to attack another man'.[35] He also identified the structural effect of the state on the individual by suggesting, 'man becomes a soldier after he becomes a citizen'.[36] Furthermore, he saw war as a result of state interaction within an artificially constructed state system; thus he considered war, 'of an accidental and exceptional nature which can arise between two or more individuals'.[37] The approach of inherency theory to conflict firmly locates the root causes within the institution of the state, as it suggests that the creation of the state and its subsequent interaction with other states is an inherent cause of conflict.

The most significant outcome of inherency is that it makes conflict not only endemic but also an established norm in human activity. Although this is a useful starting point for understanding the causes of conflict, the disadvantage with the inherency debate is that it makes state conflict very difficult to explore with an aim to resolving it, because it will always be seen as existing naturally in human activity. Any approach to conflict which is based upon inherency will fail to epistemologically question the human element in conflict, and instead will merely accept and even dismiss the existence of conflict as 'human nature'. Reasons for conflict explained through inherency theory are liable to criticism, as Waltz points out by suggesting, 'they blame a small number of behaviour traits for conflict, ignoring more benign aspects of human nature that point in the other direction'.[38] This is the central criticism that is levelled at inherency as a cause of conflict. It is a very bleak and pessimistic portrayal of human nature and ultimately the state, which by accepting its very nature is impossible to change. Nevertheless, inherency exists as a potent cause of conflict, particularly in the state, as it regards conflict as a natural, unquestioned and accepted part of state activity.

Sovereignty

A state, under the normative understanding provided by international law; is defined in the Montevideo Convention on the Rights and Duties of States, Article 1, 1933, in relation to four criteria. These are, a defined territory, a permanent population, independent government and the capacity to engage in international relations (with other states).[39] The institution of the state is constructed on two conceptual pillars. The first is sovereignty, this enshrines the existence of the state as a unitary, rational actor, and by definition, implies that the state has sole authority over its internal population and is free from outside interference. The other is legitimacy, this is achieved through sovereignty, and implies that the government has accepted and recognised political authority over the population. This effectively means that the state has the legitimate use of violence both inside and outside of its borders in order to protect the rights of its population and the institution of the state against perceived threats.

This is the basis of the social contract, identified by Rousseau,[40] which legitimises violence by the state in the name of self-interest. If the state perceives an internal challenge to its authority from within the state territory, which is perceived as a direct challenge to state legitimacy, it can validate the use of violence. Similarly, if the state perceives a challenge to the core values of territory, population or government from outside the state, this is seen as a direct threat to its sovereignty. In a response similar to a challenge to legitimacy, the state will embark on conflict or war with other states. Suganami suggests that sovereignty provides state leaders with a discourse with which to use war as a tool. He points to 'key decision-makers' within states as 'instigators of war'.[41] Buzan however, recognises the underling potency of conflict in the composition of the state and argues that the concepts of war and state are synonymous. He suggests, 'states make war and wars make states'.[42] This argument is illustrated empirically by Wallensteen and Sollenberg, who show that out of 110-armed conflicts between 1989–1999 all involved the institution of the sovereign state in some capacity.[43]

Sovereignty is also a central concept in the existence of the realist Westphalian international system. This can also be seen as a cause of conflict because acceptance of the idea of sovereignty also implies a lack of recognition of any form of global governance or 'higher than state authority'. This causes, as Suganami points out, the rationale that makes states constantly prepared for war and indeed embark upon it at any time.[44] Richmond argues, that it is the artificial territorial and identity based construction of the individual states, coupled with the Westphalian framework in which they operate, that exist as continually replicating causes of conflict. He lists a number of reasons in his critique of the Westphalian system that relate directly to sovereignty as a cause of conflict. These are,

(1) Failure of the state to provide constitutional arrangements in representation and territory for diverse identities.
(2) Coercive and oppressive majority regime as a false representation of unity of state.
(3) Desire for impermeable borders representing an artificially constructed territory.[45]

Power

Power is a commonly reoccurring concept in the causes of conflict. Keohane suggests that power can be defined in two ways, 'power as a resource, and power as the ability to influence others' behaviour'.[46] Morgenthau, in *Politics Among Nations,* suggested that power is instrumental in deciding international relations. He argues, 'statesmen think and act in terms of interest defined as power'.[47] Power, from the state perspective, is considered to be an inherent human aspiration and is focused within the state and the state-centric world. Morgenthau argues that the intrinsic struggle for power between nations shows the limitless character of the lust for power revealing the quality of the human mind.[48] He also suggests that this insatiable human desire for power is not just a way to influence other states but is an end in itself because it is located in human nature. This he suggests is the reason for international conflict.[49]

Power is concentrated in the institution of the state and is substantiated by military strength and capability. This provides the state with the credibility for both aggressive and defensive policies. Individual states can be regarded as vying for power, relative to each other. Morgenthau convincingly argued that power underwrites the whole international process or interaction between states and that the incessant struggle for power was not only the force behind the actions of states but that it also provided a means of stabilising the international system by a balancing of relative power.[50] Dunne suggests that other sources of power can be found through non-violent authority or international status and economic or ideological influence.[51] However, it is more than apparent that the competitive and conflictual nature of the assumed power relationship between states, which is underwritten by the existence of standing armies and the availability of weapons of both low and high technology, supports assumptions that conflict is inevitable. This can be seen not only as a way to understand conflict but also as a root cause of it.

This functional instrumentalist approach to understanding conflict, which has echoes of Von Clausewitz, is supported by Quincy Wright. He suggests that power, generated by conflict and war, is used to effect policy change, redress power imbalances and maintain the status of nations and the established international order.[52] Vasquez returns to the power argument and proposes that the main cause of war is the foreign policy practice of power politics. He believes that war is state organised violence.[53] This is also the basis for understanding the hegemonic power concept, which suggests that the most powerful state builds an international system to reflect and protect its own interests. It is apparent that power is concentrated in the hands of the state and as I have argued above, can be seen as a root cause of conflict. This is primarily because the state sees conflict or war as rational behaviour, especially in regard to the distribution of power and the importance of state self-interest.

Security

Security is a concept that can be defined as protection of, or freedom from threats to core values.[54] At the state level, this is state security, which is essentially protection of sovereignty and is enshrined in the norms of international law. The realist state system by virtue of its inherent distrust of other states will be based on its own security and the protection of the state from the impending or actual conflict, which according to inherency theory is inevitable. This system, according to Susan Strange, is based on the domination of prime political authority by state governance, which has a monopoly on violence within a recognised territory and is based upon non-intervention and mutual recognition of sovereignty.[55]

The obsession with state security causes the state preoccupation with the pursuit of power. Power that is both resources related to military capability and hardware, and influence related to political and economic strength. Security is therefore directly related to power, which is clearly a problem for weak states. The state level analysis implies that states are preoccupied with state security which self-generate an international state security system. This system, paradoxically known by the misnomer 'security', is really an 'insecurity system' based on paranoia and fear, and consequently often exists as a principal cause of conflict. Although an example of this is the tenuous and precarious relationship between India and Pakistan, whose deep mistrust of each other is institutionalised in their preoccupation with security. There are very few states that do not regard security as one of their core value.

The international security system is based on the concepts of Hobbesian anarchy and relates to the unitary state, which is in direct relation to all the other states that also all fear for their own security. This suggests an obvious inequality in power between individual states and is believed to cause constant movement and realignment in order to establish a balance of power[56] and an international status quo that provides security for all states. The problem is that whilst this system is intended to provide state security, it does not necessarily mean 'positive peace'. The state 'security' system actually exists in a constant state of conflict or 'negative peace'. This implies that the state international system is not only underwritten by conflict but also generates it, as any large or even small power change, especially in relation to arms procurement, particularly regarding nuclear, biological and chemical weapons, could result in conflict to redress the balance. This is the logic of the security dilemma and the rationale behind preventative and pre-emptive war.

The state security system also benefits from a hegemon or a number of powerful states that can actively enforce international law or at least the version of it that benefits their own international (state) security. This argument is aptly illustrated by Thucydides who wrote in the fifth century BCE and pointed out via the *Melian dialogue,* that 'the strong do what they want and the weak do what they can'.[57] The international security system is undoubtedly and quite paradoxically a cause of conflict. Waltz identified this by pointing out that in international anarchy there is nothing to prevent war. He termed this structural realism.[58] Suganami continues this structural argument and calls the international system a 'causal mechanism' and suggests that states do not choose to enter into conflict but have it imposed upon them by the system.[59] This line of argument has its roots in the work of Rousseau who believed in the structural causes of conflict. He argued that the individual was not inherently conflictual but was made that way by the nature of the system.[60] The concept of security is therefore somewhat of a misnomer. Security paradoxically, is provided by conflict, which is in itself a threat to security.

Robert Keohane in his critique of realism, *Neorealism and its Critics*, suggested, 'realism helps us determined the strength of the trap but does not give us much assistance in seeking to escape'.[61] The state level approach to understanding conflict therefore provides a useful explanation of how the root causes of conflict can be explained in relation to the state and associated state system. It does not however recognise conflicts outside of the state matrix and due to its understanding of conflict as inherent to human nature and the state, makes no attempt to understand its roots from any other source. This makes it difficult to solve outside of conflict management approaches that relate only to state activity.[62]

The roots of conflict at the non-state level

The non-state level approach to conflict is a much wider theoretical approach than the state level. Its purpose is to help examine the role of all actors and not just states. This is becoming increasingly necessary in the light of the growing importance of the non-state conflict actors. This is also true of the influence of both subnational non-state actors such as Non Governmental Organisations (NGOs) and International Corporations (ICs) and Regional Corporations (RCs) such as the European Union (EU), North Atlantic Treaty Organisation (NATO) and Multi-National Companies (MNC). In this section I intend to discuss how the concepts of idealism, functionalism and human needs theory as theoretical approaches help to explain the roots of conflict relative to the non-state actor. It is important to stress that these theoretical sections are purely for ease of access and as an aid for examination and should not be considered a definitive categorisation.

Idealism

Idealism as a State perspective is motivated by the desire to prevent war, and focuses on the concepts of interdependence, collective security and the establishment of international institutions. Idealism as a normative approach to international relations also advocates the principles of self-determination and Human Rights.[63] These principles were perhaps first identified by Kant who argued that by creating a secure environment of international cooperation and interdependence among states, conflict could be eradicated. This was his theory of 'perpetual peace' and was based on the principle that liberal democracies do not fight each other.[64] This theme is continued by David Held, who identifies the cause of conflict as the lack of democratisation and individual autonomy and argues for the creation of a secure world order based upon cosmopolitan liberal democracy.[65]

However these approaches to ending conflict can also be seen a cause of conflict. Aiming to impose or instigate a world order of what 'ought to be' is highly problematic. It suggests the existence of a universal political norm that will be accepted by all cultures, if not voluntarily, then forcibly. Not only is this a direct cause of conflict and highly questionable in the context of the concept of sovereignty[66] but potentially a future source of violence as suggested by the arguments of the 'new colonialism' debate.[67] Attempting to end violence through the imposition of an order causes conflict by waging war to end war. Many of these problems and difficulties have been illustrated by the war with Iraq in 2003. The arguments used to criticise this action; in particular the neo-colonialist debate and the paradox of using violence to make peace are accompanied by the continual growth in both military and civilian casualty figures. However, the counter argument is to suggest that to fail to deal with potential conflicts early will cause greater problems in the future. This was illustrated by E H Carr suggested in *The Twenty Year Crisis*. As a critique of idealism, he suggested that the conciliatory idealist thinking of the inter-war years caused the Second World War, because it not only obscured the growing threat of war but also failed to deal with it until it was too late.[68]

Idealism can also be seen as a root cause of conflict at non-state level. This is primarily due to the ideological tools that idealism gives the non-state actor. For example, a common cause of conflict in the non-state actor is nationalism and the desire for state formation. This is brought about by the need for representation, participation and in many cases protection, of a nation, ethnic group or identity. As Ignatieff suggests, 'no human difference matters until it becomes a privilege'.[69] It is also a product of the international state system and the international guarantees and benefits that becoming a member of the exclusive state 'club' provides notably, sovereignty, legitimacy and international recognition. This is especially evident in the post-colonial era in Algeria, Palestine and Cyprus and in the post-Cold War period especially in Central Asia and the Balkans. It is also applicable to the Palestinian-Israeli conflict, where the desire by the Palestinian non-state actor to achieve a recognised state (a principle of self-determination enshrined by the UN[70]) is conceivably generating a severe and intractable conflict with Israel.

From this perspective it can be argued that idealism is an institutionalised cause of conflict. The post-World War One ideas of Woodrow Wilson, especially the concept of national self-determination, inspires groups and communities to seek self-rule by state formation, primarily through violence. Wilson believed that the way to peace was by state formation and the creation of a state system. Indeed his fourteenth point stated the need for 'a general association of nations to be formed to afford mutual guarantees of political independence and territorial integrity to all states'.[71] This encourages communities to exercise their rights and establish states if not politically then by recourse to 'legitimate' violence. So whilst the state and the state system became an institution created for peace it inadvertently became enshrined as an idealist cause of conflict.

Although the League of Nations was unsuccessful in preventing further conflict, it was the first attempt at creating an international body and it provided the blue print for the United Nations (UN). However, the UN has problems, it is a state-centric body, so it serves to reinforce the importance of the state in international relations, which is a cause of conflict. Contemporary conflict is also increasingly intrastate and frequently exists inside states or between communities along ethnic geographical boundaries that do not reflect the often arbitrarily created state borders. Whilst the UN represents a global organisation for world peace and purports an aim to end the 'scourge of war', it paradoxically recreates conflict by institutionalising the importance of the state, a proven cause of conflict.

The UN also fails, more importantly, to officially recognise the importance of non-state conflict. Despite the right to self-determination, enshrined in United Nations resolution 1514, which states, 'all peoples have the right to self-determination and membership of international society...and colonialism is a crime, which constitutes a violation of the charter of the United Nations'.[72] This implies that all non-state actors who claim to represent 'a people' have the legitimate right, sanctioned by the UN, to self-determination and state formation. This is an understanding that maintains conflicts in areas such as Palestine, Kosovo, Kashmir and Chechnya because the internationally recognised state is able to engage in conflict in order to protect rights to self-determination, sovereignty and territorial integrity. This is the basis of Chapters 6 and 7 of the UN charter[73] but it brings into question the relationship between established states and the rights of nations within them for autonomy. It also illustrates a difficult contradiction in the guarantee of the rights of peoples by the UN between the protection of peoples and their individual human rights and the maintenance of the political and geographical integrity of the established state under international law.

The principal contradiction with this situation is between the rights of the state enshrined in self-determination, legitimacy and sovereignty and the rights of the individual non-state groups who seek representation and participation and protection of their identity. There is clearly a cause of conflict between the rights of states in respect to sovereignty and the rights of the non-state group to self-determination. This is often seen in the debate over the legitimacy of conflicts in which nations struggle for independence, self-rule and the rights enjoyed by sovereign states against established states. This is clearly demonstrated by the conflict between the Palestinians and the Israelis, and is particularly problematic when institutions such as the United Nations favour established states even though they state in their charter that nations should have independence as a right.[74] Who therefore decides who can have self-rule and independence and who cannot? Idealism produces conflict because it exists in the nexus between the rights of the state and the rights of the non-state group, both of which are paradoxically and perhaps incompatibly enshrined in the UN charter.

Functionalism

By examining the location of the actor within the framework of society it is possible to view the causes of conflict within a social context. Jabri suggests that conflict is a social condition and is located in the relationship between self and society as an inevitable form of human conduct.[75] Conflict studies provide a useful and enlightening approach to explaining this form of conflict through social conflict theory and the theory of functionalism. Functionalism is a utilitarian approach to conflict and suggests that it is a purposeful and necessary procedure to enact or stimulate social change. George Simmel, who pioneered research in this field, argues that conflict is functional. He believes in an a priori fighting instinct of man towards man[76] and suggests that conflict has a positive social purpose in resolving tension and disputes. He suggests, 'Conflict resolves the tension between contrasts, and contains something positive'.[77] In a continuation of this argument Coser in *The Functions of Social Conflict,* explores the basic communicative purpose of conflict. He suggests that it is 'ranked among the few basic forms of human action' and provides an invaluable role as a form of social 'safety value' that provides a political, social and economic tension release for actors within society.[78] Coser divides conflict into two social types. The first is realistic; this is conflict directed at the source of the frustration and is stable. Second is non-realistic; this is tension release and is unstable.[79] This implies that conflict has a vital social function and is instrumental in establishing boundaries relative to identity in groups and communities. It also formulates and conserves social divisions and provides a communications channel for necessary and positive social change. This theory is also known as 'instrumentalism' and is the function of violence and conflict as societal change. Vayryen argues that whilst violence produces human suffering it is useful for providing a channel through which to express grievances. He sees violence as an inherent part of the dynamism of society and suggests that by examining the function of the violence the cause may be found.[80]

This approach can also be termed 'constructivist' and is expounded by Angell who suggests that conflict is a catalyst for the necessary progression of society, as it generates institutional political and socio-economic change and technological development. He illustrates this argument with reference to Marx's *The Communist Manifesto,* which he suggests is 'the most influential theory of social conflict' because it demonstrates the necessary social upheaval caused by the overthrow of the capitalist class.[81] He also applies the theory of Social Darwinism to the function of conflict and suggests that societies and groups are engaged in conflict as a struggle for the survival of the fittest.[82]

There are however a number of problems with functional theories of conflict, perhaps the most important is suggested by Burton, who argues that these theories assume that the developing society is homogeneous and coherent. He quotes Hobbes' 'Coercion Theory'[83] and Weber's 'Value Theory'[84] to illustrate the assumption of an integrated social system upon which the justification for functional, instrumentalist and constructive conflict is based. Interestingly, Burton differentiates between conflict within an established value system (rebellion) and conflict against it (revolution).[85] Both of these generate social conflict, but have different orientations to the existing social system. This implies that whilst conflict can have a function for society as a whole, it might have conflicting agendas within it. For example, some actors might foresee the violence as useful to enable social change within the established framework of society, whereas others may want to destroy the existing social framework.

A further criticism is that functional theories of conflict assume that violent conflict is an inherent function of society. Deutsch, identifies this and suggests that conflict has a perceived utility and that the root of conflict depends on the type of social relationship, either constructive (non-violent) or destructive (violent) and the issue is not to prevent conflict but to understand what conditions cause it to become violent.[86]

Social conflict theory is also a very useful approach for attempting to understand the actual manifestation of conflict. In a groundbreaking study on violence, Dollard developed a theory in which he considered violence to be the end result of a biological human tendency that links frustration to aggression.[87] He argues that an individual or group has a goal or objective, but if attainment of this goal suffers interference then frustration occurs. This leads to aggression, which is direct physical violence against the source or believed source of the interference.[88] In a critique of this hypothesis, Yates points out that this theory assumes aggression is always a consequence of frustration and the occurrence of aggression always presupposes frustration.[89] Nevertheless, frustration-aggression does serve as a constructive tool for exposing the potential roots of violent conflict and provides a useful basis on which to construct further theories of conflict. For example, Ted Gurr based his integrated theory of political violence on the manifestation of human aggression. He suggests that political discontent develops, becomes politicised and eventually turns violent due to the perceived discrepancy between what the individual or group expect to have (perceived value) and what they actually have (value capability). Gurr terms this 'relative deprivation'.[90] Although the theory of relative deprivation is an excellent tool for examining the generation of conflict, it is not an exact science and cannot predict instances of violence in comparison to suggested high levels of deprivation. It could also be argued that relative depravation can be an infinite cause of conflict. For example, an individual or group, regardless of their political, economic or social condition, may never be totally satisfied and will always perceive some form of deprivation, which will cause frustration and potentially, aggression. Relative deprivity is a relative perception and can serve as a discourse to justify violence, so the employment of a deprivation discourse by the actor could itself create a sense of deprivation resulting in violence.

Human needs theory

Human needs theory is further example of an approach that explains conflict from the perspective of the non-state actor. The foundations of this approach are in the work of Maslow who suggested the existence of a universal set of socio-biological basic human needs that required satisfaction on a hierarchical basis. Maslow argued that all human action and motivation was based upon the fulfilment of these (unconscious) needs of which he considered members of society to be in a constant state of partial satisfaction.[91] John Burton adopted this human needs theory and applied it to explaining conflict. He suggested the existence of a knowable set of human needs that although individual, were enshrined in the context of society. Burton argued that the roots of conflict existed as unsatisfied human needs, which were often supplanted by the power requirements of the state and society. He suggested individuals in society would pursue their needs within the confines and norms of society. If however, these needs become frustrated they will resort to methods outside of these norms.[92]

There are problems with this approach. Although it demonstrates that society has to take individual needs into account in order to avoid violence, it also reveals the potential conflictual disparities between the individuals and society. For example, the thesis of human needs and violence suggests that if individual values are subordinate to societal values and do not reflect them, then violence can occur. This implies that it is not possible to enforce values on society that do not represent individual needs. However, individual needs (as the name suggests) relate directly to the individual and are not necessarily reflective of society as a whole. Is it possible therefore for society as an expression of the collective to provide satisfaction of the needs of every individual? No society it would seem can satisfy every individual's needs. Human needs theory presupposes the existence and significance of an arbitrary list of needs, which implies a universal human application, but which takes no account of the influence of culture or history and more importantly gives no indication which needs are more influential than others. It also does not suggest how often these needs change in accordance with changing human values and requirements. In a critique of Burton's work, Hoffman questions if the human needs approach is applicable at the international level of states and if they are indeed common needs. Hoffman suggests, 'that whilst commonality might exist at the cultural level, it is at the level of values and interests that differences occur'.[93] He also adds that if they are actually universal needs in regards to culture, then this raises questions relating to human needs imbued with western-centric values, which problematises the actual notion of needs themselves.[94]

Human needs theory does however provide the point of departure for a very revealing approach to understanding conflict, and as Richmond points out 'helps to uncover the many levels of conflict through a human-needs spectrum and provides alternative tools to understand the basis for social conflict'.[95] Testament to this fact is the number of human needs related theories that have subsequently developed. In conjunction with Burton, Azar developed the theory of protracted social conflict (PSC)[96] in which he attempted to explain the manifestation of violent conflict, especially prolonged intra-state war. Azar built on Burton's work and identified that the cause of conflict was often located not necessarily in the needs of individuals but in the relationship between individuals in identity groups and the state. Azar called this 'disarticulation between the state and society'. Crucially, Azar identified that individual needs and values where represented by social groups and it is the needs of these groups in society that have to be fulfilled. He suggested, 'Protracted social conflict arose due to communities deprived of satisfaction of basic needs on the basis of communal identity'. To tackle this he developed a framework that comprised of four areas of investigation designed to expose all the possible causes of the conflict. The first area, 'communal', is an analysis of the identity groups involved in the conflict to establish racial, religious, ethnic and cultural influences and relationships. The second is based on the depravation of human needs, the most important of which Azar considers to be the 'safety needs'. These include security, identity, representation and equality. The third area scrutinises the role of the state and governance in order to examine how human needs are satisfied by the state. Finally, Azar included international linkages; an area intended to ascertain the nature of the socio-economic relationship with other states, particularly stronger ones.[97] This approach to understanding the causes of armed conflict by identifying the relationship between the needs of identity groups and (state) governance is increasingly becoming accepted into mainstream approaches to conflict. It is illustrated by the construction of a comprehensive and multi-level model for identifying the sources of contemporary conflict, recognised as 'international social conflicts' by Miall et al, which seeks to demonstrate the complexity of contemporary conflict.[98]

Structural approaches to conflict

The structural level of analysis of conflict is an investigation into whether structure is the reason why and how actors (depending on their agency[99]) behave in conflict, particularly in relation to each other and or the perceived system they are in. A useful starting point for structural theory is Marx; he argued that the worker must break the structural system of capitalist exploitation causing oppression and servitude by instigating violent revolution.[100] This theory provides a clear understanding of the influence of structure as well as a blueprint and justification for conflict by individuals and groups that perceive themselves as oppressed and subjugated because it legitimises their violent behaviour against a dominating structure. Wallerstein developed this argument into a theory of international relations by applying structural theory to the international system. He argued that a system of global capitalism exists in which the strong core states economically exploit a weak semi-periphery and even weaker periphery of states.[101] He suggested, 'the world system is a social system, its boundaries are strong member groups, rules of legitimisation and coercion and its life is conflicting forces which create the tensions that hold it together'.[102] Structuralists argue that violence is generated by the structural constraints imposed by a perceived system. This is developed by Wendt, whose constructivist arguments suggested that individuals, in this case, states, act in their own interests and develop a structure that protects their own identity and interests in direct relation to other states. Thus individual states exist in their own intersubjective and history based structures.[103] Hence the roots of conflict are in the construction of these systems and conflict is caused by the interaction between systems and actors and between actors themselves over the existence of incompatible goals. In this section I aim to investigate how the root causes of conflict can be understood using structural theories by examining the structural concepts of system, situation and culture.

System

Key structural approaches for understanding conflict have been developed by peace researchers and applied to theories of social conflict. The principal contributor in this field is Johan Galtung who has examined conflict from a human social perspective and created the conflict triangle. This is an attempt to delineate conflict, both symmetric and asymmetric, into direct, cultural and structural violence. One component or side of Galtung's conflict triangle is 'conflict behaviour' and relates to how the actors behave in relation to the perceived system and to each other.[104] In respect to this Mitchell suggests conflict behaviour can be characterised as overt actions in conflict situations intended to force the opposition to abandon or modify their goals.

This suggests that the behaviour of actors in relation to each other, and or the perceived conflict structure, can create a conflict system. Mitchell illustrates his argument by proposing different strategies of conflict behaviour; these are 'coercion, reward and settlement'.[105] All of which can produce different conflict systems.

Systems of conflict also exist due to the friction between actor and structure. Mitchell develops this structural argument and suggests that the source of incompatibility is a mismatch between social values and social structure, where the pursuit of goals as values or resources is rendered incompatible with the existing value system or structure.[106] This also suggests a correlation between how actors behave and the creation of a conflict system. Giddens identifies this and formulated 'structuration theory' in which he suggests that violent conflict is due to structural reasons inherent in every social system and although the system may change the structural causes remain.[107] This implies that conflict is inherent in social systems as the natural interaction of human action with social structure. Giddens calls this 'the institutionalisation of war as human practice'.[108] Jabri develops this theme and argues that violent conflict is a human activity, which is caused by the interaction of human action (agency) and the incumbent social system (structure).[109] This is the primary claim of her book *Discourses on Violence*, in which she locates violence in the relationship between self and society. She suggests that, 'War or violent conflict are social phenomenon emerging through social practices, rendering war an inevitable and acceptable form of human conduct'.[110]

This implies that in order to understand the roots of conflict it is necessary to examine the structural relationship created by the behaviour of actors in their natural interaction with society. Banks suggests that human behaviour can be explained by two factors: actor and environment. He argues that 'mental selves are constructed largely by what we have experienced and learned in our human-made environments'.[111] This argument is also apparent in the influential work of Fanon who identified the existence of colonialism as a structural cause of conflict, which generated the behaviour of actors. He argued that although decolonisation was a change of system, the structural violence would remain. In an Orwellian twist, Fanon stated, 'the native is an oppressed person whose permanent dream is to become the persecutor'.[112] This suggests that the roots of conflict are a reaction or interreaction of the behaviour of the actor with the structure and with one another, which can recreate the conflict structure in the form of systemic violence.

Situation

It is apparent from these arguments that the structural roots of conflict are in the interaction between actors. This is typified by conflict behaviour in the form of the pursuit of incompatible goals within the incumbent social structure or system and is created by human activity. However, is it also possible to suggest that the roots of conflict also exist in the relationship between actor and perceived goal. At the apex of Galtung's conflict triangle is 'contradiction' (conflict situation), which is the actual or perceived incompatibility of actors and is defined by Galtung as 'incompatible goal-states in a goal seeking system'.[113] Galtung argues that this is a structural cause of the conflict. He suggests, '[D]eep inside every conflict lies a contradiction – a problem that requires a solution'.[114] Bercovitch combines these ideas in 'situationalist theory' and although he recognises the importance of human involvement he stresses that it is the situation that generates incompatible goals or values among different parties.[115] In a similar theory, Boulding argues for a more general understanding. He suggests that conflict arises as a result of the stress and strain of social relationships. He lists structural variables that together with dynamic variables comprise the 'strain (war) functions', which in times of conflict outweigh the 'strength (peace) functions'.[116]

The structural roots of conflict also exist within the conflict situation provided by the mutually incompatible goals of the parties. Mitchell develops a theory on conflict situation and suggests that it is created by the pursuit of goals and from goal incompatibilities. He argues that the source of the goal incompatibility is located in the social structure and value system, and the goals exist as 'positive' and 'negative' types. By identifying the type of goals he argues that the source of the conflict will become apparent.[117] Conflict situations or the roots of conflict can exist in a structural form created from the aims and goals of the conflicting parties in relation to the structure of the society in which they are located. Although this argument suggests, perhaps too simply, that if the goals of the conflicting parties are achieved then the conflict will be solved. It does however provide a useful lens with which to scrutinise the subjective aims of the conflict actors and the nature of the social system against which they believe they are incompatible.

Culture

This structural framework suggests that in order to understand the roots of conflict it is necessary to examine the cultural reasons behind the conflict actions. This represents the nature of the socio-cultural environment and the individual, and is an attempt to locate the role of violence and conflict in the relationship between the individual and the history and culture of society. The philosophical tradition of this approach to conflict revisits the debate that deals with whether the individual is a product of society or society a product of the individual. If a society is considered anarchic, it is possible to argue that the 'normal' and accepted situation for individuals is a constant state of conflict as it is apparent that all individuals in a society are subject to some form of moral and ethical authority. As Plato argued, 'even among a band of robbers there must be a principle for justice to permit them to share the spoils'.[118] Society creates its own structural behavioural system based on the socio-political environment and shared history and culture. Rousseau argued that society influences the behaviour of individuals[119] and Marx suggested that environment determines consciousness.[120]

However, is it possible to discern the actions of individuals from an evaluation of a society as a whole? It is perhaps idealistic and unrealistic to assume that all individuals within a society share all the same norms in values, beliefs and behaviour. I suggest that in order to gain access to the behaviour of individuals the focus is not on the actual group or society but on the influences that generate its existence, the element for consideration is culture. By this I mean the particular influences, reasons and environment that create the behaviour of individuals, which in turn have an effect on both individual and group characteristics. Cultural influences on behaviour can originate from the immediate family, to tribal, group, community, nation, state, continent and even global. This incorporates the arguments of social anthropology and the need for cultural analysis[121] to attempt to establish and then differentiate between cultural frameworks in societies. Mead and Metraux believe the existence and interactions of cultural society contain the roots of human conflict and suggest a six-point framework for cultural analysis, which is intended to identify cultural structures.[122] They argue that culture equals the social environment and this is shared by all members of a given culture and regulates their relationships with one another.[123] Nordstrom and Robben argue that an examination of the anthropology and ethnography of violence is an attempt to locate conflict firmly in the realm of human society. They suggest 'violence is culturally constructed, like all cultural products it is only a potential – one that gives shape and content to specific people within the context of particular histories'.[124] Conflict can therefore be a cultural construct, which is the point Margaret Mead suggests by stating, 'warfare is only an invention'.[125]

Cultural analysis can help to identify the causes of conflict within a particular society, for example, Fanon examined the culture of colonialism and concluded that within this cultural framework violence was a natural state. He suggested that the constant atmosphere of violence inspired only greater violence, which then became a cultural norm.[126] This can also be seen when investigating the culture of a society that appears to exist only by violence, whether instigated by state ideology, ethnic groups, religion, crime or the drugs trade. Conflict and violence exist and propagate wherever it is considered culturally acceptable. This can be considered a culture of violence, so ingrained that it becomes accepted. Bourdieu calls this phenomenon 'habitus' and argues that fear, insecurity, and violence of death, torture, disappearances and rape become 'normal' and 'natural'.[127] This implies desensitivity and the socialisation of violence within conflict cultures, which culturally normalises violent behaviour.

Cultural analysis however relies upon a number of assumptions and generalisations from which it can provide a broad insight into society. It is based on a principal assumption that the behaviour of an individual in society is a product of cultural influences. This serves to provide access to the culture and the location of conflict within it, by reference to the behaviour of the individual. This is helpful in providing a useful culturally sensitive approach to conflict through which the causes of violence can be addressed. Cultural analysis may explain the permanent presence of violence in society, as a culture of violence that can be explained in relation to a particular society and exists as a structural cause of conflict. But it is not a uniform method as it fails to explain the presence of violence in peaceful societies without a history of violence and conversely cannot account for the lack of violence in cultures with a long history of violence. It also suggests that societies are insular and impervious to influences from other regions or cultures that might trigger violence.

Nevertheless, it is equally as important to avoid the trap of cultural relativism, by which I mean the explanation and acceptance of human behaviour placed in the socio-cultural institutions of a society.[128] The manifestation of conflict should still be viewed relative to a normative understanding.[129] Even in so-called civilised cosmopolitan cultures where extreme levels of open violence are culturally unacceptable, the recourse to state sponsored violence can easily regenerate conflict as socially acceptable. This is demonstrated by public support for war, illustrated by the support for the 'war on Terrorism' instigated in 2001 which effectively sanctioned conflict against 'terrorism' throughout the globe, and led directly to wars in Afghanistan in 2002 and Iraq in 2003. Fanon demonstrates this societal paradox by pointing out that double standards exist between societies that extol the virtues of peace yet still engage in conflict outside of their own society. He states in response to his understanding of colonialism; 'this Europe where they are never done talking of man, yet murder men everywhere they find them'.[130]

The problem is that cultural norms are difficult to identify, as cultural analysis gives only a general understanding on a broad scale. The application to multi-ethnic or multi-religious societies needs to be questioned, as it is misleading to impose a generic culture on a region that contains a myriad of small groups and communities. Cultural analysis is also problematic when considering the single individual because it is ultimately the individual cultural construction and subjective opinion of the human being who commits violence that will determine the appearance of conflict in a society, regardless of apparent norms and values. This suggests that the roots of conflict might exist in the behaviour of an individual who commits violence for no other reason than just for enjoyment. Nevertheless cultural analysis is very useful tool for examining the location of violence in the relationship between the individual and society and in helping to provide an understanding of the manifestation of conflict. Thus understanding will come from 'situating war and violent conflict in the constitution of the human self and human society'.[131]

The roots of conflict and the individual

According to Jabri, 'war is a consequence of human actions and human decisions'.[132] The central theme of this level of analysis is designed to locate the individual human element firmly into the roots of conflict. This theoretical approach is closely linked to the perceived rights and freedoms of individuals. The existence and protection of which can be seen as a cause of conflict, not only from inside as individuals struggle to establish their rights, but also from outside in the form of humanitarian intervention and the use of violence to enforce or protect individual human rights. The universal declaration of Human Rights adopted by the UN in 1948 is a '[D]eclaration that recognizes fundamental rights towards which every human being aspires, namely the right to life, liberty and security of person; the right to an adequate standard of living; the right to seek and to enjoy in other countries asylum from persecution; the right to own property; the right to freedom of opinion and expression; the right to education, freedom of thought, conscience and religion; and the right to freedom from torture and degrading treatment, among others'.[133] These established human rights present a considerable justification for conflict by individual actors who do not have them or by third party actors who seek to protect them. They clearly form the basis for conflict, paradoxically legitimised by the UN, as is claimed by many non-state actors.

This next section will concentrate on examining the nature and role of the human individual in the root causes of conflict and represents the lowest level of analysis of conflict according to conflict studies. This is in line with the new thinking on contemporary conflict and so-called 'new wars', whose common feature is protracted social conflict, centred on the individual, and relates to a whole range of contemporary issues, encompassing questions concerning ethnic identity, individual autonomy, sovereignty and human rights. This approach also parallels attempts to understand and resolve contemporary conflict in peace research, as Lederach argues by suggesting that the key to this new type of conflict is in its uniquely human dimensions.[134] In this next section I aim to investigate the location of the individual in conflict by examining the concepts of identity and ethnicity, ideology, issues and agendas, and social psychology.

Identity and ethnicity

At the individual level, human identity can be regarded as a principal cause of contemporary conflict. This is especially true since the end of the Cold War as regional conflicts can no longer be regarded as the by-product of the east-west ideological struggle or viewed through the state-centric positivist Westphalian prism. This argument is consistent with the apparent brutal nature of contemporary conflict typified by ethnic identity violence directed against communities and groups, some of which has developed into genocide. This horrific trend has led contemporary conflict researchers to investigate the role of individual and group identity and the ensuing rivalry as a root cause of conflict. Kaldor illustrates this gap in the understanding of contemporary conflict by pointing out that before closer scrutiny, it was assumed that violence against civilians, in particular ethnic cleansing, was a side effect of conflict and not the actual goal.[135]

Individual identity can be defined as a secure sense of self, developed from childhood, that incorporates Maslow's needs[136] into a deep rooted psychological 'identity card' consisting of values, motives, emotions and attitudes. Identity theory can be combined with theories relating to the construction of social identity via group membership and social interaction and is known as social identity theory.[137] This represents an important link as it identifies social or group interaction as an area prone to conflict. Anthony Smith develops 'group identity theory' and suggests the existence of the 'ethnic group' or 'ethnie' as a type of community with a shared sense of origin, values, individuality and history, all of which equate to culture. This is frequently supported by a sense of a shared homeland; a common language and often religion and can also include the physiological concept of race and the socio-economic definition of class.[138] Eriksen believes that the categorisation of people into ethnic groups is a classification that comes not only from inside the group or community but also from outside.[139] This is an important point as it suggests that ethnicity is not just a product of how people view themselves but how they view each other. This supports the classic identity mantra; 'we know who we are by who we are not'.

The existence of the ethnic group is based on identity, which is a concept established by group interaction or conflict. This is the argument of the Copenhagen school,[140] who suggest that identity is socially constructed and is susceptible to social change. However, the need for identity often presupposes the existence of the ethnic group, yet without the existence of the ethnic group there would be no identity. Although a very effective way to establish identity is through conflict it is only possible if a group identity already exists. Thus if a community is engaged in conflict either aggressively or defensively, the effect will be to galvanise group identity. This can act as a catalyst for cultural cohesion and ethnic bonding which in turn can develop into the formation of an ethnic group. The relationship between identity and ethnic group is therefore symbiotic, as neither can exist without the other and the catalyst for this relationship is conflict.

The importance of this concept is also apparent at an individual identity level. Enloe suggests 'the basic function of ethnicity is to bind individuals to a group, it informs a person where he belongs and whom he can trust'.[141] This understanding is exacerbated if the individual feels threatened, suffers relative deprivation or the suppression of individual needs. The existence of the ethnic group for protection of identity and satisfaction of needs is particularly observable in failed states as Ignatieff argues by suggesting 'it is the disintegration of states and the Hobbesian fear that results, that produces ethnic fragmentation and war'.[142] This identity phenomenon is also recognised by Eriksen who calls this 'the reflex of self-identification'.[143] The ethnic group exists as a cause of conflict because its existence is centred on identity, which can be both a by-product of, and catalyst for conflict.

The existence of the ethnic group, established to represent individual and community identity is also a cause of conflict in itself. The group will assume the persona of an individual and reminiscent of human needs theory will be as a cohesive community, sensitive and demanding to its own particular ethnic group needs. These needs could span the whole spectrum, from identity related political representation and participation, through demands for territory and economic equality, to social and cultural recognition and acceptance. Any one of these could result in conflict. As Fanon argued, the only recourse of a subjugated community was to violence, 'The last shall be first only after a murderous and decisive struggle'.[144] Whilst it is perhaps inaccurate to suggest that the existence of an ethnic group presupposes conflict, it is possible to suggest that it represents a useful indicator of the potential.

This argument however fails to take into account the role of the sovereign state. As the state level analysis above suggests the individual, group and community that exists within the state has a social contract of legitimacy, in which the needs of the people are met by the state in return for allegiance and protection. Hence it could be the nature of this relationship that can be a cause of conflict, especially if the state fails to provide for the individual, group or community. Smith suggests that the ethnic community has a number of strategies available to it in its relationship with the state, although these include the non-violent accommodation, communalism and autonomism; he names perhaps the two most important violent triggers to conflict, separatism and irredentism.[145] This stimulation of ethnic groups into political violence against the state can also be termed 'mobilisation theory'.[146] Richmond, in a study of ethnic conflict, identifies a 'metaphorical and physical no man's land' in which the ethnic group is trapped between the realist security fears of the state and the ethnonationalist demands of the ethnic leadership.[147] The nature of the precarious and symbiotic relationship that exists between the identity driven ethnic group and the sovereign nation-state is therefore a potent cause of conflict.

The ethnic group also grows in importance when the state (central government) is perceived to be, or actually is, no longer in a position to impose sovereignty and guarantee the security of the identity of the individual or community. At this point society can fracture as its members default from the state and transfer allegiance to the security of ethnic groups. This reversion to tribalism is known as 'Balkanisation'. Barry Posen argues that as ethnic groups polarise along ethnic, religious and cultural lines and central state authority gives way to anarchy, the outbreak of conflict can be explained by the manifestation of the intra-state security dilemma.[148] This can be seen as a form of civil war and can explain conflict between ethnic identity groups, within an existing state, in a failed state or across established state borders. Richmond points out that state sovereignty is not only becoming increasingly challenged by ethnic security demands but also more importantly by individual human sovereignty and the concept of human security. These he suggests are beyond the remit of the traditional state-centric perspective.[149] This introduces arguments that relate not only to the needs of the ethnic group as a cause of conflict but also to the needs and autonomy of the individual in a contemporary liberal democratic world where human rights, freedoms and security for the individual is gaining in importance.

Individual and group identity is buried deep in the roots of ethnic conflict, as individual identity either under threat from the state or unprotected by it, gravitates towards the ethnic group for protection and security. The ethnic group then becomes the representative of the needs and security of the individual and the group as a whole. The satisfaction of these needs and the ensuing dynamics between other ethnic groups and the state or surrounding states will dictate the appearance of conflict. This implies that until an international body exists that can guarantee the basic rights of individuals beyond both the state and the ethnic group, ethnic conflict will remain a persistent problem.

Ideology

Ideology is perhaps the most easily understandable cause of conflict within the individual as it provides the political agenda and the motivation for conflict. The two most important examples of ideology as proven causes of conflict are nationalism and religion. Nationalism has similarities to the concept of ethnicity, as the basis for individual and group identity. However, instead of ethnic identity, nationalism is based on national identity and is centred on an affinity to the concept of the nation, which is underwritten by the existence of the sovereign state. The conflict caused by identity politics, which I examined above in relation to the ethnic group, is just as relevant to nationalism, although Connor argues that it can be even more conflictual. He suggests that whilst an ethnic group may be other-defined, the nation must be self-defined.[150] This often presupposes the manifestation of identity conflict and is reinforced by the argument that most states were created out of conflict.

Nationalism can be seen as an overtly political concept that seeks to unite all individuals, factions, ethnic groups and cultural communities inside an established territory into one single recognisable entity. Smith points out that to achieve this the identity of the individual is recast into that of the citizen.[151] He also suggests that nationalism exploits the existence of ethnic conflict, '[I]t endows ethnicity with a new self-consciousness and legitimacy as well as a fighting sprit and political direction'.[152] Nationalism is the removal of power from the ethnic group into the hands of the state for both the creation and preservation of the elites and the political. Just as so-called 'ethnic entrepreneurs' exploit and direct the power provided by ethnicity to serve their own agendas, so the state harnesses the grassroots human power generated by ethnic groups to serve the political needs of the nation. Identifying with this debate Giddens calls the nation 'a bordered power container'.[153] Viewing the state as an expression of political power can therefore be regarded as a potent cause of conflict as the nation exhibits similar characteristics to the ethnic group when under threat. Conflict can be generated not only to create a state but also to prevent its disintegration by forging internal coherence and staving off decent into ethnic fractionalisation.

Nationalism, alongside the Westphalian system can be seen as a mythical construct, a discourse or regime of truth that is essentially, artificially created to provide political power and legitimacy over a population within a defined territory. This is supported by the paraphernalia of nations, such as flags, anthems, and heroes that serve to inspire the cohesion of the people to the nation. This is especially evident during conflict and can be regarded as patriotism. Withey and Katz argue that nationalism succeeds, as does ethnicity, because it exploits an inherent identity need in the individual. They suggest nationalism is 'a compensatory feeling of security, superiority and power for psychologically weak people'.[154] This is supported by Max Weber who suggests that nationalism is the establishment of a 'prestige community'.[155] However, by inverting this argument it is possible to recognise a major cause of conflict, as nationalism aims to pull together all manner of ethnic groups into a single cohesive multi-ethnic state. Tanja Ellingsen argues that multiethnicity increases the propensity of domestic violence and links it to the condition of the state's political regime and socio-economic situation.[156] Conflict is an ever-present threat in an unstable or even stable state, as it could erupt internally due to ethnonationalism or externally as a way to provide internal cohesion and stability.

A similar argument can be applied to the second provider of conflict ideology, religion. This is a similar discourse to nationalism as it creates an ideology that can harness power for the pursuit of political agendas. Juergensmeyer sees religion as a form of political loyalty, which he terms 'ideologies of order'.[157] Samuel Huntington attributes the cause of ethnic conflict and 'identity wars' to the religious divisions or 'fault lines' that occur between different civilisations.[158] Although this is an attractive argument, it over simplifies religion and assumes a level of homogeneity within a civilisation, which is often not even present in a community. It is perhaps misleading and inadvisable therefore to view conflict as solely caused by religion as this can serve to hide other political and socio-economic triggers. Esposito cites the threat to identity and socio-cultural values from economic change and the subsequent social dislocation as the reason for the emergence of religious fervour and conflict.[159]

Nevertheless, religion can certainly play a major role in the generation of conflict. It can, if exploited correctly by the political elites, legitimise conflict, by establishing a 'just cause' in the form of a holy war. It provides both the theological motivation for individuals to enter into conflict and is a concept that can easily generate mass support. Religion, like nationalism is also linked to identity. Jeffrey Seul suggests religion is at the core of individual and group identity. His argument centres on 'identity competition' as a cause of intergroup conflict, which he suggests, that it is a product of the high level of commitment required by religious groups coupled with the ease by which group boundaries can be established through religious self-identification.[160] Religion is a key issue in conflict as it can be seen as the fuel, catalyst and spark to protracted violence.

Ideology is a central factor in the generation of armed conflict within the individual not only because it supplies a political agenda for the motivation and justification for violence but more simply because it provides something to recognise, identify with, believe in, and ultimately to fight for. The problems with nationalism and religion are their overtly political connotations, which might serve to obscure other more influential socio-economic causes of conflict. It is very easy and attractive to suggest that the cause of a conflict is nationalism or religion, but whilst this may be an important contributory factor or provide the rallying cry for the fighters, it may not necessarily be the actual root cause of the conflict. Ideology needs to be examined in context with all the other possible root causes of conflict in order to put its contribution to the generation of violence into perspective.

Issues and agendas

The examination of issues and agendas is an attempt to highlight the existence of the causes of conflict that relate directly to the individual. Although many of these have already been examined especially at the structural level, it is important to stress the emphasis conflict studies places on the issues that cause conflict, especially ethnic conflict. The central reason for this approach is because conflict studies seeks to examine the root causes of conflict and demonstrate that when conflict occurs, it is due to multifarious issues and subjective agendas, which are often underwritten by deeper root causes. Mitchell suggests that conflict issues originate as 'positive goals', such as establishing a state or economic gain and 'negative goals' which implies the avoidance of a situation.[161] Similarly, Jabri suggests a typology of conflict issues by dividing them into: 'consensual', which are values actively sought such as territory and resources, and 'disensual' which are belief systems such as religion and ideology.[162]

This approach to conflict at the individual level provides the study of conflict with a natural scepticism of broad quick fix solutions and causational assumptions, and promotes a multi-level and multi-dimensional approach to the root causes that adequately reflect the multi-level complexity of contemporary conflict. Carment and Jones point out that the term ethnic conflict reveals little about the underlying intercommunial tensions and issues that may become ethnic because that is the basis for exclusion and repression.[163] This problem has been tackled by conflict studies, which has provided a number of multi-dimensional approaches to ethnic conflict. Woodhouse and Ramsbotham suggest ethnic conflict is caused by six factors these are 'historical, religious, demographic, political, economic and psychological'.[164] Gurr and Harff suggest a framework theory for explaining conflict, which has a number of variables; these are 'discrimination, group identity, leadership, political environment, state violence, external support, economic status and international factors'.[165]

The employment of a comprehensive examination of all the possible issue and agenda contributory factors for conflict relate directly to the grassroots generation of conflict. It represents an attempt to interpret and understand the aims and goals of individuals. So whilst religion or territory might provide the issue for conflict it is the existence of other possible issue root causes, such as unemployment or loss of property that might actually generate the conflict in the individual. At the structural level I argued that conflict was caused by the structure created by the interaction of the incompatibility of these goals, this level however suggests that by examining the issues it is possible to investigate why they have become agendas for conflict. Conflict issues and agendas are related to the concept of power, not state power that was discussed above but the notion of human power, by which I mean the motivational force behind human action. Coser from the functionalist school argues that conflict is essentially a positive test of power and relative strength between antagonistic parties.[166] Foucault suggests that the mechanism of power combined with perceived knowledge is instrumental in establishing 'regimes of truth'.[167] This concept suggests that individual or group behaviour is affected by power, which consequently influences how truth is perceived. Thus by becoming aware of the source and generation of power, issues that lead to conflict can be identified. This is supported by Fetherston who suggests that the key to understanding social issues, institutions, structures and relationships is provided by understanding power relations.[168] The investigation of the issues in a conflict suggests the existence of multi-dimensional issues as root causes in conflict, which need to be addressed from multi-dimensional perspectives if the conflict is to be understood.

Social psychology

Social-psychological conflict is an examination of the psychological root causes of violence within the individual. A central element in social psychology is attitude. This is also a component of Galtung's conflict triangle,[169] and correlates to the construction of the mental condition of those in conflict. It relates particularly to how they view both the conflict and ultimately the opposition. Miall et al divides attitude into a number of components; these are emotive (feeling), cognitive (belief) and conative (will).[170] Similarly, Mitchell defines conflict attitudes as 'a set of psychological processes and conditions that accompany involvement in conflict'. He separates attitude into 'affective' (emotional, judgemental) and 'perceptual' (cognitive).[171] This implies that the roots of conflict can be exposed via an investigation of the highly subjective and relative psychological construction of the individual in conflict. Whilst this is useful in helping to theorise as to the mindset of the individual in conflict, it is difficult to actually fully understand the psychological construction of such subjective concepts. Furthermore, this theory presupposes a link between the occurrence of violence and the psychological attitude of the combatant.

In a continuation of the frustration-aggression and inherency arguments, many psychologists have argued that the roots of aggression and violence are an innate emotion. Lorenz suggested, 'aggression is psychic energy, a drive that is the basis for all human violence'.[172] He argues that it is located in a territorial and hunter based killer instinct.[173] Simmel suggested the existence, deep in the human psyche of an *a priori* fighting instinct that causes a need for hostility. He points to the ease with which it is possible to inspire distrust, suspicion, over confidence and sympathy and believes that it is this 'hostility drive' of feelings, emotions and impulses that sustains a conflict around objective causes.[174] Freud also argued for the existence of 'thanatos' or the 'death instinct', which he believed became destructive when directed outwards as aggression.[175] These arguments imply that conflict attitude, whilst it remains a potent cause of conflict, is actually an inherent human characteristic that just requires the right conditions to turn it to violence. Tidwell suggests that inherent conflict attitudes are beneficial to the individual as a self-preservation or survival instinct.[176] According to these arguments conflict attitudes existing in the emotional make-up of the individual are potent cause of conflict under the right conditions. Thus Mitchell suggests 'conflict attitudes are common patterns of expectation, emotional orientation and perception which accompany involvement in conflict situations'.[177]

The existence and construction of subjective beliefs can be seen as not only a major cause of conflict but also a factor that can sustain protracted conflict by often prolonging the violence after the original objective reasons for it have long since disappeared. A very helpful study into the underlying process and psychological construction of conflict attitudes is Christopher Mitchell's *Structure of International Conflict*. Mitchell's central argument is that conflict attitudes arise from the common human tendency to develop ways of dealing with stress. He calls this the 'protective psychological process' and suggests a 'cognitive consistency' is achieved by 'selective perception, selective recall and group identification'. Although Mitchell suggests that cognitive consistency is in response to conflict, it can also be seen as both an initial cause and reason for the continuation of conflict. Mitchell also argues selective perception and selective recall is the rejection and suppression of all information that does not conform to the most basic and simple understanding adopted by the individual.[178] The categorisation of information into black and white thinking assists the individual by simplifying a complex or stressful environment. Examples of this include stereotyping of individuals and groups, tunnel vision and dehumanisation. This psychological process also serves to exacerbate the conflict, by employing, for example, uncomplimentary (mirror) images, issue polarisation and the freedom of action differential.[179] Banks suggests that this is an identifiable cause of conflict as each party becomes 'cognitively blind' to the other, by employing different theories based on different beliefs and values, which ultimately influence perceptions.[180]

The other important part of Mitchell's cognitive consistency thesis is 'group identification'. This argument builds upon the ideas discussed above on the role of individual and group identity in the generation of conflict. Mitchell however concentrates on the psychological elements that exist in the differentiation between the 'in-group and out-group'. He suggests that the 'in-group' rationalise their actions with their own reasoned, logical and moral understanding of the situation. Consequently, from their subjective moral stance they perceive their actions in conflict as a reaction to aggression and thus fail to see how any blame for the conflict can be apportioned to them. They consider themselves defensive and seek to galvanise the in-group by projecting the stress of hostility onto outsiders, denying responsibility and avoiding any internal ambiguity of identity. Hence the maxim 'those who are not for us are against us'.[181] Fanon argues that group identity thrives on the actual existence of violence and that this is a further cause of conflict. He suggests that the practice of violence is a source of dignity and empowers the repressed individual and draws members of the group into a cohesive element.[182] Individuals, through acts of violence, can establish their own identity, that of the group and of the enemy, all of which is assumed to be cohesive and homogeneous. This is especially important for the enemy, which is then seen as an uncomplicated focus of hostility. Mitchell suggests that in order to deal with the psychological difficulty of alienating a complete 'people' the 'black top' image is often employed to demonise the leadership and separate it from the repressed or indoctrinated masses.[183]

Further social-psychological causes of conflict are suggested by Vayryen. He highlights the psychological perceptions and resultant misjudgements inherent in the causation of conflict such as the perceived incompatibility of goals and the expected gain or perceived utility of conflict.[184] Lederach suggests that it is the social-psychological perceptions, emotions and subjective experiences that trigger the cycle of violence that leads to deep-rooted self-perpetuating conflict.[185] Dollard in a development of the frustration-aggression theory suggests the existence of 'displaced aggression', as a cause of conflict, which he argues is a cathartic expression of violence against a target other than the actual source of the frustration.[186] Mitchell calls this 'transfer' and 'displacement' and suggests that the generation of aggression might be redirected against something completely unconnected to the original source of aggression.[187] This is the basis for the concept of the scapegoat.

Social-psychological factors or conflict attitudes serve to illustrate important sources of conflict that are encompassed in the entrenched nature of the subjective understanding of conflict by the actors. These factors can serve to not only generate the conflict, but can also cause an increase in the intensity and duration of violence, especially as cognitive opinions over time can become even more polarised and self-fulfilling. This implies that in order to fully understand the roots of conflict it is necessary to penetrate the minds of the actors in conflict.

The multi-level roots of conflict

This chapter has focused on attempting to explain the root causes of conflict by investigating the approaches to it supplied by conflict studies, when viewed from the different perspectives provided by a multi-level analysis. This survey of literature has not produced any definitive reasons or conclusive scientific explanations for the manifestation of conflict nor has it suggested ways of solving it. It has however demonstrated how conflict can be explained and understood from a number of different perspectives. These perspectives or discourses, when taken together provide a very useful multi-level and interdisciplinary approach to understanding conflict. However, it is important to stress that this is a theoretical exercise and these theoretical frameworks are not necessarily complimentary. Each approach provided by each level has a particular use and function. This is argued by Robert Cox, who suggests, 'theory is always for someone and for some purpose'.[188] The state level understands state conflict but cannot recognise non-state or intra-state conflict. This however is provided by the non-state level of analysis, which seeks to explore the role and importance of other actors in conflict as it highlights the nature of the conflictual relationship between the individual and society. This is particularly evident in the examination of functionalism and human needs theory. Further to this approach is the structural level of analysis, which provides an alternative approach to conflict. This discourse is designed to highlight the nature and purpose of the systems in which the actors' perceive they exist; this is demonstrated by considering the structural arguments provided by Marxism. The final level of analysis is the individual; this is intended to focus on the role of the individual and the group in conflict. It allows for example, an examination of the construction of the identity and the effects of ideology as potent conflict generators.

Despite the relative strengths and weaknesses of these different multi-level approaches, whichever perspective or theory of conflict is employed to explain the root causes, regardless of how helpful or illuminating they are in understanding particular causes of conflict. They are all based on particular assumptions and therefore suffer from limitations and restrictions in their approach to conflict.

The conclusion of this roots survey therefore suggests some important findings. First, the causes of conflict, especially contemporary conflict, can be more clearly understood from a comprehensive, multi-level and multi-dimensional perspective. This implies that although different perspectives are employed to understand the roots of conflict, by combining these approaches into a single multi-level framework it might be possible to establish an all-inclusive and wide-ranging explanation of the root causes of conflict. From the perspective of solving conflict this would be invaluable, as it will allow the deep-rooted reasons for conflict to be engaged, addressed and potentially answered. Second, like the survey of terrorism literature in Chapter 1, the survey of conflict studies suggests a general differentiation between approaches for explaining conflict. These can be classed as follows,

1. Orthodox conflict theory is a state-centric approach and relates to the traditional understanding of conflict as inter-state war. It is found in historical texts such as Machiavelli and Von Clauswitz and conventional work by Waltz. It is also the basis for conflict management approaches.
2. Moderate conflict theory can be seen as the conflict resolution approach to conflict. It is a multi-level approach and incorporates theories such as human needs. Its main proponents are researches such as Boulding, Azar, Burton and Galtung.
3. Critical conflict theory is a radical, holistic and multi-dimensional approach to explaining conflict and is found in the work of Linklater, Lederach, Jabri and Richmond.

Thirdly, conflict studies do not really deal extensively with the subject of terrorism, even though it has made considerable advances into explaining non-state conflict it still focuses primarily on war. Conflict studies would definitely benefit from incorporating some of the approaches to explaining terrorism, which were discussed in Chapter 1. This is dealt with in the construction of a comprehensive theoretical framework and is the subject of the next chapter.

3
Conflict and Terrorism: A Comparative Analysis

Introduction

The studies of terrorism and conflict both have a great deal to contribute to helping explain each others root causes – but only if their respective approaches can be applied together. This is particularly significant for the study of terrorism. In this chapter I intend to demonstrate how the root causes of terrorism can be more clearly explained and understood by combining the different approaches of terrorism and conflict studies that were discussed in Chapters 1 and 2. This theoretical exercise is in response to the explanation of terrorism provided by orthodox terrorism discourse. This discourse, as I have argued, monopolises the comprehension of terrorism and has particularly limiting shortcomings in relation to understanding it. The intention of this synthesis therefore is to rethink terrorism by deconstructing the orthodox understanding of the root causes and instead present a broader, more holistic and multi-level approach. This should provide a wider explanation and ultimately a more useful understanding because it will furnish the study of terrorism with greater access to an extensive range of analytical tools that can be used to understand the roots of the problem of terrorism and hopefully help to resolve it.

Part 1 of this chapter will combine the strengths of the different methods for approaching and examining terrorism whilst highlighting the shortcomings and gaps that exist. This will then be compared to conflict studies to discuss how the gaps in terrorism studies can be filled by the approaches and theories provided by conflict theories. As with the first two chapters this will be conducted on a multi-level basis. The result of which should be a comprehensive, multi-level and multi-dimensional study of the roots of terrorism. From this survey it should be possible to construct a theoretical holistic framework that can be applied to terrorist conflicts in order to gain a more advanced understanding of the root causes. This will comprise Part 2 of the chapter. The comprehensive theoretical framework will be 'applied' in Chapter 5 to the Palestinian-Israeli conflict to illustrate how theoretically rethinking terrorism can have a useful practical application for understanding of the roots of the problem. Prior to this comparative multi-level analysis however I will re-establish definitions for terrorism and conflict and briefly discuss if they can be accommodated by each other.

Terrorism and conflict defined

To facilitate a definitional point of departure for this comparative study, it is necessary to compare the definitions of both terrorism and conflict to ascertain if terrorism can be suitably located in conflict, and also if the dominant understanding of conflict encompasses terrorism. In Chapter 1, I defined terrorism as a specific form of violence motivated by a political agenda or more simply as 'lethal political violence'. Simply this is an act of lethal violence that is perpetrated in order to further a political cause or achieve a stated political objective. This definition, as I argued, is useful as it separates the act of violence from the political legitimacy debate, whilst still differentiating it from non-political lethal violence, such as that based on greed or personal gain. It is a definition of a particular type or method of violence and can appear quite narrow in its application. However its usefulness is in explaining the act of violence itself and the relative political consequences. It does not necessarily seek to explain the wider implications, such the context in which the violence occurs, the actors involved or indeed the roots of the violence, as its focus is predominantly political. Notably, the definition I employ does not refer to terror, which is seen by orthodox theory as the basis of the understanding of terrorism. Terror is not used in my adopted definition because it is so closely associated with orthodox terrorism theory and the problems inherent in the subjective moral legitimacy debate, which is synonymous with orthodox terrorism discourse.

In comparison, the classification of conflict I employ for this study seeks to incorporate 'actual or potential violent conflicts which range from domestic conflict situations that threaten to become militarised beyond the capacity of domestic civil police to control, through to full-scale inter-state war'.[1] It is immediately apparent that the application of conflict suggests a much more wide-ranging and broader approach to the manifestation of violence, than terrorism, this is primarily because more advanced approaches to conflict, such as conflict resolution and peacebuilding, seek to incorporate all types of violence, including terrorism, into an extensive definition that can aid multi-level investigation into the causes of the conflict.

Terrorism by the adopted definition of lethal violence in conflict can be relocated into conflict studies. The principal advantage of this would be to open up terrorist conflicts to the multi-level and inter-disciplinary approaches to understanding violence that I discussed in Chapter 2. This relocation would also bring with it the tools of conflict resolution, such peacemaking and peacebuilding, with which progression could be made into understanding the manifestation of terrorism beyond the constraining influence of subjective politics. There are however, tremendous difficulties with this manoeuvre; accepting terrorist violence as conflict could mean in effect bestowing some form of legitimacy on the perpetrators of the violence. Using the above definition of conflict, a state dealing with a group that employs terrorist violence would be forced to concede that the group might have a legitimate reason for the anti-state violence. It could then be classed as a form of asymmetric conflict and could imply recognition of the cause of the group, legitimacy of their actions and combatant status to group members as legitimate soldiers. This would give the group the protection afforded to lawful combatants provided by the Geneva Convention. Arguably, it is this desire for legitimacy that is the principal aim of the majority of terrorist groups. The implications of this are highly problematic, as it would have an immense and probably unacceptable political impact on the formation of state policy, especially anti-terrorist and counter-terrorist strategies, as these policies are based on the monopoly of legitimacy. It is also possible to argue that whilst states might be aware of the roots debate when dealing with terrorist groups, it is in fact incompatible with orthodox terrorism theory, which is employed by states to maintain and defend the political and socio-economic status quo.

Conflict studies are also subject to a legitimacy debate where typically both sides refuse to accept the legitimacy of the other or recognise their claims and are locked into seeking a zero sum solution to the conflict.[2] Terrorist conflicts, without even attempting to relocate the violence, can be seen as conflict involving the use of terrorism between groups contesting the rights to legitimacy. A situation not unlike one found in most conflicts. Despite this conclusion, the question that needs to be asked is can orthodox conflict studies actually accommodate terrorism? Terrorism by definition is violence with a political object-ive, and conflict or war, as Von Clausewitz famously stated, is the con-tinuation of politics by other means and is intrinsically 'an act of violence intended to compel our opponent to comply with our will'.[3] Although this initial comparison suggests an easy symbiosis, the prob-lem arises in the method of violence. In the subjective moral debate, conflict and war is legitimised 'legal' violence whereas terrorist violence is 'illegitimate' and 'unlawful'. This line of argument suggests that ter-rorism can only exist outside conflict, where the legitimacy of conflict is recognised by both sides. Terrorism cannot by the normative definition of unlawful violence, occur in a declared war that is accepted by both parties. This suggests that in the normative understanding of terrorism both sides might be employing terrorist violence against one another in the form of terrorism and counter/anti-terrorism and because it is not a recognised legitimate conflict both sides claim the other is acting illegit-imately and unlawfully and therefore feel able to justify their own actions. Conversely, in war, both sides might be employing terrorist tactics but this is seen as legitimate violence within in the realm of conflict.

However, not all conflict is recognised as legitimate by all those involved. Although the main arguments inherent in this subjective debate of terrorism were discussed in Chapter 1, it is important to re-iterate here that terrorism is often characterised by the relative differ-ence in how it is defined and understood. Typically each side defines and understands terrorism relative to the others actions and not their own, hence they can both define terrorism as illegitimate and unlawful but as both claim legitimacy through their relative understandings, they see the others' action as terrorist and not their own. Furthermore, terrorism and conflict are subject to an inside/outside debate.[4] Those on the 'outside' viewing the violence deem it as terrorist in nature while those who employ it on the 'inside' see it as conflict.

It would seem that orthodox conflict cannot accommodate orthodox terrorism unless it sheds its relative and subjective understanding, but then it will cease to be orthodox terrorism. This debate then poses the question, if terrorism studies cannot be accommodated by conflict studies should it be left in its own subjective and relative moral under-standing and not relocated? Although this approach aids the forces of state and underwrites the policies of counter and anti-terrorism, it will leave the phenomenon of terrorism where it has been since the study began: without a roots debate and in an intractable, unapproachable and largely unsolvable position.

Perhaps orthodox conflict can in fact accommodate terrorism under the alternative definition of terrorism as 'lethal political violence' by considering the targets of violence. Lethal violence directed against 'civilians' (those who are neither uniformed combatants, militias or members of the establishment and who for the purpose of this argument, can be regarded as 'innocent civilians',) can be deemed violence or even crime against humanity.[5] This is a characteristic often solely attributed to terrorism and is where the link between terrorism and conflict exists, at the root of an ambiguous relationship located in the legitimacy debate.[6] Lethal violence against individuals outside the matrix of legitimised conflict can be seen as terrorism, however lethal violence against individuals or in this case civilians or non-combatants within conflict is not necessarily viewed as terrorism. O'Sullivan points out that 'World War Two did much to eliminate distinction between combatant and non-combatant by legitimising the deliberate massacre of civilians'.[7] Although a form of legality does exist in conflict, as war crime under the Geneva Conventions and Human Rights Acts, without doubt the greatest casualties of war and conflict are civilians. In a study of armed conflict since 1945 it was estimated that eighty-four per cent of those killed since 1945 were civilians.[8] It would seem that deliberately targeting civilians in 'legitimate' conflict, subjective or otherwise is acceptable but outside of this it is not. Wilkinson argues that terrorist campaigns inherently involve deliberate attacks on civilian targets and are analogous to war crimes.[9] This suggests that if some form of legality is invoked, either the violence is occurring outside the framework of legitimate conflict or inside a subjectively legitimised conflict. Within this argument the deliberate targeting of civilians within a legitimate conflict or war can be seen as 'legitimate' terrorism, which is in fact conflict. This is supported by the claim that deliberate attacks on civilians in all forms of conflict is fast becoming an accepted norm of contemporary conflict. Mary Kaldor points out that in the past civilian casualties in war have often been assumed to be a consequence or side-effect of the conflict between combatants. However the prevalence of genocide and ethnic cleansing in contemporary conflict suggests that attacking, terrorising and destroying the civilian population might in fact be the actual aim of the conflict.[10]

This comparative definitional debate can be brought up-to-date by considering the 'new' war 'new' terrorism debate. As I have already alluded to, the 'new' war debate[11] suggests the existence of contemporary conflict that is characterised by unstructured, informal and postmodern violence fuelled by hate and fear. In recent contemporary conflicts, legitimised by one side at least, such as Afghanistan in 2002 and Iraq in 2003, combatants in uniform were denied the rights of prisoners of war, and were viewed instead as terrorists suggesting that even with the involvement of structured state armies it is no longer viewed as formal conflict.[12]

This coincides with the 'new' terrorism debate,[13] which suggests that terrorism is perpetrated by unidentified amorphous and nebulous groups and or organisations, who claim no responsibility, seek maximum lethality and are driven by hate and anger. High lethality suggests that the intention of new terrorism is synonymous with the intention of conflict, to maximise the number of people killed. Although it is consistent with the orthodox understanding of terrorism that non-combatant individuals are often the targets of terrorist violence, it is perhaps important to question who actually sees them as innocent civilians or non-combatants. The perpetrators of the violence may not consider the targets innocent civilians, as is often the case in conflict. This is certainly characteristic of the Palestinian-Israeli conflict, and as Rubenstein points out, 'attacking unarmed civilians makes perfect sense to nationalists at war'.[14] It is the recipients of the violence whose relative claim to legitimacy and non-recognition of the conflict lead them to employ the traditional terrorism discourse, and try to delegitimise the violence away from conflict and towards the orthodox understanding of terrorism. This is particularly a state employed discourse, but is also employed by non-state groups.[15]

The question remains how the actors themselves see their acts of violence. As symbolic acts, intended to engender fear, intimidation and terror in a population, as orthodox terrorism theory suggests, or simply as acts of violence in a perceived conflict, the asymmetric nature of which forces them to resort to a particular method of violence to kill as many of the enemy as possible. Conclusions to this are often contradictory. Some Palestinian actors state that the aim of violence is to 'establish a balance of fear',[16] which is concurrent with orthodox terrorism theory. Others state that it is simply to 'fight and defend the homeland',[17] which is perhaps orthodox conflict theory. This question is also relevant to the relative understanding of the killing of civilians. Buzan argues that the 'exclusion of civilians from the definition of the enemy contrasts markedly with the West's behaviour until recently'. He illustrates this argument with reference to Hiroshima, Nagasaki and Vietnam.[18] In addition, in a translated video interview following the destruction of the World Trade Centre, Bin Laden states; 'we calculated in advance the number of casualties from the enemy who would be killed'.[19] This implies that the study of acts of terrorism and a great deal of terrorism literature is more applicable to the study of conflict. Terrorism has become a substitute for war as it allows an asymmetric conflict to exist by providing low cost, high yield violence via modern technology and communications that can almost achieve parity with conventional forces. Bowyer Bell argues, '[T]o divide up the war, the campaigns, as military or conspiratorial, protracted popular war or urban terror is to mingle intensity and means, time and opportunity'.[20] Interestingly, all but one of thirty-one major armed conflicts in 1993–95 listed by Schmid and Jongman featured the killing of non-combatant civilians.[21]

Conflict and terrorism studies are both in crisis. This is revealed in the uncertainty of the post-Cold War, post-September 11th and post-modern world, which is exacerbated by the globalisation debate, the decay of the dominance of the state as an institution, and the rise of the identity and importance of the individual. This is ushering in the possibility of a post and late-Westphalian world order where only by moving away from the rigid state-centric Westphalian system will it be possible to recognise the roots of contemporary conflict, new wars and new terrorism.[22] Conflict studies I would argue, especially moderate and critical approaches, have begun to identify change and have initiated the transition to recognising and dealing with conflict outside of the traditional state-centric and realist understanding. The study of conflict has moved into employing more sophisticated and comprehensive approaches to deal with this so-called new type, such as third and fourth generation multi-dimensional approaches, found in conflict resolution and peacebuilding. Although these approaches are not yet mainstream they exist in the literature as a critical approach and focus on the roots of conflict found in human security and the needs of individuals and non-state actors. Terrorism however, is still locked in the restraints of the moral legitimacy debate and the Cold-War state-centric orthodox and positivist understanding.

The aim of this study is to relocate terrorism out of this relative moral quagmire of 'subjective' politics and into the realm of conflict where it can be seen simply as an act of violence within a wider context. This will allow the understanding of terrorism to develop alongside changes in contemporary conflict and will provide it with access to a roots debate and the whole spectrum of multi-dimensional techniques available for conflict resolution. In the next section (Part 1 of this chapter) I will briefly debate the strengths and weaknesses of the respective theoretical approaches to understanding terrorism and conflict used in Chapters 1 and 2, with the intention of establishing theoretical levels of analysis with which to rethink the roots of terrorism.

Part 1: Rethinking the roots of terrorism: a comprehensive approach

The state level

'States are the creation not of nature but of men'.

Napoleon Bonaparte[23]

The state level of analysis represents the high level, top down, political approach to understanding the phenomenon of terrorism. It is also the most revealing area for investigation because terrorism studies is inextricably linked to the concept of the state. This is clearly shown in orthodox terrorism theory which views terrorism primarily as a threat to the existence of the state. The United States Federal Bureau of Investigation (FBI) defines terrorism as, 'the unlawful use of force or violence against persons or property to intimidate or coerce a government or the civilian population...in the furtherance of political or social objectives'.[24] This understanding is due to the centralised power and the primacy of the state, which enshrines the discourses of sovereignty, and legitimacy, concepts over which the state has a monopoly. From the state perspective the roots of terrorism and the subsequent manifestation of violence lie in the protection and preservation of these concepts. Orthodox terrorism discourse is designed for this purpose, to allow the state to view terrorism as an illegal and illegitimate challenge to authority. This is applicable 'internally' – within a state (governed population) and directed against the state (governing authority), and also 'externally', as a threat to the security or political integrity of a state from another state. It can also exist as terrorism by the state, as a response to perceived internal threats. This is enshrined in the social contract and is enforced by what Eugene Walter calls 'regime terror theory', or state rule by violence and fear.[25]

The difficulty with employing orthodox terrorism theory however is that it is not open to a roots debate[26] and therefore does not engage with or recognise any the underlying causes. It is a mono-dimensional approach that responds to the symptoms and manifestation of violence with the machinery of the state. (Notably, this can often have the reverse effect by increasing the level of reactionary violence and exacerbating the original problem that was causing the violence).

As a result orthodox terrorism studies is trapped at state level by the constraining nature of the legitimacy debate. This is an identifiable gap within the study of terrorism, but one that can be complemented by the approach of conflict studies because a number of conflict theories, applied at state level, question the nature and role of the state in the generation of violence. A debate which terrorism theory fails to engage in.[27] An outcome of this debate regards violence as synonymous with the state and intrinsic to its existence. The implications of this however, suggest that terrorism and violence are so ingrained in the state that the only way to approach and deal with terrorism and conflict on a long-term solution basis is to revaluate the role of the state and even suggest a completely alternative form of political governance and international system.[28] This is clearly a controversial argument, given the primacy and dominance of the state.

Nevertheless, the main implication of employing this hybrid approach of terrorism and conflict studies is to exploit the new approaches for understanding terrorism that arise in the space that is created. The first of these is based upon an examination of the responses the state employs to deal with terrorism. This argument suggests that the state has a primary role in the generation of terrorism due to the response it adopts. In this discourse, terrorism is part of the natural condition of the state, as it is generated, paradoxically, as state terrorism, in response to the threat of terrorism and is used essentially to create order and maintain political power. States that counter the threat of terrorism with the military and legal apparatus of counter terrorism not only deal with terrorism but also simultaneously strengthen and consolidate the power of the state, (although this approach can also generate terrorism in response).[29] The implication of adopting this argument for the roots of terrorism suggests the existence of *inherent terrorism* within the state, implying that terrorism is not only endemic but also vital for the existence of the state and is an engineered commodity that is propagated by orthodox terrorism discourse.

Orthodox terrorism and conflict studies have definite parallels at the state level, as both conflict and terrorism can be employed by the state to bolster its political position and as legitimate military means against opponents. They are both state orientated tools and focus on the political implications of violence by concentrating on state power and the challenges to it from within the state and by other states. Paradoxically, it is also the main response of the state to the threat of conflict and terrorism. By examining the state approach to terrorists it is possible to identify a further cause of terrorism. This is the employment by the state of orthodox terrorism discourse in order to pursue a hidden agenda as a policy of *secondary gain or devious terrorism* against political opponents. Orthodox terrorism theory designates violent political opponents, who have illegitimate designs on state power, as terrorists. The state is therefore able to employ a 'free hand' and legitimately pursue an agenda to eradicate this state opposition, regardless of whether they are actually the cause of the terrorism. This monopoly of legitimised violence allows states to pursue policies of terrorism (counter-terrorism) against their opponents both inside and outside state boundaries because of the legitimacy bestowed on them by terrorism discourse. By examining how a state approaches actual terrorists it is possible to demonstrate how instrumental the state is in propagating the manifestation of *devious terrorism* – a policy of secondary gain to eradicate and neutralise any threat to the state with whatever means are available.[30]

The employment of a recognised understanding of terrorism by states in order to tackle political dissention within its borders is becoming increasingly apparent in many countries after the declared 'war on terrorism', which effectively legitimised state violence against 'terrorists'. *Devious terrorism*, is perhaps most apparent in the Palestinian-Israeli conflict, where legitimised state violence is extensively employed inside and outside established state borders. But it is also evident in Indonesia (against Jemaah Islamiyah), in the Philippines (against the Abu Sayyaf), and in Russia (against the Chechens). It is also possible to suggest that many states are free riding the terrorist discourse of al Qaeda in order to allow the employment of devious terrorism against their own indigenous terrorist groups. This is again illustrated by Israel's use of pre-emptive assassinations against Hamas, which they justify as the 'war on terror'.[31] It is also apparent that in state polices of counter terrorism, human and individual rights and freedoms are often sacrificed in the fight against terrorism. This suggests that if a state employs an approach to terrorists that is terrorist in its nature, the state can be firmly located in the root causes of terrorism.

A third area of examination that becomes apparent when conflict theories are applied to the state is located in how the state approaches terrorism. The existence of a terrorist threat is useful for the state as it helps bolster its political standing and bestows on it extra political powers over and above those existing in the social contract. For example, terrorist situations often see the introduction of emergency powers.[32] These give the state authority to pursue the threat using methods that might ordinarily undermine the basic individual human rights and freedoms. The threat of terrorism in a state has a similar effect to a state in conflict; it makes it more cohesive and powerful, implying that states can employ terrorism discourse in order to pursue a policy of *terrorism management*. This is a controversial argument and suggests that the state does not employ a roots debate with the intention of facilitating terrorism resolution, as this would loosen the state grip on political power. Instead the state aims to propagate terrorism and manage it in order to maintain tight political control of the population. By examining how the state actually approaches terrorism and what methods it adopts to deal with it, it is possible to ascertain the role of the state in the root causes of terrorism.

It is evident that the current approach to understanding terrorism adopted by the state and enshrined in orthodox terrorism discourse is beneficial to the state as it fails to question the role of the state in the generation of terrorism. It also bestows absolute legitimacy on the state to justify its actions against a terrorist threat regardless of the reasons or root causes. The application of conflict theories questions the role of the state and in particular the response and approach of the state to terrorism and terrorists. Conflict studies identify and locate the roots of terrorism in the institutions of state, particularly in the relationship between the state (governing authority) and the governed population, and the state and other states. This produces a number of important implications for the understanding of the roots of terrorism, and suggests the existence within the state of *inherent, devious* and *management terrorism*.

The non-state actor level

> The condemned social order has not been built up on paper and ink and a combination of paper and ink will never put an end to it.
>
> Joseph Conrad, *The Secret Agent*[33]

The non-state actor level of analysis moves the focus of the roots debate away from the centrality of the state, although not completely, and onto the role of the non-state actor. As I discussed above, orthodox terrorism discourse locates the cause of terrorism in the violent challenge or threat to the state, which it sees as originating from within the state itself or from another state, (the non-state group is not seen as a separate entity from the state). The non-state level however is an approach that allows recognition of the actor as a terrorist player independent of the state.[34] This level of analysis has become increasingly important in the contemporary world, particularly since the end of the Cold War, where the perceived role of the non-state actor in the generation of political violence has greatly increased. Hoffman proposes theories associated with the Grey Area Phenomenon[35] to suggest that terrorism can be located in 'threats to the stability of nation states by non-state actors and non-governmental processes and organisations'.[36] This is also particularly prevalent in the light of the threat of terrorism from al Qaeda type organisations, who seems to exist as nebulous networks of individuals and groups who bear no relation to their indigenous state or nation. The role of the state however should not be overlooked as it represents the central obstacle to the ambitions of the non-state group and is a major determinant of armed struggle.[37] This is supported by Wilkinson, who differentiates between *state* and *factional* terror, but focuses on the challenge of non-state groups employing terrorism against the liberal democratic state.[38]

The emphasis of understanding terrorism is often seen as a political battle where the power seekers target the power holders, who are predominantly represented by the state. Although more moderate approaches in terrorism studies have pointed to attempts to use terrorism to influence political communities or social behaviour,[39] the ramifications of this still reflect on the holders of political power. So whilst it is valuable to examine the political causes of terrorism first, the understanding of the roots of terrorism needs to move beyond the constraints of the political. This is because despite the ability of orthodox terrorism studies to locate terrorism in the conflict generated by the dynamics of intra-state interaction and the relationships between non-state groups, it takes little or no account of any other reasons why the violence might occur, other than the pursuit of political power. This detracts from identifying the individual motivations of groups and from consideration of the political and socio-economic situation, which might be something other than a direct challenge to political authority.

This gap in the understanding of terrorism can be filled by applying social conflict theories contained in conflict studies because although conflict manifests itself in the political, it has its roots in the relationship between self and society and is therefore a social condition and that needs to be located in the realm of social conflict. Social conflict theory applied to terrorism studies suggests that terrorism has a constructive purpose and a political and social utility. This is supported by the conflict theories contained in functionalism,[40] instrumentalism[41] and constructivistism.[42] All of which argue that violence can have a purpose, such as acting as a catalyst for necessary and positive social change, or forming a channel through which to express and alleviate political, social and economic inequality. The implications of this approach for the roots of terrorism suggest that the causes of the violence can be located in political, social and economic grievances. Therefore by questioning the nature of the social order and the broad economic, social and political perspectives and by analysing the function of the violence it may prove possible, as Vayryen argues, to provide the key to understanding the cause of the violence.[43]

This discourse suggests that conflict is a function inherent in society and can be located in all social relationships. Terrorism can therefore be understood by an investigation of the established social order. This might help to explain the character and intentions of the actors and the nature of goals they seek. For example, terrorism, viewed through the prism of functionalism is the demand for social change located in the interaction between actors in society where human action is a product of human decisions within the context of social relations.[44] The approaches of social conflict theory effectively provide space in which it is possible to re-examine terrorism and project the potential cause of the violence outside the political realm and into a social spectrum.

However, there are a number of assumptions associated with applying the conflict theory discourse to the roots of terrorism debate. For example, by investigating the function of the terrorism the assumption is made that terrorism has a purpose. This presupposes the existence of a social grievance or perceived injustice within the non-state actor that perpetrates the violence. It also suggests that if terrorism exists in the relationship between actors seeking change in society then it is an inherent part of society. According to Vayryen, 'society is like conflict; dynamic and in constant change'.[45] Also, by examining further the function of the terrorism, it is possible to establish if the violence is intended to destroy the existing framework of society or merely change it, as violence for reform or revolution.[46] By implication therefore it is possible to identify the existence in functional social conflict of either *revolutionary terrorism* or *reactionary terrorism*, which have an agenda for either destroying or reforming the existing social system.

An additional conflict theory that can be employed at this level is human needs theory. This represents a further attempt to move away from the political and relocate the roots of terrorism in the socio-economic framework of society. Human needs theory suggests the existence of a set of socio-biological human needs that require satisfaction on a hierarchical basis; if these needs remain unfulfilled the actors will resort to violence. As Burton suggests, 'If attempts are made to sub-ordinate individual values to social values because it is not possible to enforce social values that are inconsistent to human needs, the response will be damaging both to the individual and the social system'.[47]

The advantage with human needs theory is that it reveals the rela-tionship between the individual (or the particular non-state group) and society. Individual needs are pursued within the confines of a value system or society, if these needs become frustrated, methods such as violence are employed that are outside the established norms. It also concentrates attention on the needs and values of the individuals who make up different communities and organisations within society and questions their individual aspirations and their subsequent relation-ship with society. Human needs theory has also featured in a number of useful approaches for understanding conflict by providing a focus on the nexus between the individual and society in the roots of conflict debate. For example, Azar suggests, 'grievances resulting from need deprivation are usually expressed collectively and thus failure to redress these grievances by the authorities cultivates a niche for pro-tracted social conflict'.[48]

The application of human needs discourse to the gap identified in roots of terrorism debate, provides a useful way to unlock the stale political contest and provide a route into the causes of terrorism located in the non-state group. The implications for reassessing the roots of terrorism by applying this theory are revealing. They suggest that the manifestation of terrorist violence implies that individual needs are in some way frustrated, suggesting society can no longer satisfy these needs and the established norms of society have been transcended. By employing the basic safety needs identified by Azar, which are security, identity, representation and equality,[49] and apply-ing them to a terrorist non-state actor it is possible to suggest a possible correlation between these needs and the manifestation of terrorism. This implies that if the suggested safety needs of individual non-state actors are unsatisfied they might generate *grievance terrorism* which requires inclusion and consideration in the roots of terrorism debate.

Another useful social conflict theory is relative deprivation.[50] This discourse complements human needs theory and suggests that vio-lence develops in society between groups or individuals who perceive a relative imbalance; politically, economically (and) or socially between what they should have and what they actually have. This discourse is useful because it focuses attention on the perceived differences in the status of non-state actors suggesting that if the actor feels deprivation in relation to society as a whole or another actor then this is a cause of conflict. As Gurr suggests, '[C]onflict is a condition in which the source of the discrepancy between value expectation and capabilities is another group competing for the same values'.[51] The theory of relative deprivation can also be applied to terrorism in an attempt to fill the gap produced by the lack of explanation of the socio-economic roots causes of the political violence. The implications for explaining terrorism by using the relative deprivation discourse are such that the manifestation of terrorism can be attributed to some form of disparity between actors in society, (human needs discourse is subjective to the individual, whereas deprivation is a perceived situation relative to others). This suggests that the cause of terrorism could be located in the relative perceptions of the belligerent actors to each other and society in general, thus existing as *deprivation terrorism*. Hence, '[T]he potential for political violence is a function of the degree to which such discontents are blamed on the political system and its agents'.[52]

The roots of terrorism at the non-state actor level can be clearly illustrated by the application of discourses from conflict studies, particularly social conflict theory. It is perhaps important to point out here that this study is also a critique of orthodox terrorism theory and whilst some of these approaches, particularly relative deprivation, appear in terrorism studies, albeit as moderate terrorism theory[53] they are not adopted by the mainstream orthodox approach. This is primarily because they are incompatible with the relative legitimacy debate upon which orthodox terrorism theory is based. Wilkinson dismisses them by arguing that theories of frustration and aggression and relative deprivation are too general and cannot explain why some groups in similar conditions become violent and others do not.[54]

Although it is very important not to completely discount the influence of politics on the generation of terrorism, it is helpful, as I have illustrated above, to widen the debate and relocate conventional terrorism theory into the realm of social conflict. This will allow identification of possible causes of violence that exist in the relationship between actors in society as a social phenomenon involving governments, communities and individuals.[55] The implications that exist for understanding terrorism by applying conflict theories highlight the roots of terrorism as existing in the nature of the socio-economic relationship between individuals, groups and communities within society and imply alternative root sources of terrorism, these are *functional (revolutionary/reactionary)*, *grievance* and *deprivation terrorism*.

The structural level

> Colonialism is violence in its natural state...and will only yield when confronted with greater violence.
>
> Franz Fanon, *The Wretched of the Earth.*[56]

This section represents an examination of the roots of terrorism at the structural level of analysis. This approach complements the last two levels and seeks to explore the nature of the relationship between the actor (state/non-state) and the structure, a link identified as influential in the causes of conflict.[57] Orthodox terrorism discourse locates the structural roots of terrorism firmly in the political sphere, often in the guise of ideology, and associates the structural roots of terrorism as existing as a violent reaction to an oppressive political system or situation. Terrorist theorist-practitioners such as Mao, Che Guevara and Marighella recommended employing terrorist violence to over-throw repressive regimes and gain independence or freedom. This ideology has its roots in the work of Marx and the struggle between the oppressed and the oppressor. Unsurprisingly Marxism has featured heavily in the political ideology of many terrorist groups.[58] This theme of violence in response to political oppression was also con-tinued by Sorel,[59] Fanon,[60] Sartre[61] and Camus,[62] all of whom pro-vided an attractive justification for the use of terrorism to overthrow an oppressive political system and gain personal freedom. Fanon sug-gested, 'the last shall be the first only after a murderous and decisive struggle'.[63] These writers however are not entertained by orthodox ter-rorism theory and be can be classed in terrorism studies as radical ter-rorism theory. For example, Wilkinson dismisses and heavily criticises Fanon, Sartre and other 'situationalists' for having a great significance in the development of terrorist thought and for glorifying violence and terror as an end in itself. Sartre, he suggests, 'created a positive ideology of terror'.[64]

Although orthodox terrorism discourse is useful in explaining the influence of the political structural causes of terrorism, it does not often venture any further and fails to provide sufficient analysis of any other potential structural causes. Areas that lack consideration in orthodox theory are the possible structural influences inherent in society, history, culture and socio-economics. Although routes into these areas have begun under moderate terrorism discourse,[65] they are far from extensive and still display a large void in comparison to the approaches provided by conflict studies.

This gap in the understanding of terrorism can be bridged by conflict studies, which provides a number of useful approaches. The first example of this is an examination of the historical and cultural context of conflict. This is provided by structural conflict theory, which identifies causes of conflict that are based on the culture and history of a region and the possibility of the existence of a culture of violence. Both Fanon and Sartre argue for the endemic existence of violence as an omnipotent structural force in society, one that is the cohesion to all social and political relationships and gives meaning and purpose to political action. Fanon uses the colonial relationship between native and settler to suggest that violence is an inherent part of the culture.[66] This permanent structural undercurrent of violence represented by a spiral of violence and counter violence can also be exacerbated by the historical and cultural context. Bowyer Bell describes this as an 'arena' or 'ecosystem', in which 'violence is generated due to history, culture, vulnerability and possibility'.[67] This implies that violence can be generated and prolonged by the continuity provided by historical and cultural memory,[68] which suggests that some regions are more historically and culturally conducive to the generation of terrorism and conflict than others. Conflict studies employs the techniques provided by cultural analysis[69] to approach this question, which although established on a number of assumptions, suggests that an analysis of the cultural influences inherent in a particular society can reveal how much influence they have on the manifestation of violence. This implies that the particular history and culture of a region enshrined in a society might exist as the primary cause of conflict and terrorism. This is an area of particular relevance to the Palestinian-Israeli conflict and will be discussed at length in Chapter 5.

Establishing a culture of violence debate as a structural cause of terrorism and employing cultural analysis as a tool for examining societies in conflict, draws attention away from the political debate and into an investigation of cultural and historical influences, which can be very powerful in the generation of terrorism and the natural recourse to violence. The implications for using this approach is to suggest that the manifestation of terrorism presupposes the existence of structural historical and cultural influences for the use of violence in the form of a *cultural terrorism*. Any investigation into the causes of terrorism in a particular region therefore requires the careful examination of the cultural and historical influences of violence in order to understand the roots of terrorism.

A further structural cause of conflict is systemic. This relates to the relationship and interaction of the actors with one another and is characterised by actor behaviour. This creates the apparent system when viewed from the 'outside', such as the interaction of states with one another and the creation of a perceived international system. An examination of the actors in conflict from 'outside' is provided in conflict studies through the study of 'conflict behaviour'.[70] By investigating how the actors relate to each other, the nature of the system and the structure of the causes of conflict can be investigated. The implications of this approach suggest that by adopting an 'objective' examination of the behaviour of the actors involved it is possible to develop an understanding of the structural nature of the system in which terrorism is being generated. The difficulty with this approach however is that the interpretation of the behaviour of the actors depends upon which ontological framework or discourse is adopted to understand the actions, by this rationale it is not possible to have an 'objective' view. As Walker points out 'attempts to think otherwise about political possibilities are constrained by categories and assumptions that contemporary political analysis is encouraged to take for granted'.[71] This argument is illustrated by the problems inherent in the methodology of positivism and suggests that although the roots of terrorism can be attributed to the interpreted behaviour of actors and the assumed system in which they operate, it is perhaps important to be aware of the theoretical framework that is used to interpret the behaviour of terrorist actors. This approach means that it is the observed behaviour of the actors, within an acknowledged discourse, that creates the system in which the roots of terrorism are located, and if this is the case, it suggests the existence of *systemic terrorism*.

A complementary approach to this is an assessment of the 'inside' structural causes and is facilitated by an examination of the situation or the subjective understanding of the causes of terrorism by investigating the terrorist view of the conflict. In this approach, provided by conflict studies, structural influences are examined from the point of view of the actor and how their perception of the system or structure of the conflict influences their actions. Mitchell argues that conflict situations develop due to 'mutually incompatible goals that are mismatched against social values and structures'.[72] This implies that actors perceive the existence of a conflict occurring between the attainment of their goals and the opposing incompatible nature of the system that cannot accommodate these aims. By applying a further part of

Galtung's conflict triangle, 'contradiction', which is 'conflict situation', and is defines as 'the actual or perceived incompatibility between actors',[73] it is possible to investigate the conflict structure from the inside. This approach examines the relative and subjective understanding of the conflict as a perceived situation that is created by the interaction of the actors' goals or aims and the perceived existing structure of the system. This it can be argued can create the structural reasons for conflict and terrorism that can exist as *situational terrorism.*

The problem with this approach is that the conflict can become a subjective reality for the actor, as both the goal incompatibility and the nature of the incumbent 'system' are perceived. The conflict may be unintelligible to those outside the society or to those employing a different theoretical perception; this is identified by della Porta who suggests the existence of a 'social construction of reality'. She argues that terrorism cannot be understood unless the interaction is taken into account between the structural conditions and the subjective reality.[74] This argument is also endorsed by Wardlaw[75] and Bowyer Bell.[76] However, it is a useful conflict approach to apply to terrorism studies as it advocates an examination of the terrorist's view of the conflict and therefore intends to establish the cause of the violence directly from the actor. This will help to explain the perceived structural causes of terrorism, as it will cast light on both the nature of the perceived goal incompatibility and the structure of the perceived system. Examination of this area is vital if a route is to be established for understanding the root causes of terrorism.

The final area of investigation into structural issues is an examination of the socio-economic environment or socialisation. This is an attempt to investigate the structural causes of conflict from a socio-economic perspective and is an examination of the relationship between the actor and the socio-economic environment. Terrorism studies, particularly the moderate approaches, have suggested socio-economic factors that can potentially contribute to the manifestation of violence, such as social dislocation, urbanisation, modernisation, immigration, unemployment and poverty.[77] Although some of these factors also relate to the satisfaction of human needs discussed above, establishing human needs or relative deprivation as a cause of terrorism implies that the actors are perhaps aware of the socio-economic disparity and therefore identify it as unsatisfied needs or social inequality. By investigating socio-economics as a structural cause of terrorism, the assumption is made that the actors are affected by the system or structure but are perhaps unaware of the forces acting on them. An examination of the structural environment should help to identify deep-seated and underlying socialisation issues that generate long-standing conflicts and acts of terrorism, such as institutionalised socio-economic discrimination and inequality.

By applying some of the approaches provided by conflict studies it is possible to explore the structural influence of socio-economics on the causes of violence. As Azar suggests protracted social conflict is rooted in socio-economic depravity and underdevelopment.[78] In addition Maill et al suggest that there is a direct correlation between absolute levels of underdevelopment and violent conflict.[79] Also, economics in the form of a weak economy, poor resource base and relative deprivation can be cited as a direct cause of conflict.[80] The implications of this for understanding the roots of terrorism suggest that by examining the nature of the socio-economic environment it is possible to claim the existence of *socio-economic terrorism.*

However, there are problems with this approach, as the link between terrorism and low socio-economics is not continually proven. Krueger and Maleckova suggest that any direct connection between poverty and terrorism is probably weak and they attribute the cause to political conditions.[81] There are also a number of examples of manifestations of terrorism that have appeared in developed first world.[82] But whilst this does not repudiate the theory it is possible to argue that socio-economic depravity can exist for a particular group regardless of the socio-economic condition of the host state. This debate will be examined further in Chapter 5, in the example of the Palestinian-Israeli conflict.

Orthodox terrorism discourse at the structural level is predominantly located in the political. This is complemented by the application of some chosen theories from conflict studies that lead the roots of terrorism debate into the realm of political and socio-economic structure. This helps to provide an explanation of the roots of terrorism in relation to the historical and cultural context, as *cultural terrorism.* Also the nature of the system, viewed from 'outside' and generated by the behaviour of the actors, is *systemic terrorism.* Complementing this is an examination of the conflict situation, which focuses on the terrorist view of the conflict and explores the perceived understanding held by the actors of each other and the incumbent system. This yields an 'inside' view of the roots of terrorism, which it can be argued, produces *situational terrorism.* Lastly, an investigation is provided into the environment in order to establish if socio-economic structural forces are generating terrorism, as *socio-economic terrorism.*

The individual level

> Warfare's finality lies in the work of the hands
>
> Homer, *The Iliad*[83]

The individual level is the final level of analysis in this examination of the roots of terrorism. This approach seeks to investigate and ultimately locate the role of the human individual in the generation of terrorism because '[W]ar is a consequence of human actions and human decisions'.[84] Although moderate terrorism studies develops an investigation into the individual human causes of terrorism[85] it is predominantly concerned with explaining the political role of the individual. Bowyer Bell suggests that the ideological motivation of the individual is a useful way to understand the cause of terrorism. He argues that all terrorists have an ideology of action that is encompassed in what he calls 'the dream' which is the root of the ideological motivation and is the source of the perceived legitimacy of the political claim and justification for the use of violence.[86] This approach allows for a direct examination of the ideological motivation or belief system and ideas of the individual terrorist.

Whilst this ideology or mindset might identifiably exist as the individual or group political motivation and can be seen as the cause of terrorism, investigation into the roots of terrorism requires an examination of further motivations in order to establish if there are other deeper socio-economic or structural forces that create the necessity for the generation of a political ideology of action. Orthodox terrorism studies focus on the political ideology of individual terrorists, such as religion, which is often portrayed as the sole cause and in some cases a substitute for political ideology.[87] The problem with the approach of orthodox terrorism theory is that it concentrates on the political dimension of religion and fails to investigate other possible areas that might prove to be an underlying cause of terrorism.[88] Although it is important to consider the importance of religion as a cause of terrorism it does provide an easy and quick fix solution to explaining the manifestation of terrorism, without recourse to a roots debate. Although this might be the intention of the users of the orthodox terrorism discourse, who may seek to obscure the underlying socio-economic causes of the violence or who intend to discredit religion itself. The criticism remains that orthodox discourse does not adequately consider the deeper social or cultural roots of the individual in violence.

Applying conflict studies can fill this gap in the understanding of terrorism by providing a number of alternative approaches. These have a far greater socio-economic and cultural emphasis than the political orientation of terrorism studies and seek to locate the causes of violence firmly on the individual in society. The most useful approach for examining the ideology and mindset of the terrorist individual is incorporated into identity theory.[89] This is based on the existence of individual identity and forms the basis of social identity theory,[90] which is a very useful tool for exposing alternative reasons for violence between groups of different identities. Social identity theory can be applied to religion,[91] as the considered mainspring of terrorism, in order to uncover the roots of terrorism. Consequently, the causes of violence can be just as easily located in the identity of the individual and the group as with the immediate and often more obviously stated cause, such as religion. This suggests that it is possible to locate the causes of religious terrorism not just in the existence of religion itself but also in the identity needs of those individuals involved in religious violence. The problem with this approach is similar to the criticism levelled at human needs theory, that the identity needs represent a theoretical set of socio-biological needs that are difficult to substantiate. However, merely by suggesting that the roots of terrorism might exist beyond the political, progress is made into examining the deeper root causes.

Identity theory is also useful for approaching the subject of ethnicity and ethnonationalism and is often cited as a further central cause of terrorism and violence in both terrorism and conflict studies.[92] However, terrorism studies whilst recognising the influence of identity is preoccupied with the political motivation of ethnonationalism, which although important is not necessarily the sole cause of terrorism. Conflict studies highlights the existence of the ethnic group which exposes the existence of a collective culture, and can encapsulate shared origins, values, language, religion, homeland, and history.[93] Importantly, this categorisation of people occurs from both inside and outside the group.[94] By examining ethnic violence with identity theory it is possible to suggest the existence of political or socio-economic threats that galvanise group identity, as It can be argued that the existence of an ethnic group suggests a group with security fears, unfulfilled needs or a political or socio-economic agenda.[95]

The approach of conflict studies is important as it serves to highlight the existence of social forces in the generation of violence. Nevertheless, it is also important to consider the influence of political ideology, such as nationalism, which is a powerful motivator of terrorism. This can mobilise and in some cases radicalise the socially deprived and threatened individual or group with a political ideology, giving a sense of direction and justification for violence. Just as ethnicity is a grassroots phenomenon, so nationalism can be seen as a top down controlling and motivating political influence. The value of combining terrorism and conflict approaches in this study is in the wider debates drawn in by a holistic approach. For example, in the manifestation of ethnic terrorism, consideration must be made of the political ideology employed to generate and justify the violence, such as religion or nationalism but at the same time an examination must be conducted of the social forces that are generating the grassroots movement of the individual that is committing the terrorism. A holistic approach helps to identify how terrorism can be generated by ethnic entrepreneurs, who under the guise of nationalism or religion are exploiting the unfulfilled needs of an ethnic group for their own political agendas.

The implications for explaining terrorism at the individual level suggest that terrorism can be generated by a political ideology that is employed with the express intention of motivating and justifying the violence of the individual for the pursuit of political power. Foucault calls these regimes of truth.[96] By examining the existence of regimes of truth or ideological belief systems it is possible to understand the manifestation of violence because by identifying the source and generation of power the root causes of terrorism can be unearthed. This suggests the existence of *ideological terrorism*. In addition, it is also possible to argue for the existence of *identity terrorism*, which is violence, generated at the socio-economic and cultural grassroots level that is based on unsatisfied identity needs and can underwrite religious or ethnonationalist violence.

A further cause of terrorism within the individual is the generation of a mindset or individual ideology that relates directly to a particular issue, this generates violence by a particular group for a specific cause. Individuals can feel so affected by a single issue that they are provoked into acts of terrorism in order to remedy it. This is often how orthodox terrorism theory views a terrorist, and argues controversially that this type of political violence, as single-issue terrorism;[97] is not open to a roots debate.[98] Whilst it is very important to examine the existence of an actual issue or particular cause of the violence, it is debatable if the contribution of orthodox terrorism theory in this area is useful, if it eschews a roots debate. Whilst consideration of a single issue should not be overlooked, it can often obscure other underlying reasons or causes of violence that might be located at the individual level, such as socio-political issues. However, this might be the intention of the employment of the orthodox discourse, to focus concentration on a particular issue in order to deal with it and thus avoid the difficulties involved in opening up a wider roots debate.

The application of conflict studies is intended to move away from this mono-dimensional interpretation and look for roots in a multi-dimensional approach. The study of conflict can provide an approach into understanding this area by establishing 'consensual'[99] issues as conflict issues, which can be seen as the goals, aims, objectives or intentions of combatants and can range from specific localised issues that trigger violence to large scale disputes such as those over land or resources. Although this approach considers the conflict issues, the important difference is that this approach allows the roots of the terrorism to be investigated beyond any immediate and obvious cause of violence. A roots debate can also provide alternative methods for dealing with the violence; attempts at conflict resolution for example, look beyond the intractable issue that is believed to be causing the conflict.

There is a problem however with the conflict study approach because altering the focus of the terrorism may only serve to detract from the real cause of the violence, which might simply be a single issue. Also single issues that generate terrorism may simply be a particular issue existing within the mind of the individual and are therefore unintelligible to anyone attempting to deal with the violence. It is perhaps also important to question and problematise the multi-dimensional approach, as it is essential to ensure that the vast array of other potential causes of terrorism considered in this study do not obscure the motive which could prove to be the main driving force behind the violence: the impenetrable reason of an individual. The middle ground between terrorism and conflict studies, which is the advantage of this holistic study, is to include in any examination of the causes of terrorism an investigation into the existence of issues and to include them into any analysis of the violence alongside the other potential factors that generate terrorism. A holistic framework for approaching terrorism should therefore include an examination of the actual or perceived conflict issues suggesting that *issue terrorism* might exist alongside other reasons that generate terrorism in the individual.

The last area for investigation at this level is the social-psychological causes of terrorism. This is a continuation of the examination of the mindset of the individual and probes for psychological causes.

Moderate terrorism theory in this realm provides useful investigation into the psychological composition of the individual terrorist. It concentrates on the existence of the construction of a subjective or perceived reality within the individual and serves to provide an understanding and justification for the actions of the terrorist in pursuit of the subjective and relative truth.[100] This process of investigation of the roots of terrorism has also progressed into group dynamics and examines the dynamics of like-minded individuals existing in an enclosed and socially isolated subjective world which serves to strengthen and self-perpetuate the collective understanding and alternative reality.[101] Terrorism studies also suggests violence is generated by individuals as, displacement and diffusion of responsibility,[102] cathartic symbolism – as a substitute focus of aggression for more complicated political or socio-economic reasons[103] and also as violence as an end in itself, to strengthen the political cause and cohesion of a group.[104] In addition to these rational psychological explanations it is also important to incorporate irrational psychological emotions as a cause of terrorism such as fear, hatred, rage and vengeance.

These psychological approaches for understanding the roots of terrorism are very helpful, but as 'moderate terrorism theory' explanations for the root causes they remain on the periphery of terrorism studies. What is required is a complementary theoretical approach in order to apply these theories to the manifestation of terrorism. Conflict studies helps on this area by providing a comprehensive psychological roots of conflict debate. These are represented by Galtung, who integrates this area of examination into the conflict triangle and explores it under the title conflict attitude.[105] Mitchell also examines conflict attitude and divides it into two areas of analysis. 'Emotional', which are irrational judgemental feelings and also 'cognitive', which are perceptual beliefs and a cognitive process for construction of the violent attitude.[106] The emotional approach is useful as it can be used to examine the existence of irrational emotions in the generation of terrorism such as hatred, fear and vengeance. Cognitive is useful because it analyses the development and construction of the subjective or perceptual terrorist understanding, which is a major cause and sustaining component of violence. The formation of terrorism attitude is responsible for the Manichean polarisation of issues and the production of a number of psychological consequences such as scapegoat, tunnel vision, stereotyping and dehumanisation.[107] The implications for the study of terrorism from combining and applying conflict and terrorism psychology theory is to suggest that within the roots of terrorism, psychological attitude can exist as *emotional terrorism* and *cognitive terrorism*.

As a complement to investigating the psychological construction of the individual in violence, it is also possible to apply the approaches of conflict studies to the psychological understanding of group dynamics. In addition to the approach discussed above in terrorism studies, conflict studies suggest that group identification[108] is a primary cause of conflict. An examination of the formation of the in-group and out-group and the subsequent group dynamics can provide a helpful insight into the causes of terrorism. Associated with this theory is the creation of a subjective reality or underground that is shared by members of the group and which exists to reinforce their subjective understanding of the world. This serves to justify their actions, especially as the group becomes increasingly insular from society or begins to construct its own society.

The group can also become completely controlled by violence, not only in their actions against their opponents but also to ensure group loyalty and maintain their sense of identity.[109] Individuals become so consumed by violence within the group that it soon develops a self-sustaining dynamic of violence and becomes the main driving force behind their actions and in some instances even eclipses the original reason for violence. Although this has problematic implication for the roots of terrorism debate, it serves to reinforce the belief of Fanon and Sartre, as it implies that individual actors commit acts of violence for the sake of violence.[110] The implications for the study of terrorism by adopting this argument is to suggest that by examining the psychological roots of terrorism in the individual it is possible to discover the existence of *group terrorism* which exists within the realm of the dynamics of the subjective understanding and reality of the terrorist group.

The role of the individual is highly influential in the roots of terrorism debate. By combining the approaches of terrorism and conflict studies it is possible to construct routes into examining the manifestation of violence at the level of the individual. This holistic approach provides a close investigation into the ideology, mindset, and system of belief or regimes of truth that the terrorist uses in order to motivate acts of violence and which might generate *ideological terrorism*. This is complemented by an examination of the identity of the individual to test the existence of *identity terrorism*. Furthermore, it is also important to explore the existence of any specific issues at the centre of the violence in order to ascertain its relevance to the plausibility of *issue terrorism*. Terrorism and conflict studies both suggest a thorough examination of the psychological elements inherent in violence existing in the conflict attitude of the individual and forming *emotional* and *cognitive terrorism*. Investigation is also required into group dynamics to establish if any potential deep underlying psychological forces are generating *group terrorism*. Examination and reassessment of the roots of terrorism is therefore invaluable at the level of the individual as it provides a wealth of possible causes of terrorism to consider.

It is apparent from Part 1 of this study that by combining the best approaches provided by terrorism and conflict studies it is possible to compile a comprehensive and holistic survey of methods for understanding the roots of terrorism that incorporates all the useful approaches at all the levels in the roots debate. Part 2 of this chapter will examine how these approaches can be formatted into a workable and practical comprehensive framework for rethinking the roots of terrorism.

Part 2: A comprehensive framework for rethinking terrorism

Construction

The main reason for establishing this roots of terrorism debate and the comparison of terrorism and conflict studies is to challenge and ultimately deconstruct the mono-dimensional approach to terrorism provided by orthodox terrorism theory. This challenge can be achieved by incorporating the alternative approaches or perspectives of the root causes of terrorism, as discussed in Part 1, into a hybrid comprehensive framework. This 'alternative theoretical' approach is intended as a holistic framework that incorporates a wide-ranging, multi-level and multi-dimensional approach to explaining and understanding the root causes of terrorism. The framework can be constructed from the implications for understanding terrorism that were deduced in Part 1, and can be represented for ease of application in levels of analysis. See Table 3.1 for a graphic representation of this comprehensive framework.

The first level of analysis is the state level and concentrates on the political by focusing on the state approach and state responses to terrorism and terrorists. A number of implications for the roots of terrorism debate emerge from this perspective. The most important is that terrorism can be seen to exist inherently within the institutions and policy construction of the state. This suggests terrorism is synonymous with the institution of the state. As a result, the theoretical root causes of terrorism at the state level are *inherent and devious terrorism and terrorism management*. The next level is the non-state actor. This provides an understanding of terrorism based on social conflict theory and suggests terrorism is caused by the perceived function and utility of terrorism, unsatisfied human needs and relative deprivation. The implications of this perspective for understanding the roots of terrorism suggest the existence at the non-state level of *revolutionary* or *reactionary terrorism, grievance terrorism* and *deprivation terrorism*.

The structural level approach concentrates on the structure of society, and in particular the relationship between the actor, the structure and the socio-economic environment. The implications of this perspective suggest that the roots of terrorism can be located in the historical and cultural background of a region and the behaviour and objectives of the actors. This implies the existence of *cultural, systemic, situational* and *socio-economic terrorism*. The final level of analysis is the level of the individual; this perspective of the root causes suggests that the individual has a central role in the generation of terrorism, implying that terrorism can be found in the ideology, identity and composition of individual and group psychology. This approach suggests the root causes of violence exist in *ideological, identity, issue, emotional, cognitive and group terrorism*.

The objective of this synthesis of terrorism and conflict studies is to combine all these perspectives and levels of analysis in the construction of a single, holistic and more wide-ranging framework for approaching the roots of terrorism. The aim of which is to suggest a more sophisticated understanding of terrorism than the orthodox approach, (although the orthodox approach is included).

Application: Why a multi-level framework is required

The employment of a theoretical framework is intended to provide, as I suggested above, a wider understanding of the phenomenon of terrorism. It is my intention to apply this framework in Table 3.1, to the Palestinian-Israeli conflict in Chapter 5, as a case study example. The aim of this is to compare the comprehensive approach with the conventional one provided by orthodox terrorism theory. It will also provide an opportunity to test the assumptions, claims and implications for rethinking terrorism that have been developed in the construction and application of this holistic approach. In the next section I will briefly explain how I intend to apply the multi-level framework developed above and graphically represented in Table 3.1.

First, a terrorist conflict is selected. This can be defined as one that contains terrorism in the form of 'lethal political violence'. This is the value neutral definition I constructed in Chapter 1 and have employed

Table 3.1 Comprehensive framework for re-thinking the roots of terrorism

Level	Terrorism studies approach	Conflict studies approach	Approach/method of examination	Implications
State	Political (anti-state)	Political (state as cause)	State response to terrorism (internal/external). State approach to terrorists. State approach to terrorism.	Inherrent terrorism. Secondary gain (devious terrorism). Terrorism management.
Non-state	Political (anti-state)	Social conflict theory	Function of terrorism. Individual safety needs of agencies. Relative-deprivation of agencies.	Revolutionary/reactionary terrorism. Grievance terrorism. Deprivation terrorism.
Structural	Political (ideology)	Society (agency and structure).	Contextual: historical/cultural background. Systemic: behaviour (actor/system relation). Situational: contradiction (actor/goal relationship). Environmental: (actor and socio-economics).	Cultural terrorism. Systemic terrorism (outside). Situational terrorism (inside/terrorists view). Socio-economic terrorism.
Individual	Political (ideology)	Individual (socio-economic and cultural)	Ideology or belief system (regime of truth). Nature of identity. Conflict issues. Conflict attitudes. Group dynamics.	Ideological terrorism. Identity terrorism. Issue terrorism. Emotional terrorism/cognitive terrorism. Group terrorism.

in this study in order to move away from the constrains of the political legitimacy debate contained in the definitions of orthodox terrorism theory. This definition is also selected because, as I argued at the beginning of this chapter, it allows access to the analytical tools of conflict resolution approaches provided by conflict studies. The Palestinian-Israeli conflict is a clear example of this because it is subject to an orthodox terrorist theory understanding that is typified by relative and subjective interpretations of what constitutes terrorism. These relative understandings are represented by a political conflict over legitimacy, coupled with an actual conflict that is characterised by both sides employing terrorist methods but each claiming they are acting legitimately in response to the use of illegitimate violence. As a consequence, the Palestinian-Israeli conflict has become typical of an intractable, deeply entrenched and highly acrimonious political struggle, characterised by an increasing spiral of extreme violence. The purpose of this study and comprehensive framework is to theoretically rethink the roots of terrorism and focus attention on the possible existence of deeper multi-level and multi-dimensional causational factors.

In the next sections I intend to outline how I propose to apply the framework at each level to the case study. This technique involves an adopted approach or method of examination created from the synthesis of terrorism and conflict studies and will produce a number of implications relating to the root causes of terrorism. These implications or forms of root causes of terrorism will be tested in Chapter 5 to illustrate how it is possible to rethink the roots of terrorism. This format is clearly displayed in Table 3.1.

Approaching the roots of terrorism

State level

This approach examines how the state responds to terrorism, both internally within the state and externally with other states. It can be achieved by examining the nature of the *intra-state* and *inter-state* relationships. This will help to ascertain at the state level how terrorism is understood and where it is perceived to exist. It also involves examining the state definition of terrorism and how it applies to members of the state and other states. This will also be apparent by observing and inquiring how the state understands what a terrorist is. A state can perceive a terrorist threat to exist between itself and its own population as a very serious threat to the internal security of the state. It can also see it as an external security threat between itself and another state; official state policy and the observable actions of the state will reflect this. If this is the case it is possible to argue, by implication that the roots of terrorism are in fact inherent within the state and therefore exist as *inherent terrorism.*

An examination also needs to be conducted into how the state approaches terrorists, in other words what methods do states employ to deal with terrorists. For example, do states employ a criminal legal method underwritten by orthodox terrorism theory or do they approach it from a conflict perspective and use military solutions. Are terrorists prosecuted and imprisoned under state law, assassinated without trial, held as prisoners of war or viewed as oppressed minorities with a legitimate cause. The implications of these will suggest how and also if, the state might employ terrorism discourse in order to pursue a policy of secondary gain. By maintaining a relative political and moral understanding of terrorism the state can utilise counterterrorism and anti-terrorism techniques in order to legitimately eradicate terrorist opponents, which suggests that the roots of terrorism can be found as *devious terrorism* in state action.

At this level it is also necessary to investigate how the state approaches terrorism. Does it employ a roots debate and attempt to find political or socio-economic solutions to the violence and foresee a long-term solution to the problem? Or does it use an approach based on terrorism theory, which sees the violence as a threat to the state and leads to the employment of the machinery of state to deal with the threat in the short-term? If the latter is the case it is possible to argue that the state sees terrorism as unsolvable and therefore endemic and inherent. If this is apparent, then by implication it is possible to suggest that the roots of terrorism can be located within the state, as the state is employing a method of *terrorism management.* This implies that terrorism will never be completely eradicated but instead maintained at a manageable level to suit state objectives. The outcome of this policy it that terrorism management can be observed by the use of terrorism legislation and military approaches to the problem, which can either help solve it or actually serve to aggravate it. This includes examining emergency legislation and special powers and the actions of the police and military in regards to political accountability, which might actually serve to bolster the political power of the state.

Non-state level

Application is focused on social conflict theory and deals directly with the wants and needs of the non-state actor as a cause of terrorism.

Initial investigation needs to examine the utility or function of the terrorism. Why terrorism is employed by the actor and for what reason. What is the function of the violence and how does it relate to the nature of the relationship between the state and the actor. The implications for this understanding of the roots of terrorism suggest that terrorism can be located in the relationship between the state and the non-state actor as methods to either completely transform the existing socio-political system (*revolutionary terrorism*) or reform it (*reactionary terrorism*).

Investigation at this level also needs to be focused on individual human needs, particularly the individual safety needs of the actors. Hence the security, identity, representation and equality of the actor vis-à-vis the state need to be examined, because if left unfulfilled or unsatisfied it could be a cause of terrorism. Similarly, the potential relative deprivation of actors also requires investigation. If actors perceive a relative imbalance, politically, economically and or socially, between what they want (perceived value) and what they actually have, (value capacity) violence as terrorism can occur. This suggests that *grievance* and *deprivation terrorism* can be generated by the non-state actor.

Structure

Structural approaches to the roots of terrorism are mainly concerned with attempting to examine the nature of the society in conflict, which can be understood as the relationship between the actors and the structure. This involves an examination of the context of the conflict; this is the historical and cultural background of the region. From this it is possible to ascertain connections between culture and violence and identify causes of violence as *cultural terrorism*.

Analysis at the structural level can also reveal the systemic nature of the conflict. This involves a structural investigation of the system created by the relationship between the actors and the system and is observable in the behaviour of the conflict actors. It is essentially an 'objective' examination of the conflict from outside and is a cause of *systemic terrorism*. In addition to this approach Is the view of the terrorists' perspective from 'inside' the conflict. This can reveal the way the actors perceive the nature of the structure or system that they are in and why they resort to violence. This can be achieved by examining the conflict situation or the complex set of inter-relationships between, the actor and their desired goals, vis-à-vis their actual or perceived goal incompatibilities, and between the actors and the perceived existing structure. Hence, the presence of other actors or the type of structure that obstructs an actor from achieving their goal and therefore generating violence is *situational terrorism*.

Finally, it is necessary to examine the socio-economic structure of the conflict. This is the nature of the relationship between the actor and the socio-economic environment. This requires a careful appraisal of the socio-economic background in which the violence is occurring, if interaction with the actors and their socio-economic situation is creating violence, then *socio-economic terrorism* exists.

Individual

The roots of terrorism at the individual level is primarily concerned with the mindset of the individual. The initial point of entry is an examination of the ideology or belief system used by the terrorist individual. The intention is to establish if their ideology or mindset creates a regime of truth in which violence has a purpose. If this is possible it implies the existence of *ideological terrorism*. However, ideologies like religion can often obscure other reasons for the causes of terrorism inherent in the nature of the individual. It is perhaps useful therefore to examine the identity of the individual. This can be more useful in revealing the belief system employed and the nature of the regime of truth that the terrorist has adopted in order to generate motivation and justification for the acts of violence. If this proves to be an established connection *identity terrorism* can be located within the individual.

Also examined in the individual is the existence of actual or perceived single issues or agendas surrounding the conflicts that can be considered a mainspring of violence. These need to be examined in order to assess just how much influence they have as a single cause in actually directly generating the violence. This will determine the influence of single issue or agenda in the generation of *issue terrorism*.

A particularly valuable area of study in this individual level approach relates to the socio-psychological construction of the individual and is found in an examination of conflict attitudes. This can be divided into an examination of the presence of *irrational* emotions such as fear, hate, anger and vengeance and *rational* emotions or cognitive processes. These relate to the construction of a subjective or perceived reality and cognitive perceptual belief and process for the justification of violence. The existence of either of these forms of a subjective reality of violence implies the existence of *emotional* and *cognitive terrorism*.

It is also very important to consider the influence of group dynamics on the generation of violence because the processes of action within a group, such as acts of violence to initiate group members or enhance the group cohesion or even cathartic violence, can often exist as a self-sustaining dynamic for the generation of violence as *group terrorism*.

Towards a comprehensive framework

In the above section I attempted to explain how the multi-level framework in Table 3.1 can be applied to a particular terrorist conflict. The technique is to apply each level to the mechanics of the conflict by employing the approaches and methods of examination suggested. This will test the theoretical implications, and serve to substantiate, or not, the claims to the existence of the roots of terrorism. In the next two chapters I intend to examine the case study example of the Palestinian-Israeli conflict. This will represent a working example of a terrorist conflict and it is to this example that I will apply, in Chapter 5, the comprehensive theoretical framework I have constructed above.

4
Discourses on Conflict and Terrorism: The Palestinian-Israeli Case

Introduction

The Palestinian-Israeli conflict is a protracted social conflict and a complicated internationalised dispute that is characterised by terrorism. It also typifies the relative legitimacy debate on the use of terrorism that is so enshrined in the orthodox understanding. It is therefore an ideal case study for applying the comprehensive framework for rethinking the roots of terrorism that was constructed in the last chapter; this will be the subject of the next chapter. The purpose of this chapter is to frame the Palestinian-Israeli conflict within a historical context by evaluating the historical and subjective discourses that are used to understand the conflict. The aim is to critically examine the discourses employed, and evaluate how and why they are used to interpret and understand the suggested historical facts and events of the conflict. This will help determine the relative understanding of the roots causes of terrorism.

The evaluation of historical events and the generation of facts is a precarious venture from the outset as E H Carr points out in *What is History?* He suggests that the facts can often exist as untenable theories of history.[1] Foucault argues that historical facts are often seen as the truth, or regimes of truth, that can be easily established by a combination of power and perceived knowledge.[2] This suggests that the perceived roots of conflict and terrorism are often enshrined in subjective historical realities, established through relative facts and the construction of regimes of truth. The events of the Palestinian-Israeli conflict are no exception, as they are also the subject of a fierce historiography debate. The intention in this chapter is not to discover the universal 'truth' of the conflict as this may well prove to be a quixotic quest;[3] instead I aim to examine the history of the Palestinian-Israeli conflict by employing a critical theory and discourse analysis approach to the events. I intend to scrutinize the particular theories, frameworks and historical structures through which the facts are perceived and established. This is in order to examine what tasks they are designed for and ultimately for what purpose the interpretation of the facts and the creation of perceived truths are required. This study will focus primarily on illustrating how these different discourses relate to the understanding of the roots of the conflict and ultimately of terrorism.

Before moving to an examination of the creation of the history of the Palestinian-Israeli conflict, I would briefly like to outline the current historiography debate that surrounds the conflict. As I have suggested, the manipulation of history for the creation of facts that can be employed to vindicate a particular policy, or reinforce an ideology, are a common feature of conflicts where adversarial interpretations of historical events are employed. This suggests a battle of history can often ensue that aims to negate the opponents claim to legitimacy whilst asserting ones own, often characterised by a propaganda war. As Kimmerling explains, history is a powerful tool in both domestic and external conflict and is used to form meta-narratives that determine legal, political and territorial claims as well as being responsible for establishing individual and collective identities.[4] Without doubt both the Palestinians and the Israelis employ their own collective and relative understanding of history upon which their claims to legitimacy and justice are based. This not only sustains the conflict, as each actor believes they have sole legitimacy of action and the exclusive right to justice, but it is also a barrier to peace, as recognition of the others claims casts into question the validity of their own history upon which the conflict and the inherent ideologies of action are based. This is the basis of the current historiography debate within Israeli society. It is an academic debate essentially re-thinking Israeli history focusing particularly on 1948 and how the 'Arab' is perceived in established Israeli history, with specific reference to the refugee situation. Ilan Pappe outlines this debate, which he suggests began in the 1980s with scholarly works by the 'new historians' or 'revisionists' that strongly challenged the Israeli public's self-image, collective memory and established historical 'truths'.[5] Flapan, for example, recommends the re-examination of certain myths surrounding the birth of Israel that have become accepted historical truth and which are central to the creation of structures of thinking and propaganda.[6] Although this 'new history' began by focusing on the events of 1948, as Finkelstein points out, it has now spread to include a rethinking of all Israeli history.[7]

The implications of this revisionism however, whilst useful for a critical examination of the history of the conflict and the creation of space in which to work towards reconciliation, can be considered highly problematic for Israel. As Hazony suggests, Jewish society is now in crisis as the state is under attack from its own cultural and intellectual establishment because the new historians are threatening the national narrative.[8] A re-examination of Israeli history and the sacred 'myths' that underwrite it suggest a deconstruction of Zionism, Pappe identifies this as the post-Zionism critique or debate. Although not widely accepted and often dismissed as a largely academic exercise, it is a potent challenge to the traditional Israeli historical version.[9] Nevertheless, the post-Zionist debate is a useful point of departure to begin a critical examination of Israeli history and one I will be employing during this chapter, whilst using a similar approach for the Palestinian version of history.

This historical and discourse evaluation of the Palestinian-Israeli conflict will be divided into two parts. Part 1, will be an examination of the construction of the two conflict discourses and Part 2 will be an examination of the application and development of these discourses by investigating their role in the major conflicts between the Palestinians and Israelis from 1948 and will include the wars of 1948, 1956, 1967, 1973, International conflict, the Lebanon War, and the first and second Intifadas (until April 2003).

Part 1: Construction of conflict discourses

From time immemorial: the ancient history debate

The Palestinian-Israeli conflict is often referred to as simply a conflict over land or territory; this is the root of the ancient history debate and one that is woven into the fabric of the conflict. From this perspective the central question in the conflict is whose claim to the land is the oldest. However, since both parties claim to have been there since time immemorial, there is no easy answer to this. The Israeli's claim is located in Biblical narrative, which dates to the Old Testament period and the story of the twelve tribes, who it is believed were led by Moses out of Egypt to the promised land of Canaan, where they established the Israelite era in about 1300 BCE. After this the region became known as Judea, Samaria and Galilee, and later included the kingdoms of David and Solomon. Despite the weakening and decline of the kingdom following successive assaults by regional powers, it was the Roman Empire that finally ended the Israelite kingdom in 63 BCE, and following two unsuccessful rebellions in 66 and 70 BCE, the Jews were driven into exile and dispersion. The main purpose of this narrative will become more apparent in the discussion below on Zionism. However, if the crux of the conflict is the land of Palestine, then the role of this historical discourse is to establish for the Jewish people claims and even rights to ownership of the land by enshrining the principles of legitimacy and justice. Legitimacy because it relates to the validity of the claim to the land, which for the Jews is reinforced by divine law because they believe God promised them the land. The claim to the territory is therefore enshrined in religious belief and has an unquestionable authority and legality for the Jewish people. Secondly, justice, a powerful motivator for violence, is a theme in the historical narrative because the basis of the ancient Jewish historical claim is the divine right to land of which they were wrongfully dispossessed (by the Romans) and exiled from in the first century BCE. The Jews believe the land of Israel, the 'promised land', is rightfully theirs. This is the foundation for a claim based on the right to return of all Jewish people to a homeland they were driven from. In the context of the modern conflict, Israel is exercising its historical and divine right to reoccupy land that it originally inhabited and controlled.

By comparison the Palestinian ancient historical narrative stresses the continuity of the Palestinians as original inhabitants. It suggests that the Palestinians were descendants of two ancient peoples, the Canaanites and Philistines, which according to the Bible were the earliest known inhabitants of Palestine or the Land of Canaan from 3000 BCE. During the Israelite period they existed as a minority but were regenerated by the arrival of Islam in 610 CE, which according to Tessler 'created currents of change and a fundamental transformation of existing political and cultural patterns'.[10] Coupled with this is the inextricable link to Arabism, which is the central and unifying theme in identity and political outlook of peoples in the Arab world. Palestinian historical discourse is therefore intertwined with the history of the Arabs.

The Palestinian historical narrative is employed in a similar manner to that of the Jews. Palestinian legitimacy for action is based on their legal rights as not only the original but also the continuous occupants and inhabitants of the land. The Palestinian claim to justice stems from legitimacy and the right to maintain an unbroken inhabitancy of their homeland. This is a legal claim to permanent residency, which in the context of the modern conflict is injustice by the Israelis who have occupied and forced them out of their homeland.

From both ancient historical narratives, legitimacy and justice can be employed to endorse methods to re-claim the land, such as just cause and just war theories, which are often engaged to justify violence, conflict, terrorism and holy war. Whilst the roots of conflict are often regarded as existing in the material dispute over land it is often the associated rationale supported by historical narrative and religion that can provide the ideological polarity of conflict understanding and the incentive for violent action. This is the basis for the construction of conflict discourses.

Historical narratives not only provide the validation and motivation for violence in defence of the historical claims, but also contain a counter narrative, which is intended to discredit the opponents' account. An example of this is the 'time immemorial' debate. Thus in order to counter the Israelis claim that they were established since time immemorial, the Palestinians, as Kimmerling points out, have invented their own time immemorial in reference to their Canaanite and Philistine roots, which according to the bible preceded the Jewish tribes.[11] The intention as I suggested above, is not to debate the truth of these narratives but to investigate how they are employed. For example, both parties employ the Bible to substantiate their historical claims not only because they are applicable to their own religions, but also because they are comprehensible to each other and are accessible enough for the international community to recognise. Biblical terminology is freely interspersed with modern geographical regions and contemporary lexicon in order to create an established historical narrative. As Masalha points out, terms such as 'promised land', 'holy land', 'Palestine' and 'greater Israel' (Eretz-Yisrael) all have important modern political implications. The knowledge of the geography of the 'land of Israel' is often a precondition for understanding its history.[12]

The ancient historical narratives, whilst useful for generating propaganda and to project claims and counter-claims, also help to sustain historical memory; an integral part of protracted social conflict. According to Flapan, 'The Jews and Arabs possess a long historical memory and suffer trauma and tragic events unable to forgive or forget'.[13] However, the use of historical narrative can also create memory, thus only by examining the narrative is it possible to ascertain and question the claims in historical memory. Tessler argues that it is only in the last century that Jews and Arabs have viewed each other as enemies. He suggests a necessity to 'dispel the common misconception that the current struggle in Palestine is an extension of an ancient blood feud, fuelled by ethnic or religious antagonisms, dating back hundreds of years'.[14] Historical narrative is clearly an influential factor in the formation of conflict memory and the continuation of violence as it forms the basis for the construction of conflict discourses.

History and the formation of discourses

Historical narratives help establish, sustain and maintain discourses and are an integral element in the construction of conflicts as they often contain the incompatibles that lead to violence and the institutionalisation of conflict. However, the question in this context is the location of history in the formation of a discourse or indeed the effect of a discourse on the creation of history. The Palestinian-Israeli conflict is characterised by two opposing discourses, Zionism and Palestinianism (Palestinian Nationalism). These are fluid concepts and open to varying definitions, but at their most extreme interpretation they are mutually exclusive, hence the perceived zero sum nature of the conflict. Discourses are central to understanding not only the historical narratives of the Palestinian-Israeli dispute but also the actual dynamics of the conflict. Throughout the modern period both discourses develop in reaction to and from events. Unsurprisingly, the history of the discourses is also debated by the opposing discourse. For example, the central pillar of orthodox Zionism is to deny the existence of Palestinianism. Orthodox Israeli history argues that Zionism created modern Palestinian Nationalism,[15] whereas Palestinian history suggests it always existed and developed relative to the other Arab states.[16] It is immediately apparent that there are a number of similarities in the claims and progress of both movements. Due to this many scholars suggest a mutual development and stress the impossibility of explaining one discourse without the other.[17] However, whatever the nature of their progress, the existence of a discourse is central to the causes of the conflict, so what are the discourses and what historical claims do they make? In the next section I intend to explore the perceived historical development of both discourses prior to 1948.

Zionism

Israeli historical narrative suggests that Zionism originated in Eastern Europe in the late nineteenth century and was given a political voice by Theodore Hertzl, with the publication of *The Jewish State* in 1896. Zionism is an ethnic Jewish identity based discourse that supports the secular movement for a national home for the Jewish people in Palestine. It is a type of Jewish nationalism and is built predominantly on ancient historical narrative. As Laqueur suggests, 'it is a belief in the existence of a common past and common future for the Jewish people'.[18] Zionism requires acceptance of the historical narrative and the belief that Jewish people all over the world have a right not only to belong to a nation but also to live in an established homeland. Also, as Zionism originated in Europe it is infused with the ideas of the European enlightenment and the French Revolution, and is rooted in European political and social culture, especially the existence of the nation-state and the protection that it can afford its ethnic citizens. This theme of protection is perhaps the central thread of Zionism and is as relevant now as it was then. Hertzl embraced and developed Zionism not only in response to increasing levels of anti-Semitism in Europe at the time,[19] but also to counter chronic anti-Semitism throughout Jewish history. The implications of the existence of Zionism for the first wave of Jewish immigrants who arrived in Palestine in 1902, is that these people accepted a discourse that promised them a return to the national Jewish homeland where they could exist in safety and security from threats to their ethnic well-being. This in hindsight was the motivation for the unique and unprecedented creation of the nation-state of Israel by importing an ethnically homogenous community from all over the world into a bounded, governed, and secure national territory.

Zionism is subject to various interpretations and exists in a number of categories, the most important for this study are, Classical, Labour and Revisionist. Classical Zionism is based upon the continued and unbreakable tie of the Jewish people to Palestine and the formation of Eretz Yisrael (Greater Israel).[20] As Lewy suggests, '[D]espite the dispersion of the Jewish people, the true home of the Jews remained in the land of Israel, the idea of eventual return from the four corners of the earth was never abandoned.'[21] This is the ideological extension of the ancient narrative, the implications of which suggest that those employing this discourse firmly believe in the unwavering right of the Jewish people to live in Palestine. Zionism also represents the belief in the creation of a new society. According to Shlaim, 'Zionism is a secular movement orientated to Palestine not merely to create a new Jewish state but also a new society based upon universal values, freedom, democracy and social justice.'[22] The second main interpretation is Labour Zionism. This is an understanding of Zionism according to Socialist working class principles and is based on equality and social justice. Labour Zionism focused on agricultural settlement of the land and emphasised self-reliance by encouraging immigrants to populate and cultivate a new state based on socialist principles. Tessler points out that this is consistent with the concept of the Kibbutz or collective farm, notable for its autonomy, social cohesion and ability to provide security.[23] The labour Zionist movement provided a universal and appealing ideology for immigrants and a possible vision of the new Israel by Labour Zionists.

The main implication of Zionism is the acceptance of Palestine as the new state of Israel. This employs the assumption that Palestine was either unoccupied at the time of the arrival of Jewish immigrants, or that it was accepted that the indigenous population would be subsumed. As Finkelstein suggests, 'the mainstream Zionist movement never doubted its historical right to impose the Jewish state through the 'right to return' on the indigenous Arab population of Palestine'.[24] Zionism, coupled with the ancient historical narrative provides a discourse for the Jewish settlement of the land. So even if the early Zionist pioneers recognised the indigenous population, the Zionist discourse provided the necessary justification for action. As Finkelstein explains, the Zionist ideology provided a pre-emptive right to Palestine that outweighed the Arabs residential claim. It is based on the unique Jewish bond with the land; their historical 'right' and the belief that the indigenous Arabs were not a separate nation and were therefore part of the wider Arab community, and as a consequence could settle anywhere.[25]

The existence of an indigenous Arab population in Palestine seems incompatible with the Zionist discourse, as Zionism requires an ethnic Jewish state that belongs solely to the Jews, implying that non-Jews were not intrinsically part of it. Zionist history suggests that there were no indigenous Palestinian Arab people, as a result the Zionist discourse does not recognise their existence. Contemporary orthodox Israeli history maintains that when the first Jewish immigrants arrived from Europe in the nineteenth century, the land of Palestine was a deserted country and had no native population. Netanyahu argues, '[U]p until the Twentieth Century the name Palestine referred exclusively to the ancient land of the Jews. It has never yet been argued that there existed a Palestinian people after the Jews.'[26] Joan Peters produced an extensive work called *From Time Immemorial* in which she argues that before Jewish immigration, Palestinian land was a barren and unoccupied land and it is only after the start of Jewish prosperity when Arab migration to Palestine began.[27] This historical argument produced the Zionist rallying cry 'a land without a people for a people without a land'. An important implication for the Palestinian people from this Zionist belief of non-existence is that the Palestinians are not seen as people rooted to the land of Palestine but instead as rootless Arabs and part of the wider nomadic Arab continent. This is illustrated by Netanyahu who states, 'It was not the Jews who usurped the land from the Arabs but the Arabs who usurped the land from the Jews.'[28] It also relates to the belief in Zionist discourse that Arabs are generic and can be re-located to anywhere in the region, hence the 'transfer' of Palestinians to other Arab states.

Despite these arguments Palestinians existed in the region and were unwilling to submit to Zionism and by the 1920s were becoming increasingly hostile to immigration. Zionism dealt with this problem by widening its discourse to incorporate Revisionist Zionism, which was formulated by Ze'ev Jabotinsky in 1925. Revisionist Zionist discourse provided the justification for the use of force to achieve Zionist objectives. It is a discourse established on the assumption that the Arabs would not peacefully accept the formation of the Jewish state of Eretz Yisrael in Palestine. Flapan, a 'new historian' suggests that Jabotinsky implanted in the Jewish psyche the image of the Arab as the mortal enemy and established the idea of inevitability of conflict and the impossibility of a solution except by sheer force.[29] Shlaim also points out that Jabotinsky wrote an article entitled '*The Iron wall*' in which he suggested revisionist theory understood that the Arabs would never voluntarily give up land they saw as their own. He therefore recommended settlement by the use of force to construct a metaphorical iron wall, which they would be powerless to break down.[30]

The principal implications of employing the revisionist discourse is that it provides a framework for dealing with the Palestinian Arab problem by suggesting that the Palestinians do not want peace, will never accept the Israeli state and seek both its destruction and that of its people. This discourse allows Zionism to take by force what they perceive is rightfully theirs and subjugate the opposition. It can also serve to reinforce any number of Israeli policies especially involving domestic and foreign security decisions, as it can generate a climate of fear within the Jewish population by employing a positivist approach to Palestinian and Arab violence. It also justifies violence in defence of their land and the reoccupation and settlement of others. The Zionist discourse, as Finkelstein points out, requires the existence of a Jewish state which belongs to the Jews, non-Jewish inhabitants are not part of this and are therefore not only superfluous but antithetical and a threat to Zionism.[31] This implies that the transfer or expulsion of indigenous non-Jewish people from the land of the Jews is a legitimate action under the revisionist discourse.

This vision of Zionism is one that represents the establishment of a Jewish state in Palestine, and when confronted with opposition to this objective, employs armed struggle to achieve it. The Zionist discourse also generates and employs its own historical narrative to justify these policies and actions as Jewish and Israeli action is enshrined in its own Zionist legitimacy, which justifies employing terrorism, violence and conflict to achieve the aims and objectives of Zionism. The construction and employment of the Zionist discourse is designed and intended to achieve its aims by whatever means are necessary and therefore exists at the very core of the conflict. As Aggestam suggests, 'History lessons, experience, analogical reasoning, cognitive beliefs, and Zionism constitute a major part of the ideological belief from which conflict is evaluated and legitimised.'[32]

Palestinianism

Palestinianism or Palestinian Nationalism is the other principal discourse in the Palestinian-Israeli conflict, and like Zionism can also be seen as an identity discourse. Edward Said argued that it is the key not only to understanding the existence of the Palestinian people but also the conflict with Israel. He suggests the principal tenets of Palestinian Identity are built upon the need for repossession of the land and realisation of Palestinian statehood.[33] Acceptance of the discourse of Palestinianism is an acceptance of the assumptions upon which it is based. These include, territory, identity, history, culture and religion. Palestinianism is not only a reaction against Zionism and British imperialism but also against the wider Arab world; it is an expression of a collective and individual entity. Schultz points out that there is no single understanding of the phenomenon and suggests that Palestinian Nationalism can be understood by employing a number of different discourses, from ethnographic, through religious to nationalist.[34]

The Palestinian historical narrative proposes that Palestinianism as a discourse originated during the end of the Ottoman Empire. Muslih suggests that after the final defeat of the Ottomans the old Arab order of political allegiance to the dynastic sovereign of the Islamic state was gradually replaced by one of allegiance to the county in which one lived.[35] The beginning of this movement was the appearance of political Arabism in 1908–14 in response to growing Turkish nationalism; typified by the 1908 young Turks revolt.[36] The young Turks revolt is significant for the development of Palestinianism because it freed press censorship for the Arab people and made them able to express and distribute their grievances in print. According to Muslih, 'the press was the single most effective vehicle through which the Palestinians could make their views known...especially in opposition to Zionism'.[37] Morris called the revolt a watershed, and suggests that from this period onwards the Arab resistance to the Zionist project becomes nationalistic;[38] this is the beginning of a recognised Palestinian identity.

Arabism was soon replaced by Arab Nationalism, which was drawn into the vacuum created by the crumbling Ottoman Empire after the defeat in the First World War. Arab Nationalism also gained in stature following the McMahon-Hussein agreement and the decision by the Arabs under Faisal to begin a revolt against the Turks in 1916. Although these nationalist movements were based on western ideas and those enshrined in the individual state, such as self-determination and individual rights and freedoms, Muslih points out that Arab Nationalism envisioned the establishment of a pan-Arab system based on a united Greater Syria.[39] However, at the end of the war the hopes of Arab nationalism and Pan-Arabism were frustrated by the emergence of the 1916 Sykes-Picot agreement that created the British mandate in Palestine in 1922.

This historical narrative suggests that Arab Nationalism not only emerged as an ideological discourse but also was actively fought for. Although it is argued that the Arab campaign did not play a large role in the overall military effort,[40] the important development is that it was both recognised and employed by the Arabs and the British. This narrative also suggests the existence of an independent Palestinian identity within the Arab world. This implies the existence, recognition and use of Palestinian identity discourse, not only by the Palestinians and the British but also by the wider Arab world. The establishment of the British mandate effectively established the internal and external territorial boundaries of Palestine, thus shaping in physical reality, a Palestinian national identity. On this point it could be argued that Arab Nationalism was created by the post-war agreements. According to Morris '[N]ational movements and identities soon congealed in each mandated territory, each pressing for statehood despite common bonds of language, culture and history.'[41] Ironically, the most important political trigger for Palestinian nationalism was the Balfour Declaration 1917, which effectively sanctioned the establishment of a Jewish national State in Palestine. Palestinianism can therefore be understood through three different and seemingly contradictory but paradoxically complimentary processes, these are identity, nationalism and pan-Arabism.

Identity, according to Schultz, is associated with ethnic and cultural identity in social organisation and relates to the relative understanding of the self and the other.[42] Sayigh suggests that at the beginning of the mandate period, Palestinian social structure comprised of a fragmented mass base of agricultural peasants under the control of two potentially ruling groups competing for British patronage, the indigenous Palestinian elites and the Zionist leadership.[43] Despite the homogenous and compact nature of Palestinian society, the political identity of the peasant majority still functioned according to the Ottoman patronage through family, tribal and regional loyalties and had little grasp of Palestinian national identity.[44] The political elites were influenced by national consciousness. These elites could be divided into two groups, the Old Ottoman leaders and urban elites who wanted Palestinian independence and the Young leaders not of the Ottoman period who sought Arab unity in greater Syria.[45] Effectively Palestinian identity stood at a threshold, the majority of peasants were still in the old system whilst the elites were looking progressively forward.

The catalyst for change it seems was Zionism, which initiated a major economic and social transformation. According to Kimmerling and Migdal, Jewish land purchase and investment strengthened the economy and led to an extensive redevelopment of commerce, industry and infrastructure.[46] This caused the dislocation of Palestinian peasants from the land and increased urbanisation, unemployment and radicalisation. It led directly to a growing discontent and realisation of the threat posed by Zionism to Palestinian identity and society. Consequently, 'the notion of a cohesive society with a unique history, its members facing common threats and a shared future gained increasing acceptance among Palestinian Arabs in the interwar years.'[47] This narrative suggests that the Palestinian identity discourse was increasingly accepted within Palestinian society as a reaction to a perceived threat, and can be directly associated with incidents of Palestinian violence becoming more widespread. This is typified by the growth of Islamic resistance groups, populated from the urban slums, the most important of which was led by Sheikh al-Qassam.[48] The consequence of this was the establishment of Palestinian identity in the form of violent resistance groups such as the Black Hand, political nationalist groups such as Istiqlal and the institutionalisation of heroes and martyrs for the cause, such as al-Qassam. As Khalidi suggests, 'the resistance of Palestinian peasants to Jewish settlers underlines the role of the peasants in making Zionism central to Arab political discourse'.[49]

Nationalism is the generation of the understanding of the existence of Palestine as an independent state. Muslih suggests that the generation of the discourse for an independent state in Palestine has its roots in western ideas, 'patriotism, nationhood, sovereignty, self-determination and loyalty to a specific territory greatly affected Palestinian development'.[50] Palestinian nationalist discourse was employed to counter the imperialism of the British Mandate, and the nationalist threat posed by Zionism, which from the outset intended to establish a state in the European form. This outcome was supported by the British because nationalism is an internationally recognised discourse for the protection of identity because 'it provides collective security and is emancipatory, inclusive and exclusive'.[51] The nationalist discourse portrays the Palestinian-Israeli conflict as a clash of nationalism, two seemingly incompatible nations in one territory.

Finally, Arabism is the gravitation towards pan-Arabism and the establishment of a single Arab state, similar in respects to the Ottoman Empire. Arabism is based upon similarities in culture, language, religion, history and ultimately identity. Although most scholars agree that Palestinians largely abandoned this discourse in the late 1930s because of the intensity of the localised struggle between the Palestinians, Zionists and the British,[52] it is nevertheless an important discourse and a part of Palestinianism that reoccurs through out its contemporary history. This discourse suggests a responsibility to Palestinianism by the Arab world to establish and protect Palestinian identity, and thus brings the Arab states into the conflict situation with Zionism and the West.

Palestinianism was an evolving discourse in the late nineteenth century among the Palestinians due to various internal and external influences and soon became the main element in the Palestinian-Israeli conflict. Muslih suggests that this is due to an ideological and institutional shift of political loyalty from tribal to national.[53] However, one event above all others at this time served to bring together all the elements of Palestinianism together and acted as the mainspring for Palestinianism. This was the Arab Revolt of 1936. It began as a series of spontaneous outbreaks of communal violence and waves of strikes and civil unrest, directed by the Palestinians at the Zionists and the British. Although it is suggested that these actions were spontaneous grassroots behaviour the activities were eventually coordinated by the hastily convened Higher Arab Committee. They demanded that the British Government introduce basic changes to stop Jewish immigration. The spontaneous strikes became a general strike and widespread popular demonstrations and riots became increasingly violent coupled with concerted guerrilla activity, all of which typified a period of sustained civil disorder until it was resolutely and progressively put down by the British by 1939.

Employing the discourse of Palestinianism it is possible to understand the cause of 'the great Arab revolt' as the first organised expression of Palestinian identity. Kimmerling and Migdal suggest it is 'the first sustained uprising of the Palestinian national movement and no event is more momentous in Palestinian history'.[54] The implications from this for the development of the Palestinian national movement are quite extensive. There is little doubt that the revolt politicised all levels of the already uneasy Arab community, and was channelled into support of Palestinianism. The general unrest caused by the British occupation, Zionist expansionism and chronic socio-economic difficulties mobilised the masses to the cause of Palestinian Nationalism. Schultz suggests the revolt crystallised Palestinian political identity and created a nation.[55]

Following the defeat and harsh British repression of the revolt, Palestinian forces were considerably weakened, especially the leadership elements, which lost its central command and authority.[56] The implications of this are obvious to the fighting Palestinian elements, but equally as significant, the isolated Palestinian communities and villages lost their local leadership and organisation and became dislocated, isolated and vulnerable. This development represented the loss of security of identity that Palestinianism was supposed to provide. Hence, the overwhelming power of the British and growing strength of the Zionists caused the Palestinians to look to other Arab nations for assistance and protection, thus suggesting a re-emergence of Arabism. The Arab Revolt also had implications for the Zionists. Most importantly, it radicalised the Zionist opposition and developed into almost open warfare. Smith suggests that as a result the Zionists adopted terrorist tactics equal to the Arabs and begun to prepare for concerted resistance against the Arabs and the British.[57] It illustrated to the Zionist leadership the nature of the conflict they could expect with the Arabs, and justified the development of revisionist Zionism as a reaction to Palestinian intransigence and resistance to their aims. This recognition of the core of the conflict was summed up by Ben Gurion, who is quoted as saying 'There is a fundamental conflict, they and we both want the same thing – Palestine.'[58]

The Arab Revolt created the conflict structure of the modern Palestinian-Israeli conflict. It established the framework in which the Palestinian Arabs and the Jews established their diverging positions and entrenched adversarial stances as it became clear to both communities that each other's intentions were incompatible. By 1939 both nationalist ideologies had taken form and employed incompatible and conflicting nationalist discourses that were given corroboration by the generation of the cycle of violence by both sides during the Arab Revolt. These conflict discourses continued to develop and crystallise further after 1948. This will now be examined in relation to the major conflicts between the Palestinians and Israelis since 1948 until the second Intifada.

Part 2: Application of conflict discourses

1948 – the first Arab-Israeli war

On the May 14 1948 Ben Gurion the Jewish Prime Minister declared the existence of the State of Israel. This was the culmination of a bitter civil war with the British and the Palestinians and was the precursor to victory in a conventional war with the regional Arab states of Syria, Jordan, Egypt, Lebanon and Iraq from May 1948 to May 1949. The roots of the war were in the Arab revolt of 1936 and the realisation by the Palestinians and the Israelis that they faced conflict over their incompatible claims to the land of British Palestine. In the aftermath of World War Two, an exhausted Britain could no longer sustain conflict with the Jews and Palestinians nor devise an acceptable solution and so handed the problem over to the UN, before withdrawing completely. Ernst Bevin the British Prime minister stated, 'We are unable to accept the scheme put forward by either the Arabs or the Jews or to impose ourselves, a solution of our own.'[59] The UN then devised a partition plan, but drawn into the vacuum of the departing British occupation were two increasingly militarised communities.

The war of 1948 is known to the Israelis as the war of Independence or liberation, and occupies a fundamental position in the historical roots of the Palestinian-Israeli conflict. Despite the fact that the majority of the fighting was against the Arabs, the Israeli historical narrative records it as a 'war of liberation', against the British. As Pappe points out 'Israeli terminology of the war is constructed carefully so as to confer upon Zionism the equivalent status of a third world liberation movement'.[60] This serves to legitimise the conflict for Zionism and is the basis for the modern historical narrative of the Zionist discourse. It is especially relevant to the tactics employed by the Jewish terrorist organisations such as the Irgun and Lehi, or Stern group who incorporated national liberation into the Zionist discourse in order to justify terrorist attacks.[61]

Ian Lustick argues that the Jewish terrorist groups in this period employed solipsistic violence that was intended to inspire and motivate the Jewish people.[62] This suggests that violence is an integral factor in Zionism and is inextricably linked to the foundation of the Israeli national psyche characterised by an oppressed and subjugated Jewish people struggling against adversity. The Zionist discourse configures the events of 1948 in the Israeli historical memory as a moment of resurrection of the Jewish national psyche. It is represented as 'the culmination of the teleological process of redemption and renaissance of the Jewish people',[63] and is the culmination and realisation of the ancient historical roots of the Zionist discourse – the return to the Promised Land. The Jewish national psyche was transformed from a persecuted, humiliated and defenceless people, an image, personified by the Holocaust to a powerful unified nation. In Israeli historical narrative, a tiny Israeli David overcame against all probability, the attack of the mighty Arab Goliath.

The war of 1948 for Zionism and the newborn Israel was a fight to defend the state and its people – a fight to live or die. The Israeli national psyche was transformed from a self-image of non-violent, persecuted and meek people into assertive and aggressively defensive nation, who realised that after generations of suffering they no longer had to be subservient and could defend themselves and their people. The fear of domination and the struggle for self-defence was historical continuity of the ancient historical narrative of Massada and the modern history of the Holocaust – through Zionism, never again will the Jewish people suffer at the hands of another.

A national belief emerged from the events of 1948 in the power of the Israeli state through the strength of the military, giving the Israeli state a military dominance of the region and enabling it to pursue its Zionist agenda. As the Palestinian scholar Sayigh argues, 'Israeli military and political power became a dominant factor and aided the Zionist states land clearance and displacements, as the surrounding Arab governments were powerless to stop it'.[64] Zionism and the Israeli state was established, enforced and now protected by the violence of military power.

The war of 1948 exists in the Palestinian historical narrative as al-Nakba or the catastrophe. Despite organised Palestinian resistance, the invasion of the Arab states and the UN partition plan for two separate states, the Palestinians did not gain independence; instead their society was shattered. First by the civil war with the Jewish community, and then by the effects of the entry of Arab states into the war, particularly

Jordan and Egypt, who invaded and occupied the West Bank including East Jerusalem and the Gaza Strip respectively. All of this, according to Kimmerling and Migdal, led to the virtual disappearance of Palestinian society, as those who remained were subsumed by the new Jewish state or the Arab neighbours and those who fled were dislocated in a mass exodus to the Arab states and beyond.[65]

The disaster of 1948, compounded with the defeated revolt of 1936, is at the core of the Palestinian historical narrative as a principal cause of the Palestinian-Israeli conflict and was a huge setback for the discourse of Palestinianism. For the Palestinians, not only was it was a humiliating military defeat, but it led an enormous loss of Palestinian land (including west Jerusalem) to the new Israeli state, and also created the refugee problem. The Palestinian national psyche was deeply affected by the war; as they came to believe were the victims of an immense conspiracy and monumental injustice.[36] This came from the loss of their homeland and the scattering their community, and also from bitterness at the Arab states for failing to defend them whilst concurrently occupying their land. Rosemary Sayigh suggests that these losses penetrated deep into Palestinian psychology. She points out that a sense of isolation developed that was compounded by family disruption and separation. Coupled with this was the sense of shame and loss of respect and status that accompanied land ownership. All of which had a deep cultural impact on the Palestinian communities.[67] Yezid Sayigh highlights the fact that the loss of land and other means of production undermined the sense of identity in a predominantly agrarian society and removed sources of autonomous wealth and economic reproduction.[68]

This created a Palestinian national self-image of humiliated and unjustly disposed victims. Benny Morris calls this a 'psychosis of flight.'[69] According to Sayigh the events of 1948 were both 'centrifugal and centripetal' in that it scattered the Palestinian national population whilst simultaneously forming small concentrations of exiled communities who had no identity, security, rights or recognition.[70] Al-Nakba for the Palestinian nation also meant they became the pariahs of the Arab world, characterised by a camp society in the West bank and Gaza and a scattering of satellite communities in many other countries. However, the war of 1948 crystallised Palestinian national identity and created a distinct identity based upon the common experience of loss. This focused on the right to return and the demand for a state.[71] According to Edward Said, 'behind every Palestinian there is a general fact: that he once lived in a land of his own called Palestine'.[72]

After 1948 the Palestinian community was leaderless, scattered and broken and without doubt effectively marginalised from any position of influence or authority in the region. The Palestinians community now looked to the Arab states for leadership and resolution of their problems, even if the Arab sates had other agendas. Although the post–1948 Palestinian-Israeli conflict became a predominantly state conflict, Palestinian security, the refugee situation, the status of Jerusalem and Arab public opinion vis-à-vis the Israeli state continued to dominate events.

1956 – the Second Arab-Israeli war

The period from 1949 to 1956 was a war of attrition, characterised by cross-border violence and low-intensity conflict between the Arab nations and the newly formed state of Israel. Smith called this, not war, yet not peace situation, a 'state of belligerency'.[73] This period however culminated in the Suez War, when Egypt under Nasser, moved to nationalise the Suez Canal. Israel responded by invading the Sinai, causing Britain and France to intervene against Egypt. The result was a further humiliating defeat for Egypt and the Arab world, and a complete military success for Israel, which gained Gaza temporarily and the Sinai permanently. The conflict demonstrated the declining authority of Britain and France in the region and the growing influence of the United States and the Soviet Union. It also confirmed that the Palestinian-Israeli conflict was now completely subsumed by the wider state based Arab-Israeli conflict, which in turn became subordinate to the Cold War.

The Suez campaign, according to the Zionist discourse, was a defensive and just war that achieved all its operational objectives.[74] It also vindicated Israeli security policy that focused on the high intensity threat of war posed by the neighbouring Arab states and the low intensity threat of border incursions. In addition, it encouraged security by violence and included pro-active and pre-emptive measures. This was the *'Iron Wall'* thesis of Israeli defence policy, a strategy of counterforce involving the immediate recourse to violence and direct military action as the central doctrine of Arab relations.[75]

This enhanced security policy was not just due to the Suez war but also to the increasing frequency and intensity of border conflicts. In response to these 'incursions', Israel employed 'direct action' security measures in the form of 'defensive' raids such as those on Egypt, and Gaza. The purpose was to secure its borders with the use of force against aggression by Palestinian Arab armed groups and displaced refugees attempting to return home. However, it also had the effect of further militarising and desensitising Israeli society (especially the military), who according to Shlaim adopted a 'free-fire policy', he suggested they displayed 'a growing disregard for human lives and barbaric acts that can only be described as war crimes'.[76]

Israeli security policy also had the effect of sustaining the conflict. Although this might seem paradoxical, the ongoing conflict benefited Israeli Zionist objectives. This included securing the existing borders for an ethnically homogenous state and achieving territorial expansion. As a state in perpetual conflict, Israel justified force against perceived aggression and occupied land for defensive settlements and strategic depth. Besides, a peace settlement with the Arabs would imply the surrender of land and the return of refugees, both of which are antithetical to Zionism. Morris supports this argument and suggests that Israel sought to provoke the 1956 war with Egypt.[77]

Although the war was another humiliating defeat for Egypt, the Palestinians and the other Arab nations, it paradoxically improved the political standing of Egypt and the personal prestige of Nasser within the Arab world for opposing Israel and the West. The second Arab-Israeli war fuelled Nasserism and the desire for pan-Arabism that he championed. However, from the Palestinian perspective the defeat increased the sense of isolation, frustration and disappointment with the Arab nations, to whom the Palestinians looked, probably quite naively, for rectification of their situation.

Nevertheless the most important development in this period for the Palestinian-Israeli conflict was the emergence of the Fedayeen or irregular Arab fighter. These fighters emerged predominantly from the refugee camps, initially in Gaza and were trained by Egypt. They embarked on continuous cross border guerrilla operations against Israeli military, settler and civilian targets. This development represented the beginning of coordinated and organised Palestinian military action against Israel and more importantly demonstrates the practice of the discourse of Palestinianism, Israel however, viewed the attacks of the Fedayeen as directly attributable to the state from where they originated, in this case Egypt.[78] Hence, the Zionist state-centric security discourse benefited Israeli security policy because Fedayeen attacks provided Israel with the justification for action against the perceived supplier state. Although this assumption is not without some element of accuracy, as Shlaim points out, Nasser intended to recruit, arm and train the Fedayeen in Gaza in order to conduct a guerrilla war against Israel.[79] Tessler suggests that the Fedayeen originated as a response to the continued extremism and provocation of Israel against Palestinians.[80] The appearance nevertheless of the Palestinian Fedayeen represents the beginning of Palestinian armed resistance.

1967 – third Arab-Israeli war

On 2nd of June 1967 Israel launched a devastating attack on Egypt, Jordan and Syria in response to provocative troop movements and border skirmishes.[81] This was the beginning of the third Arab-Israeli war, which ended on the 10th of June with a ceasefire between a victorious Israel and the defeated Arab states. Although the human losses on both sides were high, it was the territorial changes that were to have the most far-reaching implications for the Palestinian-Israeli conflict. During the course of defeating the combined forces of Egypt, Jordan, Syria and Iraq, Israel captured all of the Sinai and the Gaza strip from Egypt, the West Bank and the Old City of Jerusalem from Jordan and the Golan Heights from Syria. Morris put these gains into perspective; 'The IDF conquered an area three and a half times larger than Israel with one million Palestinians in the West Bank and Gaza'.[82]

The 1967 war left the Arab world in defeat was once again, and imbued with a deep sense of shame and humiliation, the effect of which was a festering anger and intense desire for revenge. But the defeat, far from breaking the resolve of the Arab world made it even more irreconcilable and hostile and furthered the state of belligerency existed between the Arabs and Israel.[83] The 1967 war also had international ramifications for the Cold War as the Soviet Union saw its two principal Middle East client states, Egypt and Syria, defeated by an American ally. Consequently, the Soviet Union sought to rebuild the shattered armed forces of both states. The events of 1967 also prompted the Arab-Israeli conflict to be transferred to the regular session of the UN General Assembly, the outcome of which was one of the most important UN resolutions of the conflict thus far, UN Security Council Resolution 242. This resolution called for the withdrawal of Israel from territories occupied during the recent conflict and the respect and acknowledgement of the sovereignty, territorial integrity and political independence of every state in the area.[84] Resolution 242 effectively enshrined the principle of land for peace or withdrawal of Israel from occupied areas in return for state recognition. According to Tessler it 'established a coherent framework within which peace could be sought'.[85] As a result of this the Arab-Israeli conflict became internationalised. Hourani suggests, 'The war (1967) left its mark on everyone in the world who identified with Jews or Arabs and what was a local conflict became a world wide one.'[86]

From the Israeli perspective the Six-Day War, was the 'most spectacular military victory in Israeli history'.[87] The war reaffirmed the Israeli Zionist discourse and the conventional understanding of the hostility of the Arab nations towards Israel, as the 'live or die' situation in which Israel exists. Morris calls this fight for survival by Israel, 'the mortal fear for the existence of the national collective'.[88] According to Finkelstein the central Israeli rationale for the pre-emptive strike (which he considers a myth) was that Israel faced imminent destruction.[89] However, the subsequent victory was a vindication of the security provided by Zionist discourse because the Six-Day War is seen as 'defensive,' and although it was initiated by Israel it is understood as an example of the importance of the pre-emptive and pro-active security policy and the necessity for a powerful defence force.

The orthodox Israeli understanding of 1967 further militarised society, it facilitated the predominance of the Army in politics, and established the security situation as the primary policy motivation. Critics of Israeli orthodox history however, argue that Israel deliberately contrived the preventative war to realise territorial gains.[90] Although there is little doubt that Israel made enormous gains from the Six-Day War there should be little surprise that Israel exploited the 1967 war to further annex Palestinian land, as this is fully conversant with the nature of the Zionist discourse. The question of Israeli territorial expansion is the subject of fierce debate, the Israeli defence minister at the time, Moshe Dayan, stated that there was no objective of conquest.[91] However, revisionist historian Benny Morris suggests that some army commanders acting without cabinet authorisation tried to drive Palestinians into exile.[92] Certainly, the aftermath of 1967 saw a second Palestinian refugee crisis and after the conquest of the Old City of Jerusalem it was stated that the 'Israeli people had returned home and would never move out'.[93]

The new territorial situation transformed Israel from an ethnic Jewish state into a mini empire.[94] This is a crucial debate and is central to the Israeli-Palestinian conflict. Israel, by occupying the conquered lands created a buffer zone of strategic depth,[95] which is fully conversant with the security discourse. However, by occupying this land, Israel had become an imperialist power because it now occupied a land with almost one million Palestinians. As a result of this territorial change, a political shift occurred in post-1967 Israel politics, relating to the resurgence of the fundamentalist and predominantly religious right. The revisionist Zionist discourse allowed the Israeli right to claim these new lands to be rightfully annexed as the regions of biblical or greater Israel, namely, Judea, Sumaria and Jericho. According to Masalha, the post-victory triumph of Zionism established a confident, dynamic, semi-military and expansionist settler society, which laid claim to the occupied territories as part of maximalist territorial expansionism.[96] Although these arguments are employed from a Palestinian perspective, Morris highlights the massive settler movement of soldiers and farmers driven by religious and ideological motives and economic incentives, who moved into the conquered lands to establish Israeli settlements and eventual annexation.[97]

The implications of occupation and annexation of these territories for Israel under the discourse of revisionist Zionism is acceptable policy for the Israeli right. However, for a Jewish state that evolved under the persecution and oppression from others, it can now be seen ironically as one that has become a society that oppresses and persecutes another people. This is a difficult and uncomfortable accusation for the Israeli left. The Palestinian writer Edward Said pointed to this shift when he suggested Israel had changed after 1967 from an 'underdog to an overlord'.[98] This debate represents the dilemma in Israeli politics, and is characterised by the left and right dispute of Labour and Likud over 'land for peace' or 'no surrender'. Shlaim calls these two intellectual movements the peace movement and the greater Israel movement.[99] The occupation also caused a further problem for Israel, one that is antithetical to the principles of the Zionist discourse. Israel is designed to be an ethnic Jewish state, yet the existence of one million Palestinian Arabs combined with the existing Arab-Israeli population, created a very serious demographic threat to the ethnic integrity of Israel. This accounts for accusations and occurrences of 'population transfer', which could represent an attempt by the Israeli right to deal with the demographic problem. Masalha suggests population transfer has a deep basis in mainstream Zionist thinking and remerged after 1967.[100]

The effect of the June war on the Palestinians was dramatic, and it fundamentally influenced the development of the Palestinianism. As Morris suggests 'the events of 1967 demolished the status quo and reawakened Palestinian identity and nationalist aspirations'.[101] This occurred for two reasons; the first was the defeat of the Arab states and the apparent realisation by the Palestinians that the Arab states were either incapable or unwilling to help them achieve their ultimate aim of a secure homeland, which led them to take up their own armed struggle. Secondly, the effect of the Israeli occupation of Gaza and the West Bank united the Palestinian people into the same territory for the first time since 1948.[102] This gave new impetus to Palestinian resistance which although originally created as a tool of foreign policy for the Arab nations, now used the Fedayeen infrastructure to develop and further its objective of autonomy, both from the occupation of Israel and from the control of the Arab states. The impetus was not just from the Palestinians, because following the defeat; the Arab states gave priority to the recovery of the occupied territories and sought to promote and institutionalise the PLO as the legitimate representative of the Palestinian people.

The new independence movement was driven primarily by the nationalist Fateh organisation. This was the strongest of the Palestinian resistance groups and sought to exploit the post-1967 situation, by seeking to quickly fill the leadership vacuum left by the defeated Arab states, and assume management of the Palestinians and later the PLO. As a direct consequence of the June War, Yasser Arafat and Fateh, who had adopted the strategy of armed resistance based on the anti-colonial example of the FLN in Algeria, presided over a renaissance of the Palestinian psyche. After the June War a transformation occurred in the Palestinian people, which was similar to the change in the Jewish people in 1948; through armed struggle the Palestinians found an identity, and were able to throw off their humiliated and defeated national psyche. The adoption of armed action inspired and motivated the Palestinians and provided a 'renewed a sense of pride and autonomy which helped rekindle Palestinian national consciousness'.[103] This phenomenon is clearly illustrated by the events of the battle of Karameh in 1968, in which Palestinian forces, predominantly from Fateh, fought a pitched battle with the Israelis.[104] Although the Palestinians suffered defeat, this battle exists in the Palestinian national consciousness as a triumph for the discourse of Palestinianism. Lustick argues that this expression of Palestinian violence was directed as much for the motivation of the Palestinians as it was against the Israelis. This psychological shift 'from downcast refugees into aroused fighters' was described by Arafat as 'one of the greatest achievements of our revolution'.[105] The effect of Karameh was not just psychological. As a result of the battle, the ranks of Fateh and other Palestinian armed resistance groups swelled with thousands of new volunteers and violent resistance became an established part of the new Palestinian identity.

The resurgence of Palestinianism inspired by violence was enshrined in the Palestinian National Charter of 1968, which established the parameters for a Palestinian state, in territory, people and governance whilst stating that the way to achieve it was via armed struggle.[106] The war of 1967 represented a re-emergence of Palestinianism; it was a shift from Pan-Arabist to Palestinian nationalist in the Palestinian nationalist movements, typified by Fateh and the PLO. Struggle became central to the existence of Palestinianism and armed struggle confirmed Palestinian national identity. The employment of a liberation discourse allowed Palestinians the justification to use violence and the ability to develop the ideas of state, such as governance and sovereignty. This was illustrated by the emergence of the Palestinian National Council (PNC), which sought to establish political, social and economic infrastructure. Employment of the revolutionary struggle and liberation discourse also propagated the appearance of other revolutionary Palestinian armed groups, such as the PFLP and DFLP many of whom employed Marxist or structural anti-colonial discourses. The events of 1967 became a watershed for both conflict actors as it established the parameters for the current Palestinian-Israeli conflict and sowed the seeds for further bloody conflict.

1973 – the fourth Arab-Israeli war

On the 6th of October 1973 the combined Arab forces of Egypt and Syria conducted a surprise attack on Israel. Although the causes of the war are rooted in the defeat and humiliation of 1967, it is widely accepted that the Arab-Israeli conflict had reached a political logjam due to intransigence on both sides. Shlaim suggests that the Arab aim of 1973 was to break this impasse and provoke an international crisis in which the superpowers would intervene to enforce a settlement representative of the pre-1967 situation, particularly regarding the Sinai and the Golan Heights.[107] The war resulted in a defeat for Syria and a partial territorial victory for Egypt. Paradoxically this amounted to a considerable moral and political success for the Arab forces, not only in regard to the legitimacy of the individual regimes in Damascus and Cairo but also for the prestige, honour and dignity of the Arab World.[108] The war illustrated the ability of the Arab nations to not only seek the initiative and attack Israel but also to inflict considerable damage, thus undermining the myth of Israeli invincibility. Herzog points out that initiating the attack represented for the Arabs a major move forward and an important political change,[109] the consequences of which led to peace between Egypt and Israel. The War also led to United Nations Security Council Resolution 338, which called for a cease-fire and an observation of the earlier UNSC Resolution 242.

For Israel the Yom Kippur war of 1973 was a continued endorsement of the Zionist discourse as it clearly demonstrated the threat to Israel from the Arab states and showed the necessity for an aggressive security policy. Orthodox Israeli history records the events as a belief that Israel sought peace and the Arabs, who only understood force, did not, so after an incredible military victory by Israel, Sadat was forced to realise that the only recourse was to diplomacy and peace with Israel. Finkelstein, a critic of orthodox Israeli history, argues that it was in fact Israel that bowed to the language of force, as following the war, Egypt was able to regain its territory in the Sinai.[110] This demonstrated to the Arab world that occupied territory could be regained from Israel by violence. The main political implication for Israel from the Yom Kippur war was a right-wing backlash. Blame was sought for Israel's lack of preparedness and the government changed to the ideologically motivated Likud party and Menachem Begin became Prime Minister. Shlaim calls this 'not just a ballot box revolution but a watershed in Israeli relations with the Arab world'.[111] The effect of this for the Palestinian conflict was quite considerable as the ideological roots of Likud are in the ideas of 'greater Israel' and are close to revisionist Zionism. Begin believed that the 'Jewish people have an unchallengeable, eternal and historical right to the land of Israel.'[112] As Morris explains Begin viewed the occupation and settlement of the West Bank and Gaza as a 'divine mission' of liberation not conquest.[113] Consequently during this period settlements increased in the occupied territories and right-wing extremist groups such as Gush Emunim appeared.

The most important development however from the 1973 war was the revolutionary peace deal between Israel and Egypt that was concluded at Camp David in 1977. Although the main developments of this treaty related to the situation between Israel and Egypt, it has important ramifications for the Palestinian-Israeli conflict. Specifically, the Palestinian issue was sidelined and the Palestinians themselves were completely excluded from the peace negotiations. This fuelled the Palestinian (and Arab World) accusations that the Egyptians betrayed them in making peace with Israel. However, Israel absolutely refused to accept the concept of linkage[114] between the Israeli-Egyptian and Israeli-Palestinian situations. This is perhaps because by concluding peace with Egypt, Israel was able to successfully exclude them from the Palestinian equation and thereby further isolate the Palestinians.

The 1973 war or October War to the Palestinians, and was an opportunity for them to express themselves as their own national entity alongside other national armies. The Palestinian Liberation Army (PLA) mobilised units and deployed them to Cairo to fight together with the Egyptian forces. This was a successful endeavour for the Palestinian leadership and the PLO as it demonstrated the existence of an independent Palestinian Army and according to Cobban won support from the wider Palestinian communities whist gaining much needed inter-Arab legitimacy and self-confidence.[115] This period is characterised by the emergence of the Palestinians as self-representatives of an independent national entity.

A further influential event in the Palestinian historical narrative at this time was the civil war in Jordan in 1970 or Black September as it is referred to by the Palestinians. In this war the Jordanian leadership embarked on a military operation to expunge the PLO and Palestinian forces from Jordanian soil and particularly Amman. Although Syria entered the fray in defence of the PLO the Palestinian forces were beaten to the point of surrender. Despite this defeat for the PLO and the loss of Jordan as a sanctuary and area for freedom of movement, the war had important consequences for the development of Palestinian Nationalism. Although Jordan targeted and considerably weakened leftist Palestinian groups such as the PFLP and DFLP, harming the Palestinian forces as a whole. It did however benefit the purely nationalist movements, notably, Fateh. According to Sayigh the primary consequences of the war in Jordan was to establish Fateh, as the undisputed leader of the Palestinian national movement.[116] A further effect of the Palestinian defeat in Jordan was the relocation of Palestinian guerrilla forces to Lebanon.

The combination of Black September, which effectively divorced the Palestinians from Jordanian control, and the October War (and subsequent peace deal), which effectively separated the Palestinians from Egyptian influence, had the overall result of establishing the PLO as the principal representative of the Palestinian people. This was illustrated by the Arab summit in Rabat in October in which the PLO were recognised and endorsed as the sole and legitimate representative of the Palestinian people and the address to the UN General Assembly by Arafat in November in which the PLO were awarded official observer status. These events also caused a streamlining of the Palestinian Nationalist movement, and produced a shift in the Palestinian discourse. Sayigh suggests that at this point the sole use of armed struggle to achieve liberation was modified to the use of military action to achieve national authority.[117] The PLO with its new status of recognition now assumed a quasi-state role where armed struggle instead of the primary focus became a function of the Palestinian 'state' to protect its 'citizens' as part of the mechanics of the wider strategy of state. This ideological shift to the acceptance of National Authority and the desire for a Palestinian state instead of destruction of Israel and liberation of the whole territory is perhaps recognition by the Palestinians of the strength and permanence of the Israeli state, as well as the limits of their own military capability. This change is apparent in the political programme of the Palestinian National council (PNC) of June 1974, which endorsed the need for a state and national authority, and by Arafat's speech to the UN General Assembly in which he stated, 'today I have come bearing an olive branch and a freedom fighter's gun, do not let the olive branch fall from my hand'.[118]

However not all Palestinian armed groups accepted this change, primarily because it was a shift from the necessity for the destruction of Israel and reclaiming the whole of Palestine. This had serious implications for the refugees and effectively implied the surrender of Palestinian land to the Israeli state, a fundamental pillar of the conflict. These implications were to have complicated and violent repercussions.

International conflict

Since 1948 the Palestinian-Israeli conflict has been fought on a number of occasions outside the immediate vicinity of the Middle East and has taken on an international dimension. Perhaps the most notable of these periods was after 1967 when Palestinian groups embarked on airplane hijacks, hostage taking, raids, sabotage and assassinations against predominantly Israeli targets around the world. Although the airline hijacks were a new development, the tactics employed showed little difference to the character of the conflict that had occurred since 1948 within the regional boundaries of Israel and Palestine. Similarly these attacks brought Israeli reprisals in the form of military attacks, assassinations and raids, just as they did in the domestic conflict. The effect of this worldwide extension of the war however was to fully internationalise the conflict.

These occurrences of international violence are understood by the Israeli discourse as international terrorism. Netanyahu states, 'The PLO is not just another territorial movement or national liberation movement but a quintessential terrorist organisation.'[119] The Israelis employ the terrorism discourse to understand this violence against them as illegitimate, unlawful and morally wrong.[120] As Palestinian scholar Edward Said argues, the Palestinians are immediately associated with terrorism, so 'stripped of context an act of Palestinian desperation can look like murder'.[121] The Zionist discourse was further supported by these attacks as they proved empirical evidence of the positivist understanding that the Palestinians were intending to destroy Israeli people wherever they found them. As Kimmerling and Migdal point out this allowed Israel to delegitimise Palestinian national claims.[122] The consequence of this was the development of the 'war on terrorism' discourse that was part of the wider Zionist understanding and incorporated all the elements of the pre-emptive and aggressive security policies employed thus far by Israel. It allowed Israel to 'legally' respond to acts or potential acts of violence, which they perceived as terrorism, with military force. As a result Israel employed offensive operations, reprisal raids, pre-emptive strikes and assassinations on a global capacity against suspected Palestinian targets. As Herzog points out, the Israeli policy rejected any form of compromise and sought to stamp out Palestinian violence wherever it occurred.[123] The war on terrorism discourse is a natural extension of the security discourse that allows Israel the legitimacy to act in any way it deems necessary to ensure the maintenance of its security, either domestically or internationally. Thus by employing this discourse Israel is able to pursue and destroy its political and military opponents with international impunity.

For the Palestinian discourse this was a period of international armed struggle, initially the Palestinian groups who embarked on international attacks were proud to be referred to as terrorists, as it bestowed on them a certain honour. However, in response to the employment of the terrorist discourse by Israel, Palestinian fighters distanced themselves from the definition and adopted the freedom fighter discourse, which aptly demonstrates the relative understandings of terrorism based on claims to legitimacy. Arafat in his UN speech in 1974 stated 'the difference between revolutionary and terrorist lies in the reason for which each fights. For whoever stands by a just cause and fights for freedom and liberation of his land cannot be called a terrorist'.[124]

The reasons within the Palestinian historical discourse for the appearance of the international attacks are related to Black September, the projection of Palestinian military power and an attempt to internationalise the Palestinian position. The leader of the Black September group, Abu Iyad stated that the purpose of the attacks was to 'make the world feel that the Palestinian people exist'.[125] However, this discourse could easily exist as a way to allow the Palestinian groups freedom to conduct acts of violence against their own chosen targets to satisfy their own ideological agendas. Although, it is also argued that the attacks were an attempt to disrupt the Israeli economy and undermine morale, O'Neill suggests that they were at best used to indirectly gain support, both domestic and international.[126] This period also saw the continual propagation and splintering of Palestinian groups into multifarious ideological factions.[127] The PLO umbrella allowed for the operation of a number of different Palestinian groups, which provided extensive and varied operations for the Palestinian cause. However, due to the ideological differences, it made coordination of a single Palestinian policy almost impossible, as some groups were nationalist others Marxist and others anti-imperialist. As a result, all the PLO member groups' retained operational and ideological autonomy.[128] Some Palestinian groups even acted against each other,[129] and others forged links and operated in conjunction with European and Asian groups.[130] The net result was to considerably weaken the united Palestinian opposition in the conflict against Israel because it continually undermined a united PLO operational leadership.

The effects of the international campaign were principally to gain prestige for the PLO within the Arab world and demonstrate that the Palestinians were capable of conducting operations against Israel and independently of the other Arab nations. This was especially relevant post-1967, when a realisation emerged within the Palestinian camp that the other Arab nations were not capable or wholly interested in helping them. After the 1973 war the Palestinians also sought to disrupt the growing peace process between Egypt, Jordan, Syria and Israel in order to prevent an unacceptable resolution to the Palestinian problem. Although they did succeed in internationalising their situation and conveying it to the world's attention, the seemly random acts of violence did not engender the support for the Palestinian cause that they had hoped for. As a result the PLO leadership, notably Fateh, attempted to move away from conducting incidents of international terrorism, but due to the diverse and fractured nature of the organisation it was very difficult to halt the violence completely. Inevitably the Palestinians suffered international condemnation especially as the west understood the orthodox terrorism theory approach employed by Israel to explain terrorism and vindicate their security policy.

1982 – the Lebanon War

In the context of the Palestinian-Israeli conflict the invasion of Lebanon in 1982 by Israel was a result of the development and implementation of the Israeli pre-emptive and pro-active security and anti-terrorist policy. This was combined with a right-wing government facing the growth of the PLO in both physical military proportions and psychological operating ability. The Lebanon War was also a culmination of the interaction of the incompatible interests of the regional actors who became embroiled into a protracted, complicated and bloody civil war between the rival religious factions in Lebanon. By the time the Israeli forces withdrew in 1983, Israel had achieved a costly though decisive victory over the PLO in Lebanon. The PLO was not however, completely destroyed and relocated into exile. The defeat also did little to reduce the Palestinian opposition to Israel and support for the PLO that existed in the West Bank and Gaza Strip. The Israeli withdrawal also allowed Syria to fill the political vacuum in Lebanon and as a result of the war; Israel confronted deadly new enemies on its northern borders in the form of the Shia, Iranian-sponsored, Hizballah.

For Israel, the Lebanon war or Operation Peace for Galilee began as a limited invasion of South Lebanon in 1982 to secure Israeli settlements in Galilee from PLO attacks. However, what actually occurred was an all out military assault on Lebanon that ended in the siege and fall of Beirut. In the Israeli discourse the invasion had two aims, first to forge an alliance with the Lebanese Christians and effectively counter the growing Muslim influence, and second to deal with the PLO in Lebanon, which had established a virtual state within a state. Shlaim suggests that there was a 'big plan' driven by Ariel Sharon, which was intended to destroy the PLO completely, and break Palestinian Nationalism, allowing the annexation of the West Bank into 'Greater Israel' and the relocation of Palestinian refugees into Jordan.[131] This demonstrates the depth of the Israeli discourse and the apparent paradox in the Israeli orthodox historical narrative, generating the reoccurring question of which discourse is driving Israeli policy. Is it the revisionist Zionist discourse of 'Greater Israel', which implies annexation of all of Palestine and relocation of Palestinians or the security discourse, which seeks to defend and secure the borders of the existing Israeli state? Invading a sovereign state is perhaps a precarious security or defence policy but as Begin argued, the security of Israel depended on it. He emphasised this by evoking the emotive memory of the holocaust; 'the alternative to attacking the PLO in Lebanon is Treblinka'.[132] Sharon also sought to link the invasion of Lebanon with the territories by stating 'we are seeking a solution for peaceful coexistence with residents of the territories, who would no longer be subject to PLO terrorism'.[133] This suggests that the Zionist discourse is a combination of achieving the aims of Zionism whilst maintaining security for the state, which as I have discussed above can be one and the same. Annexing territory means both reclaiming Palestine for the Jews and providing a security zone; the Israeli discourse does just what it purports – it justifies and legitimises Israeli actions.

The Israeli discourse is driven by revisionist Zionism but is camouflaged in part by the more politically and internationally acceptable security and orthodox terrorist discourse. Palestinian scholar Yezid Sayigh suggests that the diplomatic position of the PLO was becoming so strong that they were nearing a breakthrough in establishing direct negotiations with the US for statehood. He argues that in order to pre-empt the possibility of Palestinian statehood Israel invaded Lebanon.[134] There is little doubt that Begin was either obsessed with security or obsessed with employing the security discourse to justify politically unacceptable actions. For example, Begin justified the Israeli Air Force attack against the Iraqi nuclear plant at Osirak in June 1982, by invoking the his own 'Begin doctrine', which stated, 'On no account shall we permit an enemy to develop weapons of mass destruction against the people of Israel.'[135] Although internationally condemned as a flagrant violation of international law this attack was largely accepted and understood by the international community as a necessary action under the security and terrorism discourse.

The Lebanon war had mixed results for Israel; although it demonstrated the ability to employ the security discourse in order to successfully pursue policy objectives, which included invading a sovereign state, it created a public debate over security or expansionism that deeply divided Israeli political opinion. The Israeli international and domestic image was also tarnished by the events in Lebanon, the results of which led to an increasingly vocal peace movement. Israel also suffered large causality figures, suggesting that Israel withdrew from Lebanon the emasculated victor. Arguably, the outcome of the Lebanon War led to the election of a government of National Unity in 1984 under Shamir and Peres.

For the PLO and the Palestinians the effect of the Lebanon War was severe. According to Sayigh, 'the Israeli invasion of Lebanon and the evacuation of the PLO from Beirut effectively ended the Palestinian armed struggle and the process of state building'.[136] This triggered a shift of focus of the Palestinian struggle from Lebanon to the West Bank and Gaza Strip, which increased support for an independent Palestinian state both inside and outside Palestine. The Palestinian 'national army' was also defeated and split as a body by dispersal to various locations in the Middle East. Not only was the PLO now unable to conduct coordinated military operations against Israel but also was incapable of protecting the Palestinian communities, especially the refugee camps in Lebanon; this led to brutal massacres. The PLO leadership, considerably weakened, was forced into exile and the sub-state

infrastructure they had carefully constructed was dispersed and fractured. Sayigh suggests that the result of this was a fragmented organisational structure inhibited by bureaucracy, patronage and corruption; a
structure that he argues was engineered by, and to suit the highly
stylised and patrimonial leadership of Arafat.[137] Nevertheless, the PLO
were still well supported as their position of leadership of the Palestinian people could not have been maintained by the exiled PLO and
Arafat without the support of the majority of the Palestinians.

With their effective ability to wage armed conflict severely reduced,
the isolated, exiled and emasculated PLO were forced to shift their
strategy to include greater diplomacy, which inspired a campaign by
Arafat to solicit regional allies. The defeat of the Palestinians and the
subsequent massacres in the refugee camps had the combined effect of
eliciting international recognition and sympathy for the PLO and
Palestinian cause. Instead of destroying the Palestinian leadership and
allowing the annexation of the territories, the Israeli invasion of
Lebanon inadvertently 'groomed the PLO for the forthcoming peace
process'.[138]

Palestinian War of Independence – first Intifada 1987–92

This war began in Gaza but quickly spread to the West Bank; it is
unique in the recent history of the Palestinian-Israeli conflict because it
was a completely spontaneous Palestinian popular uprising. A mass
mobilisation of all levels and classes of Palestinian society against the
Israeli occupation and military rule, a popular movement in the mould
of the first Arab revolt of 1936. It was also a return to direct conflict
between Israelis and Palestinians in Palestine and has been called the
're-Palestinisation of the Arab-Israeli conflict'.[139] This war was fought
predominantly without firearms and was characterised by civil disobedience, strikes, protests, street demonstrations and riots between
predominantly unarmed Palestinian civilians and Israeli soldiers.
Although the cause of the war was the occupation it was the effects of
the occupation that triggered the violence. Gail Pressberg lists the root
causes as land confiscation, the asymmetric legal system, the absence
of political freedom, heavy taxation, collective punishments, and
travel restrictions.[140] Socio-economic grievances and lack of opportunity coupled with the concentration of large population densities produced the humiliation, anger and hatred all of which culminated in
the mass expression of rage. By 1992 the war was over and the
Palestinians and Israeli's had embarked on an unprecedented peace
process.

The Israeli discourse perceives this 'war' as a revolt against Israeli rule in the Gaza and West Bank. The situation was seen as an internal security problem and a threat to the existence of the state. The Israeli government employed the security and terrorist discourse and treated it as such. The Israeli army responded in a very heavy handed manner with an 'iron fist' policy and instigated harsh counter measures such as the deportation of activists, physical punishments, political assassinations, mass arrests and curfews. There were also government-led punitive economic and social sanctions that included the closing of Palestinian schools and universities. Shlaim points out that this was 'the kind of arrogant and aggressive attitude that had provoked the uprisings in the first place'.[141]

The effect of the uprising on Israel was to demonise their international position and damage their perceived national narrative as a meek nation of the persecuted. The intense media coverage of the conflict often represented in reports as being characterised by a Palestinian boy armed with rocks against an Israeli tank, had the effect of portraying the Palestinians as the weak David against the powerful and mighty Israeli Goliath. This was a complete reversal of the Israeli self-perception following the events of 1948. It not only damaged the Israeli national psyche but Israel was also the recipient of strong international criticism and almost continuous UN Security Council resolutions calling for the protection of Palestinian Human Rights. The effect of this was to widen the left–right divide in Israeli politics and deepen the crisis in Israeli society. The uprising was particularly damaging to the Israel economy because the Palestinian territories were a source of cheap labour and export products. It also had a dramatic impact on foreign and domestic tourism in Israel. Although the uprising was not a defeat for Israel and ended in a hurting stalemate for both parties, Israel did effectively lose control of the Palestinian territories and suffer an economic and psychological sense of isolation. By 1989 following international recognition of the PLO and the withdrawal of Jordan from the negotiation process, Israel took the unprecedented step of beginning direct communication with the PLO. This began the 'peace process' and led to the Madrid conference in 1991 and Oslo in 1993.

For the Palestinians the uprising became known as the Intifada, which literally translated from Arabic means, 'the shaking off'. This is highly illustrative of the aims of this spontaneous, grassroots mass movement, as it represented an attempt by the whole Palestinian population to free themselves from Israeli influence and control. Although this is how it is understood in the Palestinian discourse another interpretation is of ideologically multifarious Palestinian groups vying for leadership and control. Intifada mythology suggests that the Palestinians were united and rose as one, however, Robert Hunter argues that it began as the 'youth' rebelling against the 'elders' and then became a bloody internal struggle between factions.[142] It is claimed that nearly half as many Palestinians in the occupied territories were killed as collaborators by other Palestinians as by Israelis.[143] Nevertheless, the Intifada established a new breed of grassroots Palestinian leadership within the Gaza and West Bank, which had originated through the creation of a network of political and social organisations. These organisations were decentralised and involved people from towns, villages and refugee camps and whose leadership was predominantly young and professional.[144] Although this represented the appearance of a new political consciousness of the Palestinians under occupation, it created an inside/outside leadership situation because the indigenous Palestinian leadership of the Intifada represented those inside the occupied territories whilst the PLO exiled in Tunisia represented the diaspora outside. From the outset leadership of the Intifada was provided by the Unified National Command of the Uprising (UNC) or the National Uprising Committee who were firmly established inside the territories and who coordinated strikes and disruption plans.

Although the PLO sought to represent all Palestinians, the reasons for the Intifada also arose out of growing frustration with the inability of the PLO to alleviate the situation in the occupied territories. For the PLO the Intifada represented an opportunity to reinvigorate their waning fortunes but also a challenge to their leadership position. Acting quickly to harness this spontaneous movement and secure its leadership position, the PLO sought to establish a leadership bond with the UNC, which Pressberg suggests, 'involved a relationship whereby Palestinians under occupation decided local tactics and initiate strategic plans in coordination with the PLO'.[145] This symbiotic leadership relationship was illustrated by the issuing of the Intifada demands or 'fourteen points', which revealed that only the PLO could represent the Palestinians in formal negotiations. However, the most significant political development triggered by the Intifada and the PLO's new found political legitimacy was the Palestinian declaration of independence in November 1988, which included references to accepting a two-state solution in Palestine. This implied, although not stated, the recognition of Israel and was a clear departure from the 1968 Palestinian charter, which called for the destruction of Israel and the reclamation of all of Palestine. The Intifada helped legitimise Arafat and the PLO, and effectively paved the way for PLO representation and direct negotiation with Israel at the Madrid and Oslo peace conferences. However, Arafat now had the impossible task of convincing Palestinian hardliners that they were not retreating, whilst simultaneously persuading the United States and Israel that they had renounced violence.

The Intifada also inspired the Palestinians to take control of their own social and economic situation. Although punitive measures enacted by Israel forced the closure of social institutions, the Palestinians took the opportunity to establish their own replacements. As Schultz explains the Palestinians used the Intifada to establish grassroots civil society by institution building, in areas such as heath, agriculture, education and Human Rights.[146] The Palestinians reclaimed and re-Palestinianised their local communities into a national mould. The Intifada inspired and revitalised the Palestinian people because it was within and involved the entire community. The national psyche of the Palestinian people evolved into direct defiance of Israeli authority, rebellion and disobedience became synonymous with Palestinianism. This proved a re-birth of Palestinian self-esteem and dignity after the years of humiliation and oppression. Robert Hunter calls this sense of pride the 'end of fear in the Palestinian psyche'.[147] The implications of this fearless rejection of Israeli control were an increasing number of civilian Palestinian deaths especially among dedicated martyrs. Schultz suggests that during this period martyrdom became part of the national discourse. To die for the nation was a personal sacrifice for the land and the people of Palestine, it was a return to the memory of Sheik al-Qassam the 'revolutionary father' of the 1936 revolt.[148] Martyrdom for the cause became a great honour, families were rewarded and the martyrs became heroes and legends in the community. Although dying and being killed for the cause was common during this period, the growing martyr culture coupled with increasing Islamic radicalism is perhaps the root of the suicide trend that developed at this time.

A further important development of the Intifada, which incorporates many of the themes discussed above, was the appearance of two Islamic Palestinian resistance groups, Islamic Jihad and Hamas. Although initially part of the peaceful Muslim Brotherhood that had developed through Islamic Universities, they separated from it and radicalised to violence. Nevertheless, they continued to develop deep socio-political roots in Palestine, especially through social and religious welfare organisations and institutions. Although they initially existed outside the central command structure of the PLO, and were critical of the nationalist groups, they effectively sought the same goal of Palestinian independence albeit with an Islamic state. So developed further rival Palestinian factions with fundamental and radical Islamic agendas and a growing support base in the Palestinian territories.

Palestinian War of Independence – second Intifada 2001

In the period between the end of the first Intifada in 1992 and the resumption of mass protest and armed violence by the Palestinians in 2001, the Palestinian-Israeli conflict was engaged in the Oslo peace process. This involved complicated negotiations on the establishment of a limited National Authority for Palestinian self-rule in the Gaza and West Bank. Despite the historic and groundbreaking negotiations and the establishment of the Palestinian National Authority, the violence continued on both sides and eventually erupted into a second Intifada. This time an armed uprising that effectively signalled the end of the Oslo peace accords and the dissolution of the Palestinian National Authority. Despite the movements towards peace by 2001 the Palestinians and Israelis found themselves back in the same debilitating cycle of violence that had characterised the conflict since 1936.

In spite of the apparent successes of the Oslo peace process Israel responded to the armed uprising with the familiar security and terrorist discourse and re-imposed military rule on the Palestinian territories. This was not perhaps a departure from the policy employed before the peace process as arguably Israel had in-fact been using this discourse continually. Allied to the security discourse, the 'war on terrorism' discourse was maintained throughout the Oslo peace process. Effectively Israel was able to pursue a twin track policy of political peace with the Palestinians whilst maintaining war on their potential enemies, such as political assassinations and anti-terrorist operations. Israel never deviated from maintaining the revisionist Zionist discourse under the umbrella of the security discourse and is not prepared, it seems, to allow the existence of a Palestinian state. By maintaining the conflict with the Palestinians, Israel is able justify the use of its superior military strength to prevent any form of it appearing, together with an unremitting policy of settlement construction in the West Bank and Gaza. In response to suicide attacks Israel was able to destroy almost the entire infrastructure of the fledgling Palestinian National Authority by levelling Arafat's compound in Ramallah in September 2002. This effectively stripped Arafat of political operating ability.

Also Avi Shlaim's 'Iron Wall' revisionist Zionist theory is now a reality with the construction of a security fence that when completed will be an actual iron wall between the two communities. This suggests that far from abandoning the security discourse during the Oslo process, Israel always maintained this understanding, which is perhaps antithetical to a conflict solution. The question raised by this wall construction is familiar with the security discourse versus revisionist Zionist debate; under the policy of security is the construction of the wall in fact a disguised attempt to annex land, which will not only benefit the greater Israel movement but effectively emasculate the Palestinian territory to such an extent that they are unable to create a functioning state?

The Al-Aqsa Intifada is an expression of frustration by the Palestinian population over the failure of Oslo, the inability of the PLO to alleviate the socio-economic conditions of the territories, and the United States continual support of Israel to the detriment of a Palestinian state. More importantly it represents the return to armed struggle by the Palestinian people, either to attack Israeli targets or to defend themselves against Israeli army incursions. It also demonstrates the increasing strength and support for the Islamic groups, especially Hamas whose policy of suicide attacks against targets within Israel has raised its profile and swelled the ranks of its supporters. It also demonstrates a trend in new Palestinian armed groups, such as the al Aqsa Martyrs brigade, who are increasingly likely to operate without central command.

The second Intifada is a return to, or perhaps a continuation of, the discourse of armed struggle against Israel. This discourse in the al-Aqsa Intifada could exist in two forms, a nationalist understanding to form a state in the mould of a secular Palestinian Authority or the Islamic discourse of establishing an Islamic state not just in the accepted Palestinian pre-state area but also in the whole region. This is a return to the aims of 1936 and the Palestinian charter of 1968, which called for the destruction of Israel. This demonstrates the continued infighting and fragmenting of the Palestinian community, but also shows the continuity of the conflict discourse of Palestinianism. Despite the fact that they are ideologically different groups they all seek the same end result; Palestinian identity and a Palestinian state, and they employ violence to achieve it.

Conflict discourses: impasse

The current situation clearly illustrates the common thread of opposing discourses accompanying national narratives that have sustained this conflict from the very beginning. Israel has maintained a security policy based on the protection of the ethnic Jewish state of Israel in

Palestine: the Zionist discourse. It has occupied, annexed and settled further areas in Palestine and has sought to remove Palestinian people. It has also refused to engage with the issues central to the Palestinian understanding of the conflict, which are Palestinian lands, the return of refugees and the status of the Old City of Jerusalem. These demonstrate adherence to the Zionist, albeit revisionist, discourse. Israel can employ this discourse because it can argue that the Arabs (Palestinians) intend to destroy them, this has been clearly demonstrated since 1936. They can also maintain a security policy to justify their defensive violence against the Palestinians, which involves preventing the establishment of a Palestinian state by occupation, settlement and containment. Israel also has a vested interest in maintaining the conflict as this allows it to sustain their security discourse and keep alive their ancient historical claim to the whole region.

Similarly, the Palestinians employment of the discourse of Palestinianism, comprising of Identity, Nationalism and Pan-Arabism, requires the formation and acceptance of a Palestinian state. The Palestinians have employed a number of different tactics to achieve this but have ultimately returned to armed action and terrorism, perhaps because this is *the* discourse of a national liberation movement, which they consider themselves to be. The Palestinians fight for independence from Israel, who they claim intend to destroy them, and have empirical evidence of this from 1936. Hence they employ a national revolutionary discourse (both secular and religious) to justify and legitimise their use of violence.

The nature of the impasse between the Palestinians and Israelis is the nature of the incompatibilities of the conflict discourses, which is conflict–incompatible goals. Unless both the Palestinians and Israelis actually change their established conflict discourses it is not possible to entertain a resolution to the conflict. This survey of the historical literature of the Palestinian-Israeli conflict has shown that despite the wars, conflict and terrorism, interspersed with negotiations and peace agreements, the conflict discourses have remained largely unchanged.

The nature of the discourses employed by the Palestinians and Israelis suggest that the actors have no desire to end the conflict. Zionism is centred on maintaining an ethnically homogeneous Jewish state; to abandon the security discourse underwritten by revisionist Zionism could effectively mean the end of the Jewish state as a racially pure entity. A unified one-state solution within the whole of Palestine encompassing both Jews and Arabs cannot be entertained without the complete rejection of the Zionist discourse. Whilst the Israeli left and the peace movement have criticised the extreme policies and actions of the predominantly ruling Israeli right, their recommendations stop well short of suggesting the disestablishment of the state of Israel. The Jews fear that the Palestinians are still committed to a Palestinian state in the whole region and foresee in their own destruction the establishment of a Palestinian state. The Palestinians also have a reason to maintain the conflict, as a settlement other than that which provided them with a Palestinian state incorporating the homelands and the settlement of refugees would be a betrayal of the Palestinian people.

The purpose of this chapter was to review the historical literature of the Palestinian-Israeli conflict and develop an understanding of the employment and application of the different conflict discourses and show how they are subjectively employed to define, understand and justify conflict and terrorism. In the next chapter, I intend to apply the comprehensive framework constructed in Chapter 3 to the Palestinian-Israeli conflict in order to move beyond the constraining conflict discourses and penetrate into root causes of terrorism to demonstrate that beyond the perspectives of the mono-dimensional and political discourses the understanding of terrorism can exist in multi-level and multi-dimensional root causes.

5
Rethinking the Roots of Terrorism

> If the doors of perception were cleansed everything would appear to man as it is, infinite.
>
> William Blake[1]

Introduction

'Terrorism' needs to be re-examined because the conventional understanding provided by orthodox terrorism theory, whilst useful as a discourse for dealing with the symptoms of terrorism, is clearly inadequate for explaining and helping to understand the deeper (conflict) root causes of terrorism. The Palestinian-Israeli conflict is an ideal example of a conflict where the conventional understanding of terrorism prevails and so conceals the multifarious root causes of the violence. It is therefore a particularly useful example for the application of the theoretical framework constructed in Chapter 3. In following chapter I intend in Part 1, to explain how Israel understands terrorism through the state-centric perception created by orthodox terrorism theory. I will then challenge this approach in Part 2, by applying the comprehensive framework and rethinking the root causes to demonstrate the existence of a vast range of other potential causes. Once again, this will comprise of a multi-level examination of the conflict at the level of the state, non-state, structural and individual. The chapter will be concluded with an investigation of how and why this alternative approach might be employed and an examination of the implications it has for the understanding of terrorism.

Part 1: Orthodox terrorism discourse

Israel

Orthodox terrorism theory is based on two principal assumptions: first, the primacy of state legitimacy. This suggests that the state is both unequivocally morally and legally right, compared to the terrorist actor who is indisputably wrong. Secondly, the terrorist is considered a rational actor. According to orthodox terrorism discourse the terrorist is acting outside the law and is punishable without recourse to reasons, circumstances or root causes. The terrorist is also acting to accomplish a particular aim or tactical goal that is part of wider strategic plan into which the use of terrorism fits in order to achieve a desired political agenda. Ultimately by employing this discourse, the state is actually incapable of engaging in a roots debate and examining, publicly at least, why the violence might be occurring, as this would bestow some form of legitimacy on the terrorist and their cause, thus legitimating their violence and potentially that of any other group who decided to oppose the state. Instances of terrorist violence are understood by the conventional terrorism discourse as part of a wider strategic plan to destabilise and undermine the political position of the state. This is apparent in comparison to acts of violence, which take place within war or conflict, as it is a considered element of war to kill the enemy and not part of any particular coercion strategy.

Israel employs terrorism discourse to understand the conflict with the Palestinians because it allows them to locate the violence in an internal state security problem and external border dispute, instead of civil war, ethnic, separatist or independence conflict. It also views the conflict as 'internal', meaning between the individual Palestinian groups, and 'external' between Palestinians and the wider Arab world.[2] So whilst the roots of terrorism are not explored, they are also often separated from any understanding of potential causes of the conflict with the Palestinians. Terrorism is also seen as the act of extremists and is divorced from the wider understanding of the conflict. It is seen as 'unacceptable and not part of the conflict'.[3] This is probably due to the way Israel sees terrorist attacks against 'innocents' as impossible to understand and therefore condemned unequivocally as wrong without looking for the potential reasons why it is occurring.[4] This allows Israel to employ the full power of state machinery in the form of legal and military means to deal with the illegal security problem; this is the mainstay of Israeli counter-terrorist and anti-terrorist policies and actions.

The orthodox understanding terrorism benefits the power and authority of the state and consequently the discourse of Zionism, which is focused on maintaining an ethnically homogenous Jewish state. Whilst it is true to say that states in general employ terrorism theory to maintain the security of the state, due to the precarious ethnographic nature of the Israeli situation, it is even more useful for

Israel as it can employ orthodox terrorism theory to discredit, delegit-imise and consequently ignore any claims the Palestinians have against the Israeli state.

As I argued in Chapter 1, orthodox terrorism theory can be explained using a basic typology involving three concepts of terrorism: func-tional, symbolic and tactical. Functional terrorism is the basis for the theory that terrorist groups employ acts of terrorism in order to provoke a response from the state, such as inciting ruthless reprisals. These responses are intended to demonstrate the illegitimacy of the state and generate popular support or a rebellion against it. Laqueur calls this generalisation the 'mainspring of terrorism' and suggests, 'Seldom have terrorists assumed they could seize power but instead rely on a strategy of provocation...which is intended to trigger intended events.'[5] This theory is inverted and used by Israel to explain and justify its actions against Palestinian terrorism. Following a series of bombings in mid-June 2002, Israel announced it would change the way it responded to 'murderous acts of terror.' Within the week, eight major Palestinian towns were under direct military occupation and 700,000 Palestinian people were under curfew.[6] Also, in September 2002 Israeli forces demolished Arafat's Palestinian Authority com-pound in Ramallah. This was claimed to be in response to terrorist attacks in Tel Aviv a few days before.[7] If according to orthodox theory the Palestinians strategic intention is to elicit a harsh response from Israel then their tactics worked. Conversely, if Israel is manipulating terrorist theory to suggest that their actions are what the Palestinians intend but instead are forced to respond to 'fight terrorism', then either the Israelis are ignoring the lessons of orthodox terrorism theory, which advocate a measured response to terrorism or they are free-riding on the orthodox terrorism discourse in order to destroy their political opponents. This ambiguity was illustrated in a recent and unprecedentedly critical statement by the IDF from Lieutenant-General Ya'alon, who stated, 'In our tactical decisions we are operating contrary to our strategic interest, as it (our hard-line tactics) increases hatred for Israel and strengthens the terror organisations.'[8]

The second pillar of terrorism theory is symbolic terrorism. This sug-gests that terrorism is employed as a method or psychological weapon to coerce, intimidate, threaten, kill, and ultimately terrorise a particular target group. By this rationale the suicide bombings undertaken by Palestinian groups especially inside Israel are calculated to terrorise society. This is how terrorism is understood by Israel. For example, Hoffman suggests that 'the (Palestinian) suicide terrorists intend to make (Israeli) people paranoid and xenophobic and fearful of venturing outside their homes...in order to compel the enemy's societies acquiescence to their demands'.[9]

This delegitimises the actions of the Palestinians and allows Israeli society and government to openly condemn the Palestinians and suggest that they will not give in to the illegal and illegitimate demands of 'killers' and 'murderers'. As an Israeli politician suggested the Palestinian use of terrorism 'broke the rules of the game'.[10] Israel is then able to exploit this understanding by publicly suggesting that the aim of the terrorist is to illegally attempt to threaten, coerce and terrorise. This enables the state to justify the adoption of tough counter-terrorism measures that pointedly refuse to acquiesce to terrorism in any way. This argument is found in orthodox terrorism theory and is expounded by Wilkinson as the 'hardline approach' and relates to a set of key elements that refuse negotiations, concessions, special status or deals.[11]

The orthodox discourse is not only a way for Israel to approach the problem of terrorism and deal with the violence generated by the Palestinians but it is also a useful method to publicly delegitimise and demonise them, whilst simultaneously explaining to the public, who ultimately bear the brunt of terrorism, that the state counter and anti-terrorism policies is a legitimate course of action. The landslide re-election of Likud and the Sharon government in February 2003 in the wake of the second Intifada is perhaps testament to the belief in, or exploitation of, terrorism theory, and the understanding that the only way to deal with terrorism is by recognising it as an illegal strategy for political gain. The Sharon government also continually demonised Yasser Arafat in both the national and international media and even suggested in September 2003 following a resurgence of terrorism that it would be in Israeli state interests to 'remove' him.[12] Although the suggestion received international condemnation the government's approval ratings are indicative of the extent to which terrorism discourse is understood and accepted in Israeli society.[13]

The last concept that helps explain terrorism theory is tactical terrorism. This suggests terrorism is employed to achieve short-term tactical gains or specific objectives within the wider strategic campaign, such as prisoner releases, the generation of funds or engaging the world media. Israel understands the proliferation of international terrorism in the form of hijacks, hostage taking and sabotage (from 1967) by Palestinian groups as largely intended to generate international public opinion for the Palestinian political cause against Israel, as well as raise funds and secure prisoner releases.[14] Tactical however, can also imply a weapons system employed by groups with limited means and resources. Terrorist bombings have therefore been described as the 'poor man's air force', and Hoffman, in reference to Palestinian suicide bombers suggested they were the 'ultimate smart bomb'.[15] Israel however does not see the attacks by the Palestinians as acts of retaliation for its own anti-terrorist actions nor does it understand them in terms of asymmetric conflict. They are viewed through orthodox terrorism theory as unlawful acts designed specifically to achieve a particular tactical goal with the effect of illegally influencing the political situation. They are not seen as defence, revenge, the manifestation of vented frustrations or anger or the final desperate acts of a subjugated people. Instead these acts of violence are tactical components of a wider, calculated and rational plan to illegally influence Israeli state policies. Terrorism for Israel is 'using immoral or unjust means of coercion, forcing decisions not according to power but according to emotional stress and fear'.[16]

As I have alluded to there are a number of reasons for the Israeli employment and practice of orthodox terrorism discourse. They are all linked however to state security, which is the main application for the orthodox approach. In fact it can be seen as the raison d'etre for terrorism studies, especially in the construction of state policy. The employment of the orthodox discourse by Israel is completely understandable, because Israel, founded upon the discourse of Zionism, must remain an ethnically homogenous and racially dominant Jewish state. The political, social and cultural dominance of Jewish identity is therefore a vital core value for the existence of the Israeli state. Thus as Marc Ellis argues, a civil war currently exists in which Jews fight to maintain their separation from the 'other' as only then can the essence of their Jewish identity be maintained.[17] It is vital when considering the existence of Israel not to overlook the immense importance of a pure Jewish state as anything less than a majority in Jewish homogeneity. Ethnic Jewish security is integral to Zionism and the existence of a state because it is ostensibly an identity based nationalist discourse and is deeply founded and enshrined in the Jewish national psyche. As Netanyahu argues 'a distinguishing feature of Jews raised in Israel is the absence of the sense of personal insecurity and whilst Israel itself may come under personal attack the sense of being a Jew does not'.[18]

The threat to the Jewish ethnic security of the Israeli state is therefore particularly real as the Palestinians represent a political, social, cultural and ethnic challenge to the whole fabric of the society and the existence of its ethnic homogeneity. As Gershon Baskin suggested, the implications of annexation (of the West Bank and Gaza) would amount to 'Jewish national suicide' as the eventual assimilation of a population bigger than Israeli Jews would mean the loss of Jewish national Identity.[19] The Palestinian-Israeli conflict is viewed primarily by Israel as an identity conflict and principally by the Zionist discourse as a fight for the survival of the Jewish people, hence, the absence of a roots debate and the lack of understanding of the causes of the conflict in relation to the claims of the Palestinians. For Israel the conflict is understandably about the needs of Israeli and particularly Jewish people. This is above all the protection and security of ethnic Jewish identity, enshrined in the existence of the state of Israel. For Israel, 'the conflict is the interface between competing identities, which is not only an identity struggle but also a personal struggle'.[20] Orthodox terrorism theory is therefore a potent tool employed in this struggle.

Alternative discourses on terrorism

The comprehensive approach to terrorism is based on a comparative analysis of terrorism and conflict literature. Although it is not my intention to provide an alternative theory of terrorism, it is an attempt to offer alternative discourses or theoretical approaches to the phenomenon by means of a holistic multi-level framework. However, an examination of the Palestinian-Israeli conflict as a case study for employing this alternative discourse requires a perspective change as it requires an examination of the conflict from outside the orthodox framework. To achieve this terrorism is defined simply as 'lethal political violence'. This essentially relocates the act of terrorism out of the orthodox moral legitimacy debate and into a wider conflict context from where it can be examined in a root cause debate.

The alternative terrorism discourse is also based on a number of assumptions, the first is that the act of violence is an act of conflict and is not morally or legally accountable from the relative moral perspective of the state. Hence the roots of terrorism essentially become the roots of conflict. From this perspective the terrorist violence can be examined for what it is – lethal violence within the context of an established conflict. This is linked to the second assumption of the alternative discourse that the acts of violence are within the context of asymmetric conflict. This approach is particularly useful as much of the violence that occurs within terrorism is actually occurring within a wider conflict and is often regarded by the perpetrators as acts of war or conflict, such as 'war of liberation' or the 'war on terror'. The rest of this chapter will examine the implications of a multi-level application of the alternative terrorism discourse to the Palestinian-Israeli conflict in order to demonstrate how it is possible to rethink the roots terrorism outside the orthodox box.

Part 2: Application of the alternative terrorism discourse

The Israeli state

> Freeing the great human conflicts from the naïve interpretation of a battle between good and evil, and understanding them in the light of tragedy is an enormous feat of mind; it brings forward the unavoidable relativism of human truths.
>
> Milan Kundera[21]

Israeli responses to terrorism

In accordance with the theoretical framework in Table 3.1, by examining how the Israeli state responds to terrorism it is possible to identify a root cause of terrorism. It is important however to stress at this juncture that the intention of this theoretical study is not to judge, apportion blame or condemn or in fact suggest that Israel itself is a root cause of terrorism. The purpose of this work is to examine and theorise how the institution of the state and the dynamics of its politics and power relations leads to the manifestation of terrorism and political violence, these findings could equally relate to any state. Israel employs the powerful legal and military apparatus of the state not only as a means of dealing with challenges to the state but also a self-perpetuating dynamic for strengthening and protecting the state. The Israeli response to terrorism is terrorism, which far from dealing with the problem becomes a self-sustaining dynamic responsible for propagating the increasingly destructive cycle of violence within Israel and the Palestinian territories.[22] Abu Shanab from Hamas argues, 'Israel is killing and calling Palestinians terrorists. It is Israel who are the terrorists because they occupy the land and kill Palestinians.'[23] Yet, Yulie Tamir from the Israeli Labour party suggests, 'the power of terrorism is to disrupt liberal democracy, we fight terrorism without surrendering democracy; that is what we do'.[24]

Israel befits from the threat of terrorism as it helps to reinforce and consolidate the power of the state. Kimmerling suggests, 'The (Israeli) state institutionalises conflict not because it cannot solve it but because it is conveniently suited to its own purposes...and can augment its power and neutralise competing social political agencies.'[25] This suggests that rooted in the reality of the state and demonstrated by the response of Israel to terrorism is the existence of *inherent terrorism*. This implies that the roots of terrorism can exist in the power relationships of the state. These are against the state, from both inside and outside state boundaries. And also by the state, as state terrorism or anti-terrorism in reaction to actual threats, and as violent pre-emptive measures. Employing the legitimacy of force is a potent method of maintaining state power, marginalising potential internal political threats and neutralising or suppressing possible opposition. As a result or perhaps as an intention, the government recourse to anti-terrorism and counter-terrorism policies and accompanying legislation often infringes basic human rights.

The response of Israel to terrorism and its subsequent ability to respond and deal with the threat of terrorism provides it with a legitimate mandate to enforce a political agenda. Not only does it enforce political conformity within Israel and provide a suitable method of dealing with political dissention, it also allows for the implementation of particular political agendas, in particular the maintenance of the discourse of Zionism. The existence of a terrorist threat and the Israeli state response to it, provide definite political advantages that have been exploited by the Israeli right and can be directly attributable to their accession and dominance of Israeli national politics. By employing an alternative understanding of terrorism it is possible to see that the Israeli right has a vested interest in maintaining the employment of terrorism discourse and the existence of a terrorist threat, on which the future of the ethnic Jewish state of Israel is perceived to rest. The political power afforded to the state by the use of terrorism has been employed by Israel to maintain its political goals, from the pre-state terrorist campaigns of the Lehi and Irgun, to the ideas and policies of Jabotinsky and Ben Gurion, through Golda Meir and successively to Sharon. Furthermore, successive Likud leaderships have consecutively employed a policy of violence in order to achieve the aims of Zionism. This was starkly illustrated by the Chief of Staff in 1956, Moshe Dayan who summed up the Israeli settler mentality and the preoccupation of Israel with security, by stating: '[W]e are a generation of settlers, yet without a gun barrel we cannot plant a tree...this is the fate of our generation. The only choice we have is to be armed, strong and resolute or else the sword will fall from our hands and the thread of our lives will be severed'.[26]

Israeli state approach to terrorists

The principal consequence of the normative understanding of terrorism as illegal, unjust and morally wrong, is that it allows the Israeli state to invoke not just the criminal legal process but also extensive military operations against terrorists, and indeed any potential political opponent. Israel is therefore able to pursue legitimate and legally justified anti-terrorist and counter-terrorist policies against the Palestinians. These policies and actions are fully explained, justified and defended by orthodox terrorism discourse and are often security based in relation to pre-emptive self-defence against suspected terrorists or retaliatory actions against specific targets. These can be as varied an action as full-scale military operations, strikes by the Israeli Air Force or pre-emptive assassinations.[27] This suggests the generation of *secondary gain* or *devious terrorism* by Israel. This is because within the state understanding of terrorism it is possible for Israel to exploit and free ride on the terrorism discourse. Thus allowing it to legitimately, (justly and legally) pursue and effectively eradicate, its political enemies and opponents with impunity. Through this approach, judicial procedures and internationally recognised rights can be circumvented and ignored and terrorists can be effectively stripped of their human rights. The most recent example of this has been the killing in separate incidents of Sheikh Yassin and Dr Abdel Aziz Rantisi who were the respective spiritual and political leaders of Hamas.[28]

Israeli state approach to terrorism

This has a similar argument to the last two areas as it continues to suggest that the state as an institution is a cause of terrorism. This is due to creation of a climate of fear. Terrorism discourse suggests that acts of violence are perpetrated with the express intention of terrorising a particular target group. The psychological nature of this normative understanding of terrorism produces fear within Israeli society. The Israeli state can exploit this in two key ways. First, to generate public support for conceivably unpopular or contentious anti-terrorist and counter-terrorist measures, such as full-scale military incursions into the Palestinian areas or assassination attacks by aircraft, which result in extensive collateral damage and civilian casualties.[29] Second, this climate of fear can also be used to reinforce and support the Israeli state by the control and manipulation it naturally provides for political society. Although these two implications have been discussed above, it is the fear generated by terrorism that is the most useful to Israel and provides a vested interest not only in employing orthodox terrorism discourse but also in the continuation of Palestinian terrorism. Although this is a controversial argument, it is possible to argue that Israel greatly benefits from the existence of terrorism and the potential threat it provides the Israeli state.

The fear generated by the threat of Palestinian and Arab terrorism in Israeli society is useful for Israel because it maintains the political unity of the Jewish state especially between the right and the left. In addition it provides the cohesion for national unity between the otherwise fractious components of the composite nature of Israeli society, which is divided into seven separate collective identities: Ashkenazi, National Religious, Mizrahim (Sepharadi), Orthodox Religious, Arabs, Russian Immigrants and Ethiopians. All of whom are in constant cultural conflict with each other.[30] The existence of a threat from the conflict with the Palestinians softens the dissention between these groups, especially over immigration and status, and gives an appearance of conformity by promoting a sense of national unity. The existence of a threat also greatly benefits the Israeli right and increases the power of revisionist Zionism whilst undermining the strength of the Israeli Labour party. It also neutralises political challenges from the Israeli peace movement and stalls any possible progress of a 'peace process'. The implications of this prevent the succession of land or autonomy to the Palestinians, the return of Palestinian refugees or a compromise on the sovereignty of the old city of Jerusalem. It is possible to suggest therefore that terrorism is generated by the state in the form of *terrorism management*.

Terrorism management is employed for the continuance of the Palestinian-Israeli conflict and the subsequent acts of terrorism are sustained, managed and employed by Israel in order to maintain the specific Zionist goals. This argument is supported by Martin Woollacott who suggests that the 'ultimate effect of the suicide bomber is to keep Sharon in power and to provide him with a constant supply of reasons for his persistent and dedicated refusal to negotiate seriously about the future of the Palestinians'.[31] Sharon's hard-line actions and policies such as assassinations and incursions can be seen as an attempt to generate and manage terrorism and maintain his position in power whilst fulfilling the principles of Zionism. This argument is given further credence by Sharon's visit to the al Aqsa mosque in 2000 which triggered the second Intifada and led to the end of the Oslo peace process but which also aided his subsequent landslide re-election in 2003. Furthermore, the end of a prolonged cease-fire in August 2003 was due to an unrelenting Israeli policy of targeted killings.[32]

By employing the alternative approach it is possible to critique orthodox terrorism discourse and question the role of the state in the generation, employment and maintenance of terrorism. The Israeli state it seems needs terrorism in order to operate efficiently against its opponents, support the security discourse and further the ambitions of Zionism. All of which effectively maintain the political power and dominance of the state.

The Palestinians

> Rebellion is the common ground on which every man bases his values. I rebel – therefore we exist.
>
> Albert Camus, *The Rebel*[33]

Orthodox terrorism theory firmly locates the roots of terrorism in unlawful, illegitimate and violently coercive political challenges against the state to enact political agendas. Consequently the Israeli state employment of orthodox terrorism discourse explains the roots of terrorism as emanating from the Palestinians and their illegitimate claims against Israel. By employing this discourse Israel is able to rely on the legitimacy of action it provides and is absolved from any responsibility for causing Palestinian terrorism aside from existing as the institution of the state. Whilst this is a useful approach to the problem of terrorism because the relationship between state and non-state group is considered a major determinant of armed struggle, it is not the only root cause. In fact the principle difficulty with the orthodox terrorism theory approach is that is places too much emphasis on the nature of the political relationship between state and non-state group, particularly in this framework because the state is considered the legitimate actor. So by moving away from the orthodox understanding and embracing the approaches provided by social conflict theory it is possible to investigate functional and utilitarian conceptions of the causes of terrorism as well as examine wider roots in social and economic factors. The next section deals with these potential root causes.

The perceived utility of terrorism

The alternative approach to terrorism provides the space in which to consider and examine the reasons for terrorism that originate from the perpetrators of the actual violence. The first of these is the function of terrorism. This relates to the argument that terrorism and political violence have a necessary political and socio-economic purpose within Palestinian society, one through which it is possible to generate positive social change and provide a channel to express and alleviate political, social and economic disparity. This implies that in order to make change it is necessary to use violence against violence. Franz Fanon identified this phenomenon in Algeria and suggested, '[C]olonialism is violence in its natural state...and will only yield when confronted with greater violence.'[34] The Palestinians consider themselves in a colonial conflict against an occupier and oppressor and view Zionism like colonialism, as a culture of oppression in Palestine, which like colonialism, will eventually pass to the next form. The natural recourse to this oppression is towards deadly conflict and political violence. This has been shown by the development of Palestinianism and the adoption of armed conflict as an instantaneous response by the Palestinians to the early Zionist settlers, typified by the Arab Revolts of 1936 and 1948. Similarly significant was the formal adoption of 'armed struggle' by Arafat and the PLO against 'the occupation' to establish a Palestinian state after 1967. This was enshrined in the Palestinian charter of 1968 that stated, '[A]rmed struggle is the only way to liberate Palestine ... it is the overall strategy, not merely a tactical phase.'[35]

Despite the existence of cease-fires and the ongoing peace process in the conflict, the majority of political groups involved in the conflict support the use of lethal violence in the armed struggle as the preferred approach to achieving their political goals. This is justified as a reaction to Israeli violence and the perception by the Palestinians that Israel has consistently employed violence to achieve its political objectives. Hence, Dr Haider Abdul Shafi suggested, 'armed struggle is a useful tool to counter Israeli aggression'.[36] However, it is also understood as a way to achieve political objectives. For example, a PFLP representative suggested that armed struggle is employed 'in order to oblige Israel to withdraw and oblige Israel to pay the cost of occupying Palestinian land'.[37] Furthermore, Hamas leader Ismail Abu Shanab argued that the purpose of armed struggle was, 'to get rid of the Israeli occupiers, free the Palestinian people, establish a Palestinian state and maintain the right to return'.[38]

The implication of using the alternative framework applied at the non-state political level is to suggest that the Palestinians generate functional conflict in the form of *revolutionary or reactionary terrorism.* Hence the Palestinians actively employ violence to achieve political agendas, either with revolutionary or reactionary intentions. Revolutionary is the desire for destruction of the Israeli state and its replacement with a Palestinian or Islamic one, as demanded by Islamic Jihad (IJ) whose long-term aim after the Islamification of the whole of Palestine, is the formation of 'a union of Islamic States'.[39] Reactionary is the violent demand for the reformation of the existing system, such as a two state solution that Fateh demand. They want a 'state of Palestine beside Israel not on account of it'.[40]

Palestinian safety needs

Human needs theory applied to the question of Palestinian terrorism suggests the existence of a set of socio-biological human needs within Palestinian society that require satisfaction on a hierarchical basis in order to avoid the appearance of violence. The implications of this discourse suggest the manifestation of *grievance terrorism*. The basic safety needs of security, identity, representation and equality,[41] feature highly in the needs expressed by Palestinians involved in the conflict with Israel. Examined individually, security is perhaps the most important need for the Palestinians and one that can be seen as a root cause of terrorism and a powerful motivator of lethal violence against the Israelis. The need for security by the Palestinians can seen be in three main forms, individual, group and national. Individual security relates directly to human security and is the need for individual freedom from harm or protection from violence and is closely linked to the existence and maintenance of individual human rights. The Palestinians feel a deep lack of personal security. This is particularly evident in the second Intifada and the subsequent Israeli occupation and is clearly apparent in interviews and from observations. A survey by the Palestinian Central Bureau of Statistics found that the sense of satisfaction with personal security in Palestinian households fell by 60 per cent during the period October 2000–May 2001.[42]

The need for security can also exist at the group level, as ethnic security, which is the protection of group identity and cultural values. Coupled with this is national security; although this is usually associated with a state, it can imply the need for protection of Palestinian 'national values'. National values however, can only be secure under the protection afforded by the formation of a state. In the current normative 'international state system', only the legitimacy and sovereignty of the state can provide acceptable security under the regimes of international law and the auspices of the United Nations. This accounts for Palestinian demands for an independent state, and as a Fateh representative pointed out; although the main aim of the conflict was to 'free the Palestinian lands' the social, political and economic benefits that accompany this could only be achieved through the security provided by an independent state.[43] This need is clearly reflected in the 1968 Palestinian Charter, which stated, '[T]he liberation of Palestine is a defensive action...in order to restore the legitimate rights of the Palestinian people to Palestine, to re-establish peace and security and enable national sovereignty and freedom.'[44]

The second safety need is identity. This is closely associated with security and can be defined as 'a subjective but vital aspect of individual and group perceptions, relating to cultural, historical, linguistic and religious awareness and perceptions'.[45] The need for identity as a potent cause of terrorism is continually cited by Palestinians as a major grievance against Israel. Many Palestinians expressed the feeling that their group identity, in the form of culture, language and beliefs is not adequately protected nor represented by Israel. Consequently, the formation of Palestinian national identity has been an ongoing and violent historical process and has evolved throughout recent history into a powerful motivator of terrorism. The events from 1936 to the present day have clearly demonstrated that identity issues have propelled thousands of Palestinians into violence. This trend in the growth of the popular need for Palestinian identity reached a new height in the 1990s and was personified by the spontaneous outbreak of the first Intifada which can be seen as the Palestinians attempt to express their own cultural identity by 'shaking off' the Israeli state and creating a unified Palestinian national consciousness. It also appears that the concept of Palestinian identity is inextricably linked to freedom, which is a very enduring theme and perhaps the most cited notion Palestinians give as their reason for engaging in violence.[46]

A further cause of *grievance terrorism* is representation. This refers to Palestinian participation and representation in the political process and the personification of Palestinians in society. Without doubt the occupation of the West Bank and Gaza and the subsequent imposition of Israeli military rule have created fertile ground for political violence due to the perceived marginalisation of the Palestinians. This became even more pronounced following the outbreak of the second Intifada and the virtual destruction by Israel of the embryonic Palestinian National Authority, which represented the beginning of Palestinian self-rule and the possible satisfaction of the need for representation. Principally, it is felt by the Palestinians that Israel does not represent the Palestinian Arabs and therefore has little interest in protecting their well-being and security. The Palestinians continually stressed in interviews and conversations that what they want is participation and representation. It is clearly apparent therefore that the Palestinians have an overriding need for the protection of their identity, culture, language and beliefs, as they do not know to whom to turn to for security.

The difficulty arises however due to the Zionist discourse of the Israeli state that seeks to maintain its homogeneity as an ethnic Jewish state through religious affiliation. The nationality of an Israeli is Jewish and for a Palestinian it is Arab. Israel maintains the exclusivist nature of the Israeli state by qualifying its citizenship by religion and ethnicity and not nationality. Hence, the ethnic Jewish categorisation automatically marginalises non-Jewish nationals. The Israelis see themselves and their state as ethnically, and not necessarily religiously, Jewish. Hence, it is primarily regarded as an ethnic Jewish State, not a religious one. This clearly illustrates the consequences of national exclusivity that exist within Israel and which automatically marginalise Palestinian Arabs. The need for representation is characterised by the Palestinians demand for self-determination, which is the principle-defining theme that Palestinians use to explain and justify violence. Abu Shanab from Hamas argued, 'Resistance is to gain rights and is a message that Palestinians do not accept occupation, that we do not want to be slaves and want to live with dignity and freedom on our land.'[47]

The final safety need is inequality, this is apparent in how the Palestinian people are treated by the Israelis. Essentially, they exist as de facto second-class citizens within Israel and in the occupied territories, and are treated with derision. They routinely suffer molestation in the form of physical and psychological harm by the Israeli army, largely because they are not in a position to guarantee and protect their own basic rights. Many in the Gaza Strip had spent a period of time in prison or under interrogation and all seemed to have had a member of their family or close friend killed by the IDF. Robert Hunter suggests, '25 per cent of the Palestinian population have passed through the Israeli military court system'.[48] It is immediately apparent that the Palestinians feel a deep sense of inequality, which is caused by their inability to be able to travel freely, especially to visit friends and relations. In some regions they are virtual prisoners behind fences, barriers and armed guards, often forcibly turned away and prevented from access; even those who have the correct papers are often delayed for long periods. This was observed particularly for movement between the Palestinian regions in the West Bank such as Jericho and Ramallah and especially between Palestinian and Israeli areas in Gaza, where some check points remain permanently closed. Notably, in some areas the extreme restrictions of movement, association and expression are accompanied by harsh social and economic constraints, such as taxes and the trade tariffs.

The inequalities that the Palestinian people feel in relation to Israelis is without doubt a powerful motivation for terrorism because the daily existence of the Palestinian under Israeli occupation is dependent on the will of the Israeli army. Workers are frequently unable to travel to work, the sick or injured cannot reach hospitals and families live in terror of Israeli Army incursions into their towns, villages, refugee camps and homes. The principle grievance and feeling of inequality that materialises from this is the deep affront that the proud and self-respecting Palestinian Arabs feel to their dignity, self-worth and humanity. As a one Palestinian resident of Nuseirat refugee camp explained, 'sometimes it is better to die than to live without dignity'.[49]

Palestinian deprivation

The final area of examination at the non-state level is relative deprivation. This theory relates to the perceived and relative imbalance between what the Palestinians believe they should have, politically, economically and socially, in relation to the Israelis and what they actually have. This perceived disparity is grounds for the emergence of *deprivation terrorism*. The Palestinians can see that the Israelis have their own state, a permanent position in the United Nations, international recognition and the sovereignty, autonomy, legitimacy, security, and protection of their population that is afforded by the international institution of the state. Whereas the Palestinians perceive themselves as a people politically oppressed and under military occupation by a foreign power, who have a decimated and emasculated National Authority that cannot provide any of the benefits of a state. The Palestinians are also aware of the economic strength and standard of living experienced by Israelis that provides a relatively comfortable life with good prospects for work and financial security. It is also immediately apparent to the Palestinians, from the proximity of the Israeli settlements in the West Bank, how the Israelis live, from the new condition of their houses with running water and electricity to the expensive cars they drive on the deep banked highways that carve up the Palestinian lands that connect the settlements to the principal Israeli towns and cities. The Palestinians do not necessarily want to live like the Israelis but their grievances exist in relative deprivation and the fact that Israelis can live with freedom in relative comfort and security whilst the Palestinians suffer the ignominy of occupation, relative poverty and deep insecurity. Unsurprisingly in a recent study collated between October 2000 and May 2001, 25 per cent of 18 to 45 year olds answered that they had a tendency to violence.[50] Incidentally human needs and relative deprivation theories, employed to explain the manifestation of *grievance and deprivation terrorism,* are both based on the research in conflict studies of the assumed correlation between the appearance of frustration and the manifestation of aggression. Predictably a further survey by the Palestinian Central Bureau of Statistics found that 70 per cent of a mixed sex group aged between 18 and 45 suffered from feelings of hopelessness and frustration.[51]

Terrorism and structure

> Environment Determines Consciousness.
>
> Karl Marx[52]

The context of terrorism

The contextual approach to understanding terrorism relates directly to the relationship between the belligerents and the history and culture of violence within the region. By examining this relationship it is possible to theorise about the existence of *cultural terrorism*. Violence and conflict have existed in this region of the Middle East since the biblical period. This suggests a culture of violence connecting the present conflict with the historical legacy of violence in the region. The Jewish historical narrative believes that the Romans wrongfully deposed them of their land; this provides a legitimate two thousand year old reason for violence to defend and reclaim what is rightfully theirs. Equally, the Palestinians claim to be the original inhabitants of the region predating the Romans and maintain an even older legitimate justification for violence. Furthermore, the current modern conflict has been ongoing since 1936 and has included five regional wars.

Conceivably the current manifestation of terrorism is due to the existing cultural and structural context of violence that both sides cannot break out of. Fanon identified this structure in Algeria and pointed to the colonial relationship between native and settler to argue that violence will always exist in this type of cyclical relationship, he suggested, 'The native is an oppressed person whose permanent dream is to become the persecutor.'[53] Similarly many Palestinians rationalise the conflict with Israel as part of an ongoing history of violence, 'We have a historical and cultural legacy of violence and have seen many who come and go.'[54] The existence of historical memory in which violence is enshrined should not be underestimated in the dynamics of this conflict as a catalyst for the generation and maintenance of terrorism. It also exists as the justification for the natural recourse to violence which living generations and long dead ancestors engaged in to the settle their differences. Interestingly, in response to a question on the culture of violence, an Israeli Knesset member pointed out that it was a culture imported from Europe. She suggested, 'nationalism, ethno-nationalist conflict and the creation of the nation-state model through force is part of the culture of Europe, not of the region (of Palestine-Israel)'.[55]

Both societies are also socialised to violence; Israel is a highly militarised society. As Kimmerling points out 'the long-term Arab-Jewish conflict combined with traumatic Jewish experiences such as exile, persecution and the Holocaust have created in the Jewish Israeli collective identity a cultural code of civilian militarism'.[56] Also, the Palestinians, due to their to constant exposure to violence have become so highly socialised to violence that it has become normalised and is a routine part of their daily life. This desensitivity to violence has become institutionalised and passed on to the next generation in the creation and maintenance of memory. It is apparent that Palestinian children from a very early age are engaged in violence and are active members of the Palestinian political groups, in particular they are encouraged to carry the flags at marches and rallies to prevent the identification of adult members by the Israeli security forces.

The desensitivity to violence is also illustrated by the 'martyr to the cause' mindset and the psychological bind that makes it very difficult for groups to give up a violent cause that members have died for. It was suggested that the Palestinians cannot return to the pre-Oslo situation, because, as a Palestinian fighter remarked, 'too much blood has been spilt, it would be a betrayal of our martyrs who have laid down their lives so we can live with dignity'.[57] Coupled with this social structure of violence to which the Palestinians are exposed is the existence of the Arab revenge culture and retributionary sense of justice, which often serves to rationalise and sustain Palestinian terrorist attacks in Israel.[58] An examination of the cultural and historical structure of the Palestinian-Israeli conflict suggests that violence permeates all levels of society. The Palestinians position was aptly summed up by a PFLP representative who said, 'the occupation affects all areas of Palestinian life, way of thinking and actions'.[59] The culture of violence also exists within the highly militarised Israeli society, represented by thousands of uniformed Israeli soldiers and civilians openly carrying weapons;

from hidden pistols to automatic rifles nonchalantly slung over one shoulder. Living with the conflict has become a 'normal' perception of reality for both sides. This implies the normalisation of terror, as Nordstrom suggests, 'Routinisation allows people to live in a chronic state of fear with a façade of normality at the same time that terror permeates and shreds the social fabric.'[60] Firmly rooted in the structural level approach to the root causes of terrorism is the existence of *cultural terrorism*.

A system of terror

A further structural area for examination is systemic. This relates to the nature of the conflict system that is created by the conflict behaviour of the actors, and is linked directly to the generation of *systemic terrorism*, which is due to the relationship between the actor and the created structure. The Palestinian-Israeli conflict is characterised by recriminatory violence, where actor behaviour is typified by violence for violence, with each side claiming the justification of legitimate retaliation. This is woven into the justification for violence as both parties employ the orthodox judgemental and moral understanding of terrorism, as each calls the other terrorists for their violent actions.[61] The system of terror is as follows; in August 2003 the Hamas leader Ismail Abu Shanab was killed by an Israeli helicopter attack in Gaza. This was, the Israelis claim, in response to a Hamas bombing of a bus in Jerusalem two days earlier that killed twenty passengers. The bus bombing, Hamas and Islamic Jihad claim, was in response to the Israeli killing of Muhammad Sidr an Islamic Jihad commander the week before[62].... and so on. Such is the behavioural system of the Palestinian-Israeli conflict that produces *systemic terrorism*.

The behaviour of the belligerents, by which I mean the type of violence employed, is equally systemic in reproducing the same type of violence. Israeli Army incursions into the West Bank and Gaza often result in deaths of armed group members but also of civilians and children. In August 2002, an Israeli aircraft bombed the house of Hamas leader Salah Shehade killing him and fourteen others, including three women and nine children.[63] In response to such attacks Hamas claim the justification of retaliation to bomb domestic bus services, in cities such as Jerusalem, Tel Aviv and Haifa. The behavioural rationale from Abu Shanab of Hamas is 'We fight Israel as they fight us, they attack us in our homes we attack them in their homes.'[64] This supports the *systemic terrorism* argument and suggests that by examining how the combatants behave it is possible to identify a root cause of terrorism.

When questioned, the Palestinians see themselves as a pacific agricultural race of people forced into violence by Israel. Common statements are 'they started the violence and we are responding' and 'violence is the only language Israel understands'.[65] These statements are often repeated by Israeli soldiers and politicians in relation to the Palestinians. The Palestinians and indeed the Israelis justify their use of violence as a reaction to the violence of the other which merely reinforces the argument for the existence of a system of violence that has become a self-sustaining conflict dynamic and an ever increasing spiral into which both sides are inextricably bound. Conflict actor behaviour creates a perceived system in which the actors are forced to behave and is responsible for the generation of *systemic terrorism*. This is clearly illustrated by the actors who claim to have been unwittingly forced into violence by the behaviour of the other and substantiates the influence of the perceived system.

Situational terrorism

This relates to the structure formed by the conflict situation and the contradiction caused by the incompatibility between actors and their desired objective. It is essentially an examination of the actors' goals and how they threaten both the goals of other actors and the perceived structure in which they all exist. This is aptly illustrated by the first Israeli Prime Minster David Ben Gurion who said, '[T]here is a fundamental conflict, they and we both want the same thing – Palestine.'[66] In order to expose the existence of *situational terrorism* it is necessary to examine the actors' view of the conflict. This suggests an investigation of all the possible objectives of the Palestinians and the Israelis in the conflict. A useful illustration of my argument is to consider the aims of Palestinian groups in relation to the conflict situation, which for the purpose of this argument is created by the discourse of Zionism and is the Israeli ambition.

The stated aim of Fateh is to 'free the Palestinian land from under the control of other nations'.[67] The situational structure that produces the conflict here is the difficulty in defining what is understood as Palestinian land, a structural difficulty that will always exist. Furthermore, this Palestinian demand is incompatible with the objective of Zionism, which exists as the antithesis to this aim. Unsurprisingly, with this aim Fateh will also be drawn into conflict with other actors, especially rival Palestinian factions who are also attempting to achieve this goal. The PFLP want 'to liberate the land and form an independent state',[68] which again clashes with the situational structure and also creates further goal incompatibilities with the aims of the other Palestinian groups. For example, the long-term aim of Islamic Jihad is 'to form a unity of Islamic states'.[69] This implies not only the creation of an Islamic Palestinian state in the contested land but also Islamification of the whole region in a 'European Union of Islamic states.'[70] The conflict situation caused by the incompatibilities between these aims is very extensive, arguably involving not only surrounding states but also the whole region with the further potential for international incompatibilities. This is very obvious from the global implications of the Palestinian-Israeli conflict, particularly in the current climate. *Situational terrorism* exists through careful examination of the aims of those involved in conflict and links the goal incompatibility and the associated situational structure of the conflict.

The environment of terrorism

This relates to socialisation or the interaction of the actor with the perceived socio-economic reality and can be seen as grounds for the generation of *socio-economic terrorism*. Within this argument it is possible to suggest that poverty and social deprivation are a cause of social conflict and terrorism. Although this is disputed in some studies there are grounds to suggest that in the Palestinian territories where the poverty rate is 70 per cent,[71] the social and particularly economic environment is a positive motivation for violence. For example, a suggested cause of the first Intifada was the maintenance of a constant state of underdevelopment of the Palestinian economy by Israel in order to exploit it. As a result, the Palestinian economy is heavily dependant on Israel as it provides 90 per cent of West Bank imports and 55 per cent of exports.[72] This economic dependence has had dramatic implications for the Palestinian economy during both Intifadas, as the sealed borders prevent the flow of produce and workers to the relative prosperity of Israel. A report by the UNRWA stated, 'this has caused a near-collapse of the Palestinian economy, causing unemployment to increase to over 50 per cent and so increasing poverty, deprivations and affronts to human dignity'.[73] The unemployment situation is also illustrated in a study by the Palestinian Central Bureau of Statistics in November 2001, which found that 24 per cent of men in the Palestinian territories aged 15–55 were outside the labour force, significantly 42 per cent of these men were aged 15–24.[74]

Although unemployment figures do no necessarily suggest a direct relationship to instances of violence, it is possible to theorise a correlation between the volume of young men engaged in activity with armed groups and the very high percentage of young men out of work. Although this debate is probably the subject of another study, it is very apparent in the Palestinian territories that the structure of the socio-economic environment, in particular the perceived hopelessness due to the lack of prospects for the vast majority of men and women to find suitable work in which to earn money, is a powerful motivation for involvement in the activities of armed groups.[75] An inverted argument to this approach, which helps vindicate the theory of *socio-economic terrorism*, is that in response to a question about an improvement in the socio-economic conditions an al-Aqsa fighter suggested, 'when the socio-economic situation was good, yes we forgot the struggle for a while to make money'.[76] However, Abu Shanab from Hamas points out that whilst the socio-economic conditions exacerbate the problem that causes the violence, it is still caused by the occupation. He suggests, 'the misery of the Palestinian conditions helps as a motivation because it is caused by the occupation. But if all Palestine was rich we would still struggle'.[77]

However, those who take up armed action, especially against Israeli army incursions, are not necessarily unemployed. For example, fighters are often people with an education, jobs and prospects and who have something to lose. They are drawn into the conflict because they fight to defend and protect their families, social position and values. The majority of unemployed, it is argued, have lost the impetus to act. As Diab Allouh of Fateh suggested, 'The ones who fight are not just the ones who do not work.'[78] Nevertheless there is a great deal of visual evidence in Gaza and the West Bank to suggest that unemployment and lack of opportunity and hope is a motivator for involvement in political violence. This is especially true of Hamas who gain vast grass-roots support for their terrorist activity against Israeli as a perceived solution to the socio-economic situation. The first female Hamas suicide bomber, Reem Raiyshi, was a married mother of two children who together with her husband had been unemployed for two years prior to her attack.[79] The lack of opportunity also provides Hamas with a wide recruiting base through religion, thus it was suggested on a number of occasions, that when you have nothing and there is nothing to do, you go to the mosque. As a result Hamas has developed a network of mosques as well as sponsored social relief programmes in nursery schools, social and sports clubs, schools, hospitals and the Islamic university.[80] Hamas has penetrated deep into the socio-economic fabric of Palestinian life; this is especially evident in Gaza.

A further socio-economic environment that can conceivably exist as a structural cause of violence is the chronic refugee situation and culture of camp society. This is a constant, reminder of the perceived socio-economic dislocation that Palestinians feel. Many Palestinians still carry the keys to their former houses around their necks and when asked where they are from, they name the village or town where their family originally came from, which is typically in the modern state of Israel, even if they were born in the refugee camp. According to UNRWA there are 1.5 million registered refugees in the West Bank and Gaza, 600,000 of who live in the 27 official refugee camps.[81] As a result, Gaza is one of the most densely populated regions in the world and is characterised by grim poverty and social misery. An important socio-economic implication of the refugee situation is the loss of social status. Many Palestinian families perceive themselves as reduced from the social position of landowners to a humiliated and discriminated against minority. The continuation of the oppression and stigma of refugee status without any hope for a solution to their transient existence is a constant reminder of their socio-economic situation and a continual source of bitterness for the Palestinian people. It is clearly apparent that the Palestinians are exposed to a particularly harsh environment that imposes structural conditions that are suitable for the generation of *Socio-economic terrorism.*

Terrorism and the Individual

Men at some time are masters of their fates...so every bondman in his own hand bears the power to cancel his captivity.

William Shakespeare, *Julius Caesar.*[82]

Terrorism and ideology

This relates to an examination of the socio-political belief systems or regimes of truth that exist within the individual terrorist and which have been adopted to motivate and justify lethal violence. This is the root of *ideological terrorism*. The Palestinian-Israeli conflict has two principal ideological motivations for terrorism: nationalism and religion, in the guise of Palestinianism and Zionism, and Islam and Judaism. Probably the most important and most often quoted is Palestinian nationalism. This ideologically motivated demand for a state is the primary reason given by Palestinians for their involvement in violence and armed conflict. Out of all the Palestinians formally interviewed and informally questioned, the majority purported to understand the need for a Palestinian state and quoted this as their primary motivation for armed struggle. This is applicable to both combatants and noncombatants, who easily identify with the political 'cause' of Palestinian nationalism as it provides a natural, accessible and seemingly readily understood political concept.[83] It is the stated aim of the Palestinian nationalist parties of Fateh and PFLP and also of the Islamic parties, Hamas and Islamic Jihad.

Ostensibly, Palestinianism is a discourse that provides a unifying ideology or belief system among all Palestinians. However, as Dr Abdul Shafi points out, the Palestinians have never been as organised, single-minded and thus successful in the way that the Israelis were in their progression to statehood.[84] This is primarily due to the fact that each Palestinian group and indeed faction envisages a different type of state creation. For example, the PFLP want a Marxist state and Hamas an Islamic one. Although nationalism exists as an ideological cause of terrorism it is important to stress that the nature of the ideology whilst purporting to represent a similar outcome might in fact exist as a number of alternative outcomes, pursued by different ideological groups. These exist singularly, as a cause of *ideological terrorism* but are perhaps not resolvable with a single solution. For example, will Palestinian terrorism be halted at the creation of a Palestinian state, considering that the groups involved in the violence are so ideologically opposed over the form they want the state to take?

The second principle belief system that is a potent generator of terrorism is religion. However, religion like nationalism is often employed by orthodox terrorism discourse as the sole root cause of terrorism, to the detriment and neglect of other socio-economic and political causes. However, as this study is multi-level and the 'other' possible root causes *are* being examined, religion as a vital ingredient in understanding the construction of terrorism can be investigated within the context of other causes.

Within the Palestinian Islamic groups it is possible to argue that religion is the primary motivation for violence. This exists at the elite level as much as it does at the grassroots. For example, the aim of the Hamas leadership is to drive out the Israeli occupiers and establish a Palestinian way of life based on Islamic principals. Islam theologically defends this aim; as the instructions, actions and rewards for entering into violence can all be divinely justified.[85] For those engaged in violence this religious understanding is equally important. In a video taped recording of a Hamas (female) suicide bomber, released after her attack, she said, 'I have two children and love them very much. But my love to see God is stronger than my love for my children, and I am sure that God will take care of them if I become a martyr.'[86] Furthermore, the religious benefits of a martyr are a strong motivation for terrorism and indeed suicide attacks. As the Koran suggests martyrdom or death in jihad earns eternal bliss and rewards in paradise.[87]

Although it is important to examine religion as a sole ideological root cause of terrorism, it is important to view it within the context of its association with political and socio-economic causes of violence, as religion often coincides with the socio-economic structure, implying that the only way to escape a life of socio-economic misery and hopelessness is to go to heaven. Thus, if all dignity and humanity is taken away and life is made unliveable, those who believe are prepared to 'die with honour in order to go to a next life with dignity'.[88] This suggests that religion provides an attractive alternative for those suffering a difficult life, the link between the perceived cause of the misery, in this case Israel and the occupation, and the act of violence against it is therefore not difficult to understand. The appeal of religion also goes beyond just the Palestinian Islamic groups, even in nationalist groups such as al-Aqsa and the PFLP, the importance of religion should not be underestimated in facilitating violence. It was pointed out by an al-Aqsa fighter that although the al-Aqsa martyrs brigade does not have a religious political agenda, its members use religion as a belief system in order to motivate them into action, a fighter knows that if he dies in action he will go to heaven a martyr.[89]

Johann Goethe suggested that with religion 'death has no sting'.[90] This fittingly explains the role of religion in *ideological terrorism* and shows how religion can exist, as with nationalism, as the direct political or ideological cause of violence. However, religion can also provide indirect motivation, especially for suicide attacks by providing a belief in a better life after death.

Terrorism, identity and the individual

Although identity was discussed in the non-state section on the generation of grievance terrorism as part of human needs, this component is concerned particularly with the role of identity at the individual and group level, and examines how it becomes a cause of *identity terrorism*. Identity as a cause of terrorism has its roots in identity theory and by the exclusionist nature of the definition of the concept. Individual identity can be given form and an impetus for violence by group identity. However, the classification of identity comes from both inside and outside the group or ethnic community. Palestinian *identity terrorism* is rooted in the nature of the 'self' and the 'other'. The self relates to the development and maintenance of individual and group identity in relation to itself. For example, violence is a way in which the Palestinians can communicate their sense of self. This is argued by Franz Fanon who sees violence as an expression of individual freedom and power: 'Violence alone, violence committed by the people, violence organised and educated by its leaders makes it possible for the masses to understand social truths.'[91] Through violence the Palestinians can fight for and defend their identity, characterised by the intangible such as dignity, honour and self-respect, and the tangible, represented by state formation, land and religion. All of which are encompassed in their sense of identity relative to who they perceive themselves to be and are forms of identity violence for self-expression. Hence the pithy statement from one Palestinian fighter who said, I fight as a Palestinian for Palestinian identity therefore I am a Palestinian.[92]

This relates to how the Palestinian identity is a trigger for violence in relation to the 'other,' or in this example Israel. Shultz suggests that the nature of the struggle against the Israeli and the occupation gives the Palestinians their identity. She argues, 'the Palestinian Identity constitutes a denied and excluded entity but also a collectivity which is the struggle for statehood, independence and international legitimacy'.[93] The Palestinian conflict with the Israelis is the essence of Palestinianism. As a Palestinian resident explained, all Palestinians are involved in the struggle and all are affiliated to political groups. Lustick argues that identity violence is generated for solipsistic purposes; terrorism is employed not for what it can do *to* the Israelis but what it can do *for* the Palestinians.[94] The adoption of violence and the armed struggle against the Israeli occupation transformed the Palestinians from peasants in 1948 into militants and revolutionaries by 1967. The constant support and unity of belief in the use of violence against Israel for state creation by all the Palestinian political groups can be seen as a way to homogenise the nature of Palestinian identity, it is therefore a potent cause of terrorism.

Issues and agendas

A further cause of terrorism in the Palestinian-Israeli conflict is the existence of single or specific conflict issues. This area requires consideration because by employing the multi-level framework, focus is directed on political and socio-economic causes of terrorism. Whilst it is vital to examine these areas it is also important not to overlook the possibility of simple single-issue causes of violence. These can exist theoretically as a straightforward cause of *issue terrorism*. This section is a departure from the complicated causational web of factors discussed so far and is an attempt to penetrate directly into the perceived causes of violence in order to investigate the existence of single-issue or sole causes of political violence. Although protracted social conflicts such as the Palestinian-Israeli conflict are by their very nature highly complicated and a single-issue approach may not be applicable, it is nevertheless important to employ this lens to examine the roots of terrorism, as it may be useful in revealing sources of motivation.

An example of a Palestinian single issue is land loss, which is perhaps the single most important issue in this conflict. According to a report by B'Tselem, a Palestinian human rights organisation; since 1967 Israel has expropriated 79 per cent of the land in the West Bank and Gaza Strip territories, also in the West Bank alone, 50 per cent of the land is effectively under the control of settlements.[95] Aside from the goal of reclaiming the 'homeland' as an ethereal concept associated with national self-determination and identity, which is pursued at the political level, what the Palestinian actually wants and why they might engage in violence, is over the far more practical issue of family home and ancestral farming land, which is a powerful motivator for violence. The land situation is currently becoming even more of a potential trigger for violence following the construction by Israel of a security fence through the Palestinian territories. A UN report suggests that 2 per cent of the West Bank total land area is on the Israeli side of the barrier. This has split many Palestinian villages, causing the loss of agricultural lands, access to schools, hospitals, government services and universities.[96]

An additional example of issue terrorism could also be water. Since 1967 Israel has controlled the water resources of the West Bank and Gaza Strip, which includes the only surface water supply, the river Jordan, of which 75 per cent is diverted to Israel.[97] Israel therefore controls the water provided to the Palestinian territories. According to the PASSIA, the Palestinians asked for 450m mcm per year, they were given only 246m mcm, this is compared to Israel which uses 1,959m mcm annually, 25 per cent of which comes from the West Bank and Gaza Strip and accounts for 80 per cent of ground water resources in the Palestinian territories.[98] The Israeli control of water and the subsequent scarcity and relative deprivation of water resources for agricultural and domestic use could easily exist as an issue that generates *issue terrorism*.

Terrorism attitude

A further area for examination at the individual level is attitude. This is predominantly a psychological approach to rethinking terrorism and can be divided into two areas in which the roots of terrorism exist. The first is *emotional terrorism*, which relates to terrorism generated by irrational feelings, emotional judgements and subjective truths. The other is *cognitive terrorism*, which is terrorism caused by a rational thought process based on a perceived reality and subjective beliefs. The irrational psychological emotions of the individual, upon which the understanding of *emotional terrorism* is based, are feelings such as fear, hatred, rage and vengeance. These are all common expressions that were employed by the Palestinians throughout the interviews and as Abdul Shafi explained, are central to the conflict as 'it is very emotional, it is about issues of the family and the home'.[99]

Palestinian terrorism can be located in the emotional fear of Israelis. For example, the Palestinian subjective understanding of the conflict is based on their knowledge of Zionism, which is the creation of a Jewish state in the whole of Palestine. The Palestinians point to the Israeli flag and the 10nis coin as proof that Israeli intends to colonise the whole region and push the Palestinians out. According to the Palestinians the two blue lines on the Israeli flag represent the Tigris and the Nile and the Jewish star represents the Jewish state in between, this is also pictorially represented on the 10 NIS coin. Primarily the Palestinians perceive that they are in a struggle for their existence against Israel.[100] This perception of fear is provided with empirical evidence from the construction of settlements in the West Bank and Gaza and by the number of Palestinians killed. Estimates suggest there are 145 Jewish settlements, which in the West Bank comprise 42 per cent of the post-1967 land.[101] Conservative estimates of deaths suggest 3,650 Palestinians have been killed from 9 December 1987–May 2003.[102] The reaction by Palestinians is therefore clear, according to Khalid al-Batsh of Islamic Jihad 'the purpose of Sarayra al-Quds (the armed wing of IJ) is to establish a balance of fear: the Palestinians are afraid therefore we must make Israelis afraid'.[103]

Hatred of the Israelis is a natural emotion that exists within the Palestinians. 'The hate in my heart now is too big to describe to you. I never thought I was capable of hating so much but, day after day the anger increases.'[104] Although it is important to point out that many Palestinians make a point of explaining that is not a religious hatred or a hatred of Israeli people per se, but a hatred of the occupiers. The Palestinians perceive that all their problems – political, social and economic, emanate from the Israeli occupation. The Israeli occupiers are therefore the hated enemy, against whom the Palestinian fighters vent and express their hatred for what they perceive they do to them. As Mohammed Atitti, the leader of al-Aqsa martyrs brigade, stated, '[S]o long as Israel comes into our homes in the refugee camps, we are going to come into theirs and take action.'[105] It is possible to argue that this cycle of hatred (it is just as powerful on the Israeli side) has become for some a self-sustaining dynamic of the violence, as combatants seek to fight each other based purely on their inherent hatred of the other.

Anger against the Israelis also exists within the Palestinians as an emotional trigger for violence. Theoretically this manifestation of anger could arise due to any or indeed all of the political and socio-economic causes of violence discussed so far in this multi-level study. But as a sole cause of *emotional terrorism*, anger exists as a very natural human expression, when the daily problems and difficulties that confront the Palestinian people – which are caused by the Israeli occupation – are observed and examined. This unified expression of anger by the Palestinian people at their conditions has been clearly demonstrated by the spontaneous and unified eruption of violence and protest that has characterised the two Intifadas of 1987–92 and 2001– (ongoing). This is especially evident during organised 'days of rage,' in which all Palestinians are encouraged to take to the streets in violent protest at the occupation.

Although the first Intifada was intended as an unarmed uprising compared to the al-Aqsa Intifada in which firearms are being used, the proportion of deadly violence has notably increased. In the first Intifada (December 1987–1999), 1,338 Palestinians and 493 Israelis were killed in the Occupied territories and in Israel.[106] The figure for the al-Aqsa Intifada so far (September 2000–January 2004(ongoing)) is 2,305 Palestinians and 703 Israelis killed,[107] which can only serve to increase the deep feelings of anger in both sides. Anger is therefore a potent emotional component in the generation of *emotional terrorism* in the Palestinian-Israeli conflict.

The last important element that can be viewed as a generator of emotional terrorism is vengeance. Revenge and retribution have a deep tradition in Arab culture, and it is evident that the continued levels of violence and killing that is experienced by the Palestinians among their friends and families can only serve to maintain the conflict and even drive acts of terrorism as a reason in itself for violence. Dr Haider Shafi suggested that even after the main issues have been resolved personal or family issues such as personal grudges might still exist as a cause of violence.[108] The expression, 'an eye for an eye', is in particular, a commonly reoccurring theme used by Palestinians to justify suicide attacks within Israel. However, although it is the basis for the justification for acts of terrorism inside Israel by Hamas it is also used by Israel to justify revenge attacks on Palestinians. The former Hamas leader Abd al-Aziz Rantissi stated, attacks inside Israel were intended as a 'balance of suffering...if they stop killing our people we will stop killing them'.[109] It can be argued that these irrational conflict emotions form the basis for the spiral of violence of increasing intensity that characterises the Palestinian-Israeli conflict and account for the manifestation of *emotional terrorism*.

Conflict attitude as a root cause of terrorism is further complemented by *cognitive terrorism*, which is terrorism caused by a rational thought process based on a perceived reality and subjective beliefs. *Cognitive terrorism* is a theoretical assumption based on the psychology of how the terrorists perceive the nature of their situation. This is the form of framework they employ to understand their world and deal with the events in it and are supported by relative conflict discourses and historical narratives. Complementing this approach are cognitive consistency arguments. These are achieved through selective perception or information that does not conform to the actors' monochromatic understanding of the conflict and is rejected in the same way that information that does conform, is accepted. Importantly the Palestinians and indeed the Israelis perceive themselves in a righteous and justified struggle against the violence and injustice of the other. Both believe they are victimised, dehumanised and persecuted. The Palestinians and Israelis view each others actions as aimed at their own destruction, they perceive themselves to be in a 'fight or die' struggle. By employing this approach each side is rendered cognitively blind to understanding the approach of the other.

This psychological profile provides a coping strategy for those engaged in violence and terrorism, suggesting that it is possible to understand how the rational action of Palestinians produces *cognitive terrorism*. For example, a Fateh spokesman stated that 'it (the conflict) is an issue of justice and therefore belief will achieve victory'.[110] Mirror image perceptions also sustain the conflict, as an al-Aqsa fighter, suggested, by stating, 'I hate Israelis because they hate me, I destroy them because they want to destroy me.'[111] Continuous employment of a lexicon such as 'occupation', 'oppression', 'suffering', 'resistance' and 'freedom' together with religious legitimacy, build a 'struggle discourse', which the Palestinians can employ to justify any actions they deem necessary to achieve their aim in the struggle. As Islamic Jihad stated, 'Jihad is to bring liberty and dignity to the (Palestinian) people from the occupiers.'[112] The roots of *cognitive terrorism* are therefore apparent in how terrorists construct their psychological understanding of the conflict.

Group dynamics

This cause of terrorism in the Palestinian-Israel conflict is a further psychological approach and also relates not only to the creation and maintenance of subjective realities within the group but also investigates how the group operates. It is important to examine the external dynamics of the group, such as how it relates to both the 'outside' and other groups, as well as the internal dynamics, for instance how the group is constructed, motivated and led. All of these factors it can be argued contribute to the identification of the roots of terrorism within *group terrorism*. Although armed Palestinian groups are largely accepted within Palestinian society, they exist 'outside' or 'underground' in relation to the Israelis and to a certain extent the western world. Due to this 'outside' understanding they can be identified as one cohesive group, such as a Palestinian resistance movement, or PLO, which is intended as an umbrella organisation for all Palestinian groups. Through this organisation they gain their 'cause' cohesion, unity of action, and group justification and reasoning for the use of violence. All the Palestinian groups are pledged to fight the occupiers and justify their violence in the name of 'freedom' for the Palestinians. Furthermore there are many instances of the Palestinian movements working together, for example, a suicide attack at the Gaza crossing point was claimed by Hamas and al-Aqsa martyrs brigade as a joint operation.[113]

Nevertheless, the Palestinian movement is divided into different factions, which have their own agendas, group dynamics and justification for violence through the creation of subjective realities. These realities are relative to the other Palestinian groups, in the same way that the whole Palestinian movement has a subjective reality in relation to the conflict with Israel. The Palestinian groups are also in socio-political competition with each other. This difference or existence of the 'other' can also exist as a cause of violence as the groups vie for political control and social dominance of the Palestinian people. Hamas, it appears, is gaining in popularity among the Palestinians to the detriment of the traditional domination of Fateh, due largely to its policy of attacks inside the Israeli state. This can also account for the rise of al-Aqsa martyrs brigade and their employment of methods usually associated with the Islamic groups, as a reaction to the perceived inactivity of Fateh.[114]

A further motivational aspect of *group terrorism* is related to the internal dynamics of the group. A highly motivated armed Palestinian group can be constructed in such a way that their existence is only justified through violence. Violence must therefore be sustained in order to validate their survival. In their perception, the al-Aqsa Martyrs Brigade gained a level of prestige and dignity by joining the US State departments' list of terrorist organisations. In reaction to this its joint-founder Nasser Badawi stated, 'our reaction will be more action – the work of al-Aqsa Brigades will be accelerated'.[115] Some Palestinian fighters can only exist within the structure of a group, who train, arm and lead them, without this infrastructure they would just be Palestinian civilians.[116] One Palestinian fighter implied that he gained social kudos from membership of an armed group and from carrying a weapon,[117] and explained that it was good to have a cause for which to fight.

Although all fighters refer to the Palestinian 'cause' and belong to the whole Palestinian struggle they are recognised and identified by their particular group affiliation and allegiance, and are identified as such.[118] Consequently, it was suggested that all Palestinians are either active members or supporters of one of the groups. This suggests that some form of group dynamic structure exists that correlates group membership with identity, leading to support of violence and participation in it. Coupled with this is the nature of group leadership. It can be argued that group members carry out the acts of violence but only under a rigid group structure. It is perhaps the leadership therefore that generates the acts of violence. Abu Shanab from Hamas suggested that Hamas provides Palestinians with a way of showing their support.[119] A particular group can therefore provide Palestinians with a conflict infrastructure and facilitate routes for direct participation in the conflict. This argument is not to necessarily suggest that the onus for violence is completely with the group leadership but is a composite factor in how leadership and membership coupled with causational factors create group dynamics, which it can be argued, causes *group terrorism*.

Rethinking the roots of terrorism: the Palestinian-Israeli conflict

The purpose of this chapter has been to demonstrate with the aid of a case study, that it is possible to rethink the understanding of terrorism. This can be achieved by moving away from the mono-dimensional orthodox terrorism theory approach and engaging instead in a roots debate by employing an alternative comprehensive framework. One that reveals the root causes of terrorism in a multi-dimensional format. I have argued that by applying the alternative framework it is possible to explain the root causes of terrorism in the Palestinian-Israeli conflict quite differently to that of orthodox terrorism theory. This study has illustrated that by employing the accepted normative understanding of what constitutes terrorism and who is a terrorist, the Israeli state is able to construct a perception of the Palestinians as unlawful users of deadly violence who are attempting to influence the democratic politics of the liberal state of Israel by illegal, unjust and morally unacceptable means for their own illegitimate ends. However, by applying the comprehensive approach it is possible to recognise that the roots of political violence can exist at multi-levels within a conflict. An examination at the state level reveals just how instrumental the role of the Israeli state is in the generation and maintenance of terrorism and investigation at the non-state level illustrates how the Palestinians can employ terrorism in order to enact political, social and economic change and how it is an expression of their human needs and relative deprivation. Investigation into the roots of terrorism at the structural level show the structural pressures that cause violence in the Palestinian and Israeli societies created by the interaction between the actors and the perceived structures. Also, exploration of the individual level exposes the political, socio-economic and psychological reasons for political violence that exist within Palestinian individuals. The implication of this 'alternative' approach is a direct counter to the orthodox understanding of the terrorist as a mindless murderer. The alternative framework implies that terrorism arises from deep-rooted political and socio-economic problems that exist within all levels of society.

This study reveals a number of significant reasons, causes and motivations for terrorism within the Palestinian-Israeli conflict. It produces a far more satisfactory, comprehensive, and indeed useful understanding of the causes of political violence and terrorism than the limited mono-dimensional political and moral orthodox approach. The primary advantage of employing this alternative discourse; examined in this chapter, is to expose the root causes of terrorism at all levels. This approach however is not without problems. The main difficulty with this approach relates to how the Palestinians or the perpetrators of terrorism can employ this alternative framework in order to justify their use of lethal violence as the alternative terrorism discourse can be used as a justification for the use of terrorism. Whilst the alternative terrorism discourse might prove a useful tool with which to understand the causes of violence and perhaps attempt to deal with them, it also can provide a useful excuse for the perpetrators of terrorism. Any of the above multi-level causational or motivational factors can be employed by the Palestinians to explain their use of violence. This is perhaps a reason why the orthodox terrorism discourse, which eschews a root debate, is so widely employed. Also, the alternative framework is not a panacea for all the ills of political violence, especially nihilistic or millenarian terrorism that is directed for universal destruction and the removal of all political structures.

Nevertheless, the primary use of the alternative terrorism framework within this case study is to provide an extensive and sophisticated understanding of the roots of terrorism in the Palestinian-Israeli conflict and prove that if the root causes are to be successfully engaged, then it is necessary to move away from the orthodox understanding and employ an alternative approach. This is a comprehensive perspective that is both a multi-level and multi-dimensional approach to the problem, thereby facilitating a holistic study that is vital to the understanding of terrorism if solutions to the violence are to be found. The theoretical comprehensive framework employed in this study provides a number of keys that can be used to unlock complicated and protracted social conflicts that are characterised by terrorism. The primary purpose of this is to approach the root causes of terrorism within the conflict with the intention of solving or alleviating the deep-rooted problems and thus preventing the expression of political violence and the manifestation of terrorism.

Summary of Conclusions: Rethinking Terrorism

> The mind is its own place, and in itself can make a heaven of hell or a hell of heaven.
>
> John Milton, *Paradise Lost* [1]

Approaching terrorism

This study demonstrates that orthodox terrorism theory is the predominant discourse that is used to explain, understand and deal with terrorism. It can be recognised by an orthodox definition that is characterised by a state-centric and positivist understanding of terrorism as illegitimate and unlawful violence. It is also based on the assumption that the terrorist is a rational actor and suggests that terrorism is a carefully planned and calculated strategy directed against the state in order to influence decision-making and effect political change by the use of functional, symbolic and tactical violence. Orthodox terrorism theory is primarily based on the legitimacy of the state, although this is a relative legitimacy, it is an understanding of terrorism that has become widely accepted as the normative definition of terrorism. It exists therefore as a pejorative term adopted by actors, predominantly state actors, to create a moral justification for their claim to legitimacy.

Orthodox terrorism theory is a discourse designed and employed to legitimise the violence used by the incumbent power centre to enforce its political will whilst simultaneously delegitimising the use of political violence by opposition movements or organisations against the state. It is created and employed to deal with terrorism from the perspective of state security, without any form of roots debate, in order to legitimise governmental anti-terrorism and counter terrorism policies and actions. It is principally a state discourse engaged for the purpose of supplying a theoretical interpretation of facts and events to provide an accepted explanation of political violence that allows the legitimisation of state violence through moral and legal justifications.

The use of orthodox terrorism theory is clearly illustrated by the Israeli state, which employs the discourse to understand the conflict with the Palestinians. The discourse explains Palestinian terrorism as an internal state security problem and external border dispute, instead of civil war, ethnic, separatist or independence conflict. Terrorism is seen through orthodox terrorism theory as the act of extremists and is consequently divorced from the wider understanding of the conflict, especially in relation to the wider Arab world. The Israeli state sees terrorist attacks against 'innocents' as impossible to understand and condemns them as unequivocally wrong without looking for the potential reasons why they might be occurring. This allows the employment of the full power of the Israeli State machinery in the form of legal and military means to deal with the 'illegal' security problem and represents the mainstay of Israeli counter-terrorist and anti-terrorist policies and actions.

Political violence in Israel is understood by the perspective created by orthodox terrorism theory because it provides a highly state-centric understanding of the cause of the violence and benefits the power and authority of the state. The reason for this is closely linked to Zionism, the principle discourse that underwrites the Palestinian-Israeli conflict for the Israelis, and one that is focused on maintaining an ethnically homogenous Jewish state. Although the use of orthodox terrorism theory is principally intended to maintain the security of the state, it is even more useful for Israel due to the precarious ethnographic nature of the Israeli situation. Israel can employ orthodox terrorism theory to discredit, delegitimise and consequently ignore any claims the Palestinians have against the Israeli state.

Although the emphasis of this study is on identifying and explaining orthodox terrorism discourse, it is not the sole understanding of terrorism contained in terrorism studies. By viewing terrorism through the different perspectives provided by the levels of analysis, it has been possible to construct a multi-level survey of terrorism literature, demonstrating that the manifestation of terrorism can be caused by a multitude of different factors depending which discourse or perspective is employed. This has exposed a general differentiation between approaches to explaining the roots of terrorism.

These are,

1. Orthodox terrorism theory: this is the predominant explanation and understanding of terrorism.
2. Radical terrorism theory: this is occasionally apparent in the literature and explains and understands terrorism largely from the perspective of the terrorist.

3. Moderate terrorism theory: this is a limited approach in terrorism studies that deals with a roots debate.

Although these different approaches suggest a wide understanding of the roots of terrorism, as alternatives to orthodox terrorism theory they are marginal. The discipline is heavily dominated by orthodox terrorism discourse.

The main finding of the study of terrorism literature suggests that terrorism studies is a largely dormant academic discipline which is monopolised by a single approach that focuses on examining and justifying an already established discourse. This discourse serves only to promote the positivist understanding of terrorism and is intended to establish the 'reality' and 'truth' of terrorism and dominate the discipline in such a way that it allows no space for alternative approaches. The study of terrorism needs to break out of this mono-dimensional and pejorative moral legitimacy framework. It needs to move beyond the state-centric understanding of terrorism provided by the orthodox discourse and into a wider and more holistic approach to political violence that will provide access into the deep socio-political roots of the violence and facilitate movement towards a resolution of terrorism.

Approaching conflict

Conflict studies by comparison, is far more advanced in explaining the roots of violence and employs perspectives or discourses, that when taken together, provide a multi-level and interdisciplinary approach to understanding conflict. However, the main difficulty is that each level of analysis is rooted in its own perspective and therefore has its own particular use and function. Any interdisciplinary survey of conflict needs to take account of this when examining the discourses as root causes. For example, the state level approaches, not unlike orthodox terrorism discourse, focus on the state-centric and principally political, conflict based framework that not only generates conflict but also reproduces it via a positivist 'reality'. This realism based understanding is designed to 'explain' and 'understand' inter-state conflict and support the existence and centrality of the state and the importance of the Westphalian system.

However, the state approach fails to recognise non-state or intra-state conflict, which is becoming an increasingly important factor in the nature of the contemporary conflict. This gap in the understanding can be filled by the discourses provided at the non-state level. These are designed to understand the role of the non-state actor by revealing the role and importance of other actors in conflict, particularly the nature of the conflictual relationship between the individual and society. This is particularly evident in the examination of functionalism and human needs theory. This level is complemented by the structural approach which provides discourses designed to explain the nature and purpose of the systems in which the actors' perceive they exist. This is demonstrated by considering the structural arguments provided by Marxism. The structural level is also particularly useful in exposing the systemic and situational causes of conflict, especially actor behaviour, and is particularly valuable in examining the effect of the historical and cultural structure of violence.

The last level of analysis employed is the individual level; this is designed to focus on the role of the individual and the group in conflict. It allows an examination of the construction of the identity of the individual and an investigation into the effects of ideology and the potent conflict generators of religion and nationalism. It also provides a constructive study into the psychological construction of the conflict mindset. Each level of analysis and discourse employed to explain the root causes, regardless of how helpful or illuminating they are in showing particular causes, are all based on particular assumptions and therefore suffer from limitations and restrictions in their approach to explaining and understanding conflict.

The conclusion of this conflict studies survey of the roots of conflict suggests some important findings. First, the causes of conflict, especially contemporary conflict, can be more clearly understood from a comprehensive, multi-level and multi-dimensional perspective, achieved by combining the various discourses employed at each level. Furthermore, the survey of conflict studies suggests a general differentiation between approaches for explaining conflict. These can be classed as follows,

1. Orthodox conflict theory: this is a realist state-centric approach and relates to the traditional understanding of conflict as inter-state war.
2. Moderate conflict theory: this can be seen as the conflict resolution approach to conflict.
3. Critical conflict theory: this is a radical, holistic and multi-dimensional approach to explaining conflict.

Synthesis: rethinking terrorism

It is apparent that by combining the best approaches provided by terrorism and conflict studies into a hybrid comprehensive framework, it is possible to compile a comprehensive survey of the methods for explaining and understanding the roots of terrorism. This 'alternative theoretical approach' is intended as a holistic framework that incorporates a wide-ranging, multi-level and multi-dimensional approach to explaining and understanding the root causes of terrorism by rethinking and suggesting a number of alternative theoretical root causes. (Although these are listed in Table 3.1, as forms of terrorism within each category or level of analysis they are not a typology of terrorism but potential root causes).

The state level is the first level of analysis in the framework and focuses on the political top down state approach, by examining state responses to terrorism and terrorists. The implications that arise from this debate for the roots of terrorism suggest that terrorism can be seen to exist inherently within the institutions and policy construction of the state. Thus terrorism can be considered synonymous with the institution of the state and exist as *inherent and devious terrorism* and as *terrorism management*. This is complemented by the non-state level, which provides an understanding of terrorism based on social conflict theory and suggests terrorism is caused by the perceived function and utility of terrorism, unsatisfied human needs and relative deprivation. This perspective suggests that terrorism can be generated by the non-state actor as *revolutionary/reactionary, grievance* and *deprivation terrorism*.

The structural level approach concentrates on the structure of society, and in particular the relationship between the actor and the structure and the socio-economic environment. The discourses in this perspective suggest that the roots of terrorism can be located in the historical and cultural background of a region, and the behaviour and objectives of the actors. This implies the existence of *cultural, systemic, situational* and *socio-economic terrorism*. The lowest, grassroots level of analysis is the individual. This understanding locates the individual in a central role in the generation of terrorism. Implying that terrorism can be found in the ideology, identity and composition of individual and group psychology. This approach suggests that the roots of terrorism exist at the level of the individual in *ideological, identity, issue, emotional/cognitive* and *group terrorism*.

The aim of this theoretical synthesis is to suggest that a hybrid of the approaches of conflict and terrorism can create a more sophisticated understanding of terrorism than the orthodox approach. One that can be applied to conflicts in which terrorism exists for the purpose of generating a root causes debate and opening alternative pathways for resolving the violence. This is clearly apparent from the application of the framework to the Palestinian-Israeli conflict. The entrenched discourses employed in this conflict make little reference to the potential underlying root causes of terrorism. In fact, it can be argued, that the approach adopted by the Israeli State is actually exacerbating the political and socio-economic motivations for terrorism that have been revealed by the alternative framework. For example, Israel has maintained a security policy based on the protection of the ethnic Jewish state of Israel in Palestine, which is the Zionist discourse. It has occupied, annexed and settled further areas in Palestine and has sought to remove Palestinian people. It has also refused to engage with the issues central to the Palestinian understanding of the conflict, which are Palestinian lands, the return of refugees and the status of the Old City of Jerusalem. These demonstrate adherence to the Zionist, albeit revisionist, discourse. Israel can employ this discourse because it can argue that the Arabs (Palestinians) intend to destroy them, this has been clearly demonstrated to them since 1936. They can also maintain a security policy to justify their 'defensive' violence against the Palestinians, which involves preventing the establishment of a Palestinian state by occupation, settlement and containment. Israel also has a vested interest in maintaining the conflict as this allows it to sustain their security discourse and keep alive their ancient historical claim to the whole region.

Similarly, the Palestinian employment of the discourse of Palestinianism, comprising of identity, nationalism and pan-Arabism, requires the formation and acceptance of a Palestinian state. The Palestinians have employed a number of different tactics to achieve this but have ultimately returned to armed action and terrorism, perhaps because this is *the* discourse of the national liberation movement, which they consider themselves to be. The Palestinians fight for independence from Israel, who they claim intend to destroy them, and have empirical evidence of this from 1936. They employ a national revolutionary discourse (both secular and religious) to justify and legitimise their use of violence.

The nature of the discourses employed by the Palestinians and Israelis suggest that the actors have no desire to end the conflict. Zionism is centred on maintaining an ethnically homogeneous Jewish state. To abandon the security discourse underwritten by revisionist Zionism could effectively mean the end of the Jewish state as a racially pure entity. A unified one-state solution within the whole of Palestine encompassing both Jews and Arabs cannot be entertained without the complete rejection of the Zionist discourse. Whilst the Israeli left and the peace movement have criticised the extreme policies and actions of the predominantly ruling Israeli right, their recommendations stop well short of suggesting the disestablishment of the state of Israel. The Jews fear that the Palestinians are still committed to a Palestinian state in the whole region and foresee in their own destruction the establishment of a Palestinian state. The Palestinians also have a reason to maintain the conflict, as a settlement other than that which provides them with a Palestinian state incorporating the homelands and the settlement of refugees would be a betrayal of the Palestinian people. The approaches of conflict management in attempting to problem solve within established conflict discourses is perhaps represented by the historical survey of the conflict because it demonstrates the existence of a high level political understanding of conflict that obscures the deeper root causes that are tackled by conflict resolution approaches.

The Zionist discourse employed by Israel is based on security and incorporates orthodox terrorism discourse in order to establish Palestinian terrorism as illegitimate, illegal and unlawful violence. However, this is perhaps no different from all other states that seek the security that is enshrined in the realist positivist order of the Westphalian world. The Palestinian-Israeli conflict can be seen as asymmetric; an established state against a non-state actor that is seeking to become a state through violence. The discourses employed by the two actors although culturally significant are common political discourses for conflict, that of the state security/terrorism discourse versus the non-state national liberation discourse both of which are mutually incompatible, hence the nature of the conflict.

Re-assessing the Palestinian-Israeli conflict

By employing an alternative framework it is possible to rethink the root causes of terrorism in the Palestinian-Israeli conflict and challenge those provided by orthodox terrorism theory. By applying the accepted normative understanding of what constitutes terrorism and who is a terrorist, the Israeli state is able to construct a perception of the Palestinians as unlawful users of deadly violence who are attempting to influence the democratic politics of the liberal state of Israel by illegal, unjust and morally unacceptable means for their own illegitimate ends. However, the alternative approach at state level reveals just how instrumental the role of the Israeli state is in the generation and maintenance of terrorism and validates the existence of *inherent, devious and management terrorism*. Also an investigation at the non-state level illustrates how the Palestinians can employ terrorism in order to enact political, social and economic change and how it is an expression of their human needs and relative deprivation. This provides evidence to support the existence of *reactionary, revolutionary, grievance* and *deprivation terrorism*. Examination at the structural level shows the structural pressures that cause violence in the Palestinian and Israeli societies created by the interaction between the actors and the perceived structure. This is demonstrated by the history and culture of the Palestinian-Israeli conflict, the behaviour of the actors towards one another and the nature of the relative socio-economic conditions that the Palestinians and Israelis experience. All of this supports the claim for the existence of *cultural, systemic, situational* and *socio-economic terrorism*. Exploration of the root causes of terrorism at the individual level in the Palestinian-Israeli conflict expose the political, socio-economic and psychological reasons for political violence that exist within Palestinian individuals. They relate particularly to the nature of the conflict belief systems, identity and the psychological construction of the mindset of groups and individuals. This endorses the existence of at the individual level of *ideological, identity, issue, emotional, cognitive* and *group terrorism*.

The implication of this 'alternative' approach is a direct counter to the orthodox understanding of the terrorist as a ruthless murderer. The alternative framework implies that terrorism arises from deep-rooted political and socio-economic problems that exist within all levels of society. This multi-perspective approach to the roots of terrorism reveals a number of significant reasons, causes and motivations for terrorism within the Palestinian-Israeli conflict. This produces a far more satisfactory, comprehensive and indeed useful understanding of the causes of political violence and terrorism than the limited mono-dimensional political and moral orthodox approach.

The primary advantage of employing this alternative discourse is intended to offer a more sophisticated understanding of terrorism. The comprehensive theoretical framework provides a number of keys that can be used to unlock complicated and protracted social conflicts – such as the Palestinian-Israeli example – that are characterised by terrorism. The purpose of which is to approach the root causes of terrorism within the context of conflict with the intention of solving or alleviating the deep-rooted problems and thus preventing the expression of political violence and the manifestation of terrorism.

Legitimacy

Attempts at dealing with terrorism using the orthodox theory are focused primarily on confronting symptomatic violence with either more violence, as state force, or by criminal and legal methods. This is management of terrorism and arguably is the only avenue available because the predominance of state legitimacy eschews a roots debate. If the state intends to actually resolve the violence, it needs to move outside the orthodox terrorism discourse and bestow some form of legitimacy on the claims of the actor producing the terrorism. It then needs to engage in a roots debate to solve the deep political and socio-economic reasons that are generating the cause of the violence. This I suggest is a 'peace process' and is conflict transformation in an established procedure that is more than just a respite from violence; it is a discourse shift, potentially from the orthodox understanding of terrorism to engaging with them as legitimate actors. Examples of which have occurred in Northern Ireland, Sri Lanka and Peru. During this process there is a change in the lexicon; terrorist actors are no longer referred to as terrorists, instead they are militants or fighters in value neutral conflict language, and are engaged in negotiations as legitimate actors and in some instances pardoned for 'terrorist crimes' that they were once tried and imprisoned for. This has been particularly apparent in Northern Ireland. There is also progress in dealing with the political and socio-economic structural problems. So what changed? Although the questions that arise from this legitimacy argument are probably the subject of another study they are pertinent to understanding the role of legitimacy within the state in relation to orthodox terrorism theory and alternative root cause discourse debate, so:

1. When does the transition occur? At what point does the terrorist actor become legitimate? After a particular time period? At a certain level of violence? After a specified number of deaths?
2. Why does it happen? During a hurting stalemate? In untenable political situation? After recognition of the underlying causes of the violence? At the end of violence?
3. What is the form of the decision process that decides a group employing violence should gain legitimacy to their demands?
4. How can this occur considering orthodox terrorism theory gives no quarter to actors using violence? Is a peace process therefore a sign of victory for terrorists against the orthodox understanding? Does this show orthodox terrorism theory to be a flawed approach?

The point to stress is that a discourse transformation can occur. This suggests that at some point, a roots of terrorism discourse, incorporating the comprehensive causes of terrorism discussed in this study, can be applied by the state. It also demonstrates that orthodox terrorism theory is indeed a discourse that is employed to deal with the violent demands of illegitimate threats to the state, before they become legitimate, if they ever do. Orthodox terrorism theory is a crisis management coping mechanism employed by the state in response to anti-state violence, employed perhaps, whilst the state decides on the pertinence of the claim of the terrorists to legitimacy. However, given that orthodox terrorism theory legitimises state violence (as terrorism) in the form of anti-terrorism and counter-terrorism, which actually causes further terrorism, and also cannot recognise any form of legitimacy other that the state. Is orthodox terrorism theory, on close examination, actually incapable of dealing with terrorism? And therefore whilst it is employed, can terrorism as illegitimate violence ever be eradicated? The critique of orthodox terrorism theory contained in this study suggests this might indeed be the case.

Complexity

Orthodox terrorism theory provides a simple method of understanding the manifestation of political violence against the state. It supplies a discourse, which can be understood by the government and the governed, and it defends the core security of the state – the legitimacy to govern – and is the basis for dealing with terrorism by providing the foundation for anti-terrorism and counter terrorism methods, which to a society affected by terrorism is a vital response. In the interests of parsimony therefore the definition and understanding of the complex and dangerous phenomenon of terrorism is well served by orthodox terrorism theory. By engaging in the complicated roots of terrorism debate, the state is not necessarily dealing directly with the violence, and to deal with so many possible root causes is a long-term investment with no guarantee of the expected return of peace in the short-term. Also, orthodox terrorism theory would argue that by employing a roots debate to counter the terrorism, the perpetrators have circumvented the political process, which in a democracy is a serious problem with dangerous, precedent setting implications.

The definitions of terrorism supplied by orthodox terrorism theory also provide a relative simplicity. The implications of adopting a definition of terrorism as broad as 'lethal political violence' and redefining the phenomenon as 'conflict' will cause a complexity of understanding and immense difficulties in dealing with the violence. It also implies terrorism with out terror, which is the foundation of the accepted understanding of terrorism. Using an alternative understanding of terrorism also undermines the purpose and foundations of the state, the implications of which for the state are potentially very serious. This discourse debate can be condensed dramatically and perhaps summed up as orthodox terrorism theory and state survival versus the roots discourse and state collapse.

The difficulties of the comprehensive framework relate to its complex approach to terrorism and the multifarious nature of the root causes. These might potentially relate to a vast number of grievances, which cannot be satisfied by the state without completely undermining its position and making governance untenable. Furthermore, how is a terrorist actor, which intends to destroy the entire existing framework of society, (such as the millennial cults or fanatic religious extremists whose aim is world destruction) to be approached even within the comprehensive discourse? Surely, these types of terrorist threats suggested here require the mono-dimensional, state-centric, non-negotiable force of counter-terrorism? Although the comprehensive framework is not designed as an alternative terrorism theory: it is constructed to demonstrate the existence of alternative ways to understand terrorism and approach the root causes beyond the constraints of the political legitimacy debate. The application of the comprehensive framework could raise questions relating to whether the millennial group were actually as cohesive as orthodox terrorism theory would suggest. The violence could be investigated to ascertain the levels on which it is generated and how the causes can be approached and resolved. For example, what is the role of the state in creating the millennial violence? Do members of the group have unfulfilled needs or deprivation issues that are leading them into the cult? What structural issues are generating the violence? and what is the role of the individual? Although this is the comprehensive approach only in outline, it demonstrates how this approach can ask questions about the roots of their actions in order to penetrate beyond the immediate monodimensional understanding.

The difficulty with this approach, however, is that this may only placate a certain number of those involved in the violence, especially if is related to extreme cults such as Aum Shrinkyo[2] or particular issues that cannot be resolved by the state without its own destruction. The state is truly then in conflict with the terrorist actor, as the incompatibility of goals suggests. However, if the comprehensive approach has been employed to deal with the root causes then only a marginalised and irreconcilable minority will remain – to be dealt with by the state. Although orthodox terrorism theory already considers terrorists as marginal actors, the point to make here is that the comprehensive approach can potentially help reduce the core of violent actors by dealing with some of the peripheral causes of the violence.[3] Although this is probably the realm of further study, the point is that orthodox terrorism theory always views terrorists as irreconcilable when they take up violence, but by employing a roots approach, despite the complexity, progress could be made into helping to marginalise those involved in terrorist violence into a manageable few.

This suggests that far from being a disadvantage, the complexity of the comprehensive approach is actually very useful. As Miall et al, point out in reference to contemporary conflict, 'given the complexity of much of contemporary conflict, attempts at conflict resolution have to be equally comprehensive'.[4] Thus, orthodox terrorism theory is too narrow because it focuses on the symptoms of violence and what it perceives to be the actual cause, although its purpose is a defence of the state and an end to violence: it is a short-term solution. As Miall et al, pointedly suggest, 'although peacemakers strive to bring the violent phase of conflict to an end, long-term peace-builders who aspire to prevent violent conflict or ensure that settlements are transformed into lasting peace have to address the deeper sources of conflict'.[5]

Application

Orthodox terrorism theory has a specific role. It was created to understand a particular type of violence and as a purely academic study it provides a useful way of seeing the manifestation of political violence. However, terrorism theory has become an unchallenged discourse, its application has been hijacked, manipulated and exploited to create a regime of truth. Research in this field focuses on propagating this understanding with positivist empirical evidence, which serves to 'reinforce its own reality',[6] not necessarily challenge it. The comprehensive approach I suggest is not intended as an alternative or replacement for this approach, as this would lead to similar problems. Instead the alternative framework is designed to incorporate the orthodox understanding of terrorism and critique its position as an understanding of terrorism by providing a reflexive critique of orthodox terrorism theory.

Since orthodox terrorism theory is applied predominantly by the state it provides a useful understanding of terrorism in relation to the state and helps explain how terrorism is perceived and demonstrates how it is dealt with. The application of comprehensive understanding merely relocates orthodox terrorism theory into a wider holistic understanding or framework of the violence, and is then able, by stepping out of the orthodox box, to suggest that state application of this approach to terrorism is actually itself a cause of terrorism, whilst also implying that this might in fact be a useful side effect, or even the reason it is employed.

Despite the problems with orthodox terrorism theory, the application of the comprehensive framework as a way to deal with terrorism, instead of its intended use as a way to understand root causes, could be quite problematic. An approach employed by the comprehensive framework is to focus on liberal values, rights, needs, freedoms and requirements. However the acceptance of these concepts as a true justification for violence could paradoxically trigger greater violence. This is because elements of the comprehensive approach can exist as justification for violence, and could easily become a regime of truth or 'discourse of struggle', employed to rationalise violence. This is an inherent problem in critical theory as 'the main dilemma of such approaches, which in calling for universal inclusion also need to set normative standards for candidates to qualify for inclusion'.[7] The comprehensive approach is not intended to condone or validate the use of the type of abhorrent violence associated with terrorism, but is an attempt to offer a holistic understanding of the root causes to help identify and highlight a number of pathways to finding possible solutions to the violence.

Conclusion: Beyond terrorism

The purpose of this study has been to suggest that there needs to be a rethinking of orthodox terrorism theory. This is due to the manifestation of 'new terrorism' and 'new war' or contemporary conflict. New terrorism is characterised by lethal violence perpetrated by unidentified, often suicidal, amorphous and nebulous non-state groups. New war or contemporary conflict is structureless, post-modern, asymmetric identity warfare between non-state organisations. They are both frequently irredentist and secessionist movements with religious or ethno-nationalist agendas and are motivated by hatred and fear. These forms of warfare have been identified in chaos of the post-Cold War world and are problematic because they do not conform to the state-centric realist understanding and are also remarkably similar.

Conflict studies has embraced change and developed new approaches to understanding contemporary conflict with more critical analysis such as third and even fourth generation conflict resolution approaches.[8] The study of terrorism has not, and now needs to make the transition to multi-dimensional approaches to understanding the roots of political violence. This will mean moving beyond orthodox terrorism theory. This requires a critical approach to rethinking terrorism, recognition of terrorism theory as a discourse, and a positive engagement with multi-level and multi-dimensional root causes. This is vital for the survival of terrorism studies in the post-Westphalian and globalised world, where the emphasis is shifting from state-centric to homocentric, characterised by individual human rights, human security, and easy access to border-less travel, mega communications, high technology and membership of global society. These may potentially lead to far deeper root causes of terrorism than the state and orthodox terrorism theory can hope to understand and ultimately respond to.

Notes

Introduction

1 See, Gunaratna R, *Inside al-Qaeda: Global Network of Terror*, London: Hurst Press, 2002.

2 See, Hoffman B, *Inside Terrorism*, London: Indigo, 1999 (2nd ed.), Wilkinson P, *Terrorism Versus Democracy, The Liberal State Response*, London: Frank Cass, 2000 and Laqueur W, *The Age of Terrorism*, Boston Little Brown and Co 1987.

3 The United States Department of Defence defines terrorism as: 'Unlawful use of force or violence against individuals or property to coerce and intimidate governments to accept political, religious or ideological objectives.' Hoffman B, *Inside Terrorism*, p.30.

4 The United Nations (UN) defines terrorism in relation to international conventions, which attempt to deal with terrorism by prohibiting the method of violence used, such as Hijack and Bombing. See www.un.org.

5 Terrorism has also been defined as simply violence against civilians. See, Wilkinson P, *Terrorism Versus Democracy*.

6 See, Kaldor M, *New and Old Wars*, London: Polity Press, 1999 and Laquer W, *The New Terrorism*, Oxford: Phoenix Press, 3rd ed., 2001 and Gilbert P, *New Terror New Wars*, Edinburgh: Edinburgh University Press, 2003 and Holsti K J, *The State, War and The State of War*, Cambridge: Cambridge University Press, 1996.

7 See, Baylis J, Smith S, *The Globalisation of World Politics*, Oxford: Oxford University Press, 5th ed, 1999.

8 See, Linklater A, *The Transformation of Political Community*, University of South Carolina Press, 1998.

9 Richmond O, *Maintaining Order, Making Peace*, Basingstoke, Hants: Palgrave, 2002, p.4.

10 See, Boulding E, *Building a Global Civic Culture*, Syracuse, NY: Syracuse University Press, 1990. Vayryen R, *New Directions in Conflict Theory*, London: Sage and Lederach J P, *Building Peace*, Tokyo: United Nations University Press, 1997.

11 Laqueur W, *The New Terrorism*, Oxford: Phoenix Press, 3rd ed., 2001.

12 This debate is based on the legitimacy/illegitimacy dualism that constructs non-state violence as terrorist while state violence is deemed to be legitimate. It is summed up in the expression, 'one man's freedom fighter is another man's terrorist'.

13 See, Cox R W, *Approaches to World Order*, Cambridge: Cambridge University Press, 1996, also, Linklater A, Macmillan J, *Boundaries in Question*, London: Pinter, 1995, and Walker R B J, *Inside/Outside*, Cambridge: Cambridge University Press, 1993.

14 George J, *Discourses of Global Politics*, Colorado: Lynne Rienner, 1994.

15 Cox R W, *Approaches to World Order*, p.10.

16   Cox R W, *Approaches to World Order*, p.88.
17   Cox R W, *Approaches to World Order*, p.87.
18   Bleiker R, *Popular Dissent, Human Agency and Global Politics*, Cambridge: Cambridge University Press, 2000, p.17.
19   Linklater A, Macmillan J, *Boundaries in Question*, London: Pinter, 1995. Also see, Linklater A, *The Transformation of the Political Community*, University of South Carolina Press, 1998.
20   George J, *Discourses*, p.28.
21   George J, *Discourses*, p.29.
22   Foucault M, *Power and Knowledge*, New York: Harvester Wheatsheaf, 1980.
23   The positivist debate relates to the debate on the construction of knowledge. Positivism is based on assumptions relating to: the unity of science, the neutrality of facts, the regularity of the 'natural world' and the determination of the 'truth' by using these neutral facts in an empiricist epistemology. See, Baylis J and Smith S, *Globalisation*, p.168.
24   George J, *Discourses*, p.221.
25   Bleiker R, *Popular Dissent*, p.17.
26   Edkins J, *Poststructuralism and International Relations*, London: Lynne Rienner, 1999, p.48.
27   Foucault M, *'Intellectuals and Power: A conversation between Michel Foucault and Gilles Deleuze'*, in Bouchard D, *Language, Counter-memory, Practice*, New York: New York University Press, 1977, p.208. Quoted in Edkins, *Poststructuralism*, p.17.
28   Walker R B J, *Inside/Outside*, Cambridge: Cambridge University Press, 1993, p.29.
29   Smith S, 'New Approaches to International Theory', in Baylis J and Smith S, *Globalisation*, p.176.
30   See, Hollis M, Smith S, *Explaining and Understanding International Relations*, Oxford: Oxford University Press, 3rd ed, 1992.
31   See, Jerbis R, *Perception and Misperception in International Politics*, New Jersey: University of New Jersey Press, 1976, pp.3–7.

Chapter 1   The Root Causes of Terrorism: Orthodox Terrorism Theory

1   See, Schmid A, Jongman A, *Political Terrorism: A Guide to Actors, Authors, Concepts, Data Bases, Theories and Literature*, Oxford: North Holland, 1988.
2   Grey Area Phenomenon has been used to denote and describe the fluid and unstable post Cold War World that is beset with new conflicts, acts of terrorism, insurgency, drug-trafficking, warlordism, militant fundamentalism, ethnic cleansing and civil war. All of which form transnational threats and instability. See, Manwaring M G, *Grey Area Phenomena: Confronting the New World Disorder*, Boulder Colorado: Westview Press, 1993.
3   Laqueur W, *The Age of Terrorism*, London: Weidenfeld and Nicolson, 1987, p.72.
4   See, Reich W, *Origins of Terrorism; Foley* C, Scobie W, *The Struggle for Cyprus*, London: Hoover, 1975; Horne A, *A Savage War of Peace*, London: Macmillan, 1977 and O'Neill B E, *Armed Struggle in Palestine*, London: Westview Press, 1978.

5 For the main UN International Conventions on Terrorism, such as Hijack, Hostages taking, Bombings, and Financing of Terrorism. See, www.untreaty.un.org/English/Terrorism.

6 See for example, Clutterbuck R, *Terrorism and Guerrilla Warfare*, London: Routledge, 1990.

7 See, Hoffman B, *Inside Terrorism*, London: Indigo, 1999 (2nd ed.), and Wilkinson P, *Terrorism Versus Democracy, The Liberal State Response*, London: Frank Cass, 2000.

8 See, UN High Level Panel Report www.un.org/secureworld/

9 Silke A 'The Devil you know: continuing problems with research on Terrorism', *Terrorism and Political Violence*, vol.13, no.4 (Winter 2001), pp.1–14. Also see Malik O, *Enough of the Definition of Terrorism*, London: Royal Institute of International Affairs, 2000.

10 Quoted in, Laquer W, *The New Terrorism*, Oxford: Phoenix Press, 3rd ed., 2001, p.8.

11 Quoted by Kramer M, 'Moral Logic of Hizballah', in Reich W, *Origins*, p.148.

12 Cruise O'Brien C, 'Terrorism under Democratic conditions the case of the IRA', in Crenshaw M, *Terrorism, Legitimacy and Power*, p.93.

13 Wilkinson P, *Terrorism and the Liberal State*, p.38.

14 Cruise O'Brien, in Crenshaw M, *Terrorism, Legitimacy and Power*, p.93.

15 Wilkinson P, *Terrorism Versus Democracy*, pp.12–13.

16 Wilkinson P, *The Liberal State*, p.23.

17 Examples of this range from Palestine where 'terrorists' such as Menachem Begin of the Irgun became a respected Israeli leader to Gerry Adams and Martin McGinnis, who as active members of the Provisional Irish Republican Army are now in government in Northern Ireland.

18 Laqueur W, *The New Terrorism*, p.9.

19 Aquinas T. *Summa Theologica*, quoted in Kennedy R. 'Is one person's Terrorist another's freedom fighter? Western and Islamic approaches to ''Just War'' compared' in *Terrorism and Political Violence*, vol.11, no.1, Spring 1999, p.6.

20 Proportionality suggests the costs of the conflict must not exceed the potential benefits and discrimination requires that non-combatants be immune from direct intentional attack in Ibid p.6.

21 Wilkinson P, *Terrorism Versus Democracy*, p.101. Furthermore, the difference between attacking civilians (non-combatants) and soldiers (combatants) is often seen as the distinction in definition between Guerrilla War and Terrorism, where one is directed against the military or combatants and the other against civilian targets.

22 Malik O, *Enough of the Definition of Terrorism*, London: Royal Institute of International Affairs, 2000, p.36.

23 Stohl M, 'States, Terrorism and State Terrorism', in Slater R and Stohl M, *Current Perspectives*, p.171.

24 Wilkinson P , *Terrorism Versus Democracy*, London: Frank Cass, 2000, p. 1.

25 See, Jenkins B M, *The Study of Terrorism: Definitional problems*, Santa Monica CA; RAND Corporation, 1980, p.6563.

26 Hoffman B, *Inside Terrorism*, p.14.

27 Gurr T R, 'Empirical Research on Political Terrorism', in Slater R, Stohl M, *Current Perspectives on International Terrorism*, London: Macmillan, 1988, p.116.
28 See, O'Sullivan G, Herman E, 'Terrorism as Ideology and Cultural Industry', in George A, *Western State Terrorism*, Cambridge: Polity Press, 1991, p.44.
29 Also see, Richmond O, *Realising Hegemony? Symbolic Terrorism and the Roots of Conflict*, Conflict *and Terrorism*.
30 Bowyer Bell J, *A Time of Terror*, New York: Basic Books, 1978, p.50.
31 Bowyer Bell J, *A Time of Terror*, p.51.
32 Rubenstein R E, *Alchemists of Revolution: Terrorism in the Modern World*, New York: Basic Books Inc, 1987, p.161.
33 Laquer W, *The New Terrorism*, Oxford: Phoenix Press, 3rd ed., 2001, p.26.
34 Piscane suggested that ideas result form deeds and that violence was necessary not only to draw attention to, or generate publicity for a cause but also ultimately to inform, educate and rally the masses. From Hoffman B, *Inside Terrorism*, p.17.
35 Wilkinson P, *The Liberal State*, p.46.
36 Sun Tzu, *The Art of War*, Oxford: Oxford University Press, 1963.
37 Jenkins B M, quoted in Hoffman B, *Inside Terrorism*, p.132.
38 Much of the Literature on Orthodox Terrorism Theory suggest that the historical roots of terrorism exist in the French Revolution of 1789 when the ideology of the French Revolution and the power of the new government was enforced and consolidated by the so-called 'reign of terror', which was enacted on the population. See, Hoffman B, *Inside Terrorism*, p.15.
39 Wilkinson suggests domestic or *Internal* terrorism is confined within a single state or region while *International* terrorism is an attack carried out across international frontiers. Wilkinson P, *Terrorism Versus Democracy*, p.15, also see Hoffman B, *Inside Terrorism*, chapter 6, p.67.
40 See, Alexander Y, Latter R, *Terrorism and the Media*, McLean V A: Brassey's, 1990, and Hoffman B, *Inside Terrorism*, chapter 5, p.131 and Wilkinson P, *Terrorism Versus Democracy*, chapter 9, p.174.
41 Guerrilla Warfare is defined as 'a series of operations by irregular forces, depending on mobility and surprise aimed at harassing a regular army'. Chaliand G., *Terrorism from Popular Struggle to Media Spectacle*. London: Saqi Books, 1987, p.12.
42 'Mao developed a strategy of protracted war in three stages: the enemy's strategic offensive and the revolutionaries' strategic defensive; the enemies strategic consolidation and the revolutionaries' preparation for counter offensive: and the revolutionaries' strategic retreat'. From Wilkinson P, *Terrorism Versus Democracy*, p.11.
43 Marighela's strategy was to convert a political crisis into an armed struggle by violent acts that force the government to transform the political situation into a military one. From Chaliand G, *Terrorism from Popular Struggle*, p.87. For further information see, Marighela C, *For the Liberation of Brazil*, Harmondsworth: Penguin, 1971.
44 Schmid A and Jongman A, *Political Terrorism*, p.7. Insurgency can be defined as, 'a rebellion or rising against the government in power or civil authorities'. See, Wilkinson P, *Terrorism Versus Democracy*, p.2.

45 Crenshaw M, 'The Logic of Terrorism: Terrorist Behaviour as a Product of Strategic Choice', in Reich W, *Origins of Terrorism*, Cambridge: Cambridge University Press, 1992, p.8 and Crenshaw M, 'How Terrorists think: What psychology can contribute to understanding Terrorism', in Howard L, *Terrorism; Roots, Impact and Responses*, New York: Praeger, 1992, p.71.

46 United States Departments of the Army and the Air Force, *Military Operations in Low Intensity Conflict*, Field Manual 100-20/Air Force Pamphlet 3-20, Washington DC: Headquarters, Department of the Army and Air Force, 1990, pp. 3–1, quoted in Hoffman B, *Inside Terrorism*, p.38.

47 Schmid A and Jongman A, *Political Terrorism*, p.2.

48 Hoffman B, *Inside Terrorism*, p.211.

49 Wilkinson P, *Terrorism Versus Democracy*, p.49.

50 Laquer W, *The New Terrorism*, p.274.

51 An example of this is the Japanese religious cult, Aum Shrinrikyo who released Sarin nerve gas in the Tokyo subway system, killing a dozen people and injuring 5,000. See, Wilkinson P, *Terrorism Versus Democracy*, pp.50–1.

52 Weapons of Mass Destruction (WMDs) are Nuclear, Biological and Chemical weapons. This debate suggests that if terrorists are in fact prepared to kill as many as possible then they will not be afraid of using WMDs contradicting the arguments of orthodox terrorism theory discussed above.

53 Jenkins B M, *Will Terrorists go Nuclear?* Santa Monica: CA RAND, Corporation, P-5541, November 1975, pp.6–7, quoted in Hoffman B, *Inside Terrorism*, p.197.

54 See, Fawn R, Larkins A, *International Society after the Cold War*, London: Macmilian, p.193.

55 Legitimacy can be defined as the acceptance and recognition of the authority of the established government by the population.

56 Sovereignty can be defined as the existence of the sole authority of the state over its own population.

57 See, Stohl M, and Lopez G, *The State as Terrorist: The dynamics of governmental violence and repression*, London: Aldwych Press, 1984.

58 Calvert P, 'Terror in the Theory of Revolution', in O'Sullivan N, *Terrorism Ideology and Revolution*, Brighton Sussex: Wheatsheaf Books, 1986, p.27.

59 Walter E V, *Terror and Resistance*, Oxford: Oxford University Press, 1969, p.340.

60 Arendt H, *On Revolution*, London: Penguin, 1990, p.99.

61 Quoted in Rubenstein R E, *Alchemists*, p.236.

62 Rousseau J-J, *The State of War*, in Hoffman S, Fiddler D, *Rousseau on International Relations*, Oxford: Clarendon Press, 1991.

63 Quoted in Homer F, 'Government Terror in the United States', in Stohl M, Lopez G, *The State as Terrorist*, London: Aldwych Press, 1984, p.167.

64 Bowyer Bell J, *The Dynamics of Armed Struggle*, London: Frank Cass, 1998, p.13.

65 Hoffman B, *Inside Terrorism*, p.23.

66 Herman B and O'Sullivan G, 'Terrorism as Ideology', in George A, *Western State Terrorism*, p.77.

67 An opinion poll in Haaretz found that 70 per cent approved the attempted assassination of Hamas leader Sheikh Yassin and 60 per cent urged the Army to try again. *The Economist*, 13 September 2003, p.62.

68 Miller M A, 'The Intellectual Origins of Modern Terrorism in Europe', in Crenshaw M (ed.), *Terrorism in Context*, Pennsylvania: Pennsylvania State University Press, p.62.

69 Chomsky N, 'International Terrorism: Image and Reality', in George A (ed.), *Western Sate Terrorism*, Cambridge: Polity Press, 1991, p.12.

70 O'Sullivan N, 'Terrorism, Ideology and Democracy', in O'Sullivan N, *Terrorism, Ideology and Revolution*, p.23.

71 See, Herman B and O'Sullivan G, 'Terrorism as Ideology', in George A, *Western State Terrorism*, p.41.

72 Rubenstein R E, *Alchemists*, p.4.

73 Stohl R, Slater R, *Current Perspectives on International Terrorism*, Macmillan: London 1988, p.8.

74 Sterling C, *The Terror Network: The Secret War of International Terrorism*, New York: Holt, Reinhardt and Winston, 1983.

75 There is a profusion of recent work on al-Qeida and its believed involvement in every conflict as a Islamisist network that sponsors world terrorism. See, Gunaratna R, *Inside al-Qeida*.

76 See, George A, *Western State Terrorism*, for arguments concerning military action as terrorism.

77 See, Alexander Y, Cline R, *Terrorism as State-Sponsored Covert Warfare*, New York: Hero Books, 1986, p.38.

78 Laquer W, *The New Terrorism*, p.243.

79 Wilkinson P, *Terrorism Versus Democracy*, p.41.

80 Bowyer Bell J, *Dynamics*, p.14.

81 Schmid A and Jongman A, *Political Terrorism*, p.56.

82 This is central to Wilkinson's understanding of terrorism, which he sees as political violence against the liberal democratic state. See, Wilkinson P, *Terrorism Versus Democracy*.

83 O'Sullivan N, *Terrorism, Ideology and Revolution*, Brighton: Wheatsheaf Books, 1986, p. x.

84 O'Sullivan N, *Terrorism*, p.6.

85 Chaliand G, *Terrorism*, p.31

86 Chaliand G, *Terrorism*, p.32.

87 Laquer W, *The New Terrorism*, p.34.

88 Chaliand G, *Terrorism*, p.35.

89 Cassese A, *Terrorism Politics and Law; The Achille Lauro Affair*, Cambridge: Polity Press, 1989, p.16.

90 Della Porta D, 'Left-Wing Terrorism In Italy', in Crenshaw M, *Terrorism in Context*, p.117.

91 Rubenstein R E, *Alchemists*, p.12.

92 Marighela C (trans. Butt J and Sheed R), *For the Liberation of Brazil*, Harmondsworth: Penguin, 1971, p.34.

93 Kramer M, 'The Moral logic of Hizballah', in Reich W, *Origins*, p.145.

94 Begin M, *The Revolt: The Story of Irgun*, quoted in Rubinstein, *Alchemists*, p.127.

95 www.un.org/resolutions.

96 Yassir Arafat, 'Address to the United Nations General Assembly', 13 November 1974, quoted in Hoffman B, *Inside Terrorism*, p.26.

97 Chaliand G, *Terrorism*, p.20.

98 Bowyer Bell J, *A Time of Terror*, p.267.

99 Wilkinson P, *Terrorism Versus Democracy*, p.21.

100 Kegley J R, *International Terrorism*, London: Macmillan, 1990, p.101.

101 Kegley J R, *International Terrorism*, p.102.

102 Bowyer Bell J, *Dynamics*, p.2.

103 Rubenstein R E, *Alchemists*, p.72.

104 O'Sullivan N, *Terrorism, Ideology and Revolution*, p.xiii. (intro).

105 Friedland N, 'Becoming a Terrorist', in Howard L, *Terrorism: Roots, Impact and Responses*, New York: Praeger, 1992, p.87.

106 Clinton W, quoted in Whittaker D J, *Terrorism: Understanding the Global Threat*, London: Longman, 2001, p.204 .

107 Crenshaw M, 'The Causes of Terrorism', in Kegley J R, *International Terrorism*, p.113.

108 Della Porta D, 'Left-Wing Terrorism', in Crenshaw M, *Terrorism in Context*, p.112 .

109 Sprinzak E, 'The process of Delegitimation: Towards linkage theory of Political Terrorism', *Terrorism and Political Violence*, p.54.

110 Gurr T R, *Why Men Rebel*, Princeton NJ: Princeton University Press, 1970, p.13.

111 Coser L A, *The Functions of Social Conflict*, London: Routledge and Kegan Paul, 1968. Also see chapter 2.

112 Crenshaw M, *Terrorism Legitimacy and Power*, Connecticut: Wesleyan Press, 1983, p.21.

113 Bowyer Bell J, *Dynamics*, p.43.

114 Camus A, *The Rebel*, London: Penguin, 2nd ed., 2000, p.27.

115 Wilkinson P, 'Future of Terrorism', Valedictory Lecture, University of St Andrews, 29 April 2002.

116 Laqueur W, *The New Terrorism*, p.36.

117 Crenshaw M, *Context*, p.1.

118 See, Kegley J R, *International Terrorism*, p.101.

119 Rubenstein R E, *Alchemists*, p.228.

120 Marx K, Engles F, *Manifesto of the Communist Party*, Oxford: Oxford University Press, 1992, p.39.

121 Sorel G, *Reflections on Violence*, New York: Collier-Macmillan, 1969.

122 Miller M A, 'The Intellectual Origins of Modern Terrorism in Europe', in Crenshaw M, *Context*, p.55.

123 See, Fanon F, *The Wretched of the Earth*, London: Penguin, 5th ed., 2001, p.118 and Sartre J-P in Preface to Fanon F, *The Wretched of the Earth*. Also see, Wilkinson P, *Terrorism and the Liberal State*, p.100.

124 Fanon F, *The Wretched of the Earth*, p.118.

125 Sartre J-P in Preface to Fanon F, *The Wretched of the Earth*.

126 Bowyer Bell J, *Dynamics*, p.28.

127 Quoted in Bowyer Bell J, *A Time of Terror*, p.104.

128 Shabad G, Ramo F, 'Basque Terrorism in Spain', in Crenshaw M, *Context*, p.415.

129 Laqueur W, *The New Terrorism*, p.35.

130 Della Porta D, *International Social Movement Research*, Greenwich: Connecticut, 1992, p.7.

131 Bowyer Bell J, *Dynamics*, p.27.

132 Rubenstein R E, *Alchemists*, p.108.

133 Laqueur W, *The New Terrorism*, p.105.

134 Krueger A B, Maleckova J, 'Does Poverty Cause Terrorism? The economics and the education of Suicide bombers,' *The New Republic*, 24 June 2002, p.27.

135 Crenshaw M, *Context*, p.19.

136 Schmid A and Jongman A, *Political Terrorism*, p.111.

137 Della Porta D, *Social Movement*, p.4.

138 Wardlaw G, *Political Terrorism*, p.5.

139 Bowyer Bell J, *Dynamics*, p.27.

140 Bowyer Bell J, *Dynamics*, p.7.

141 Bowyer Bell J, *Dynamics*, p.9.

142 Dostoevsky F, *Demons*, London: Vintage, 1994.

143 Rubenstein R E, *Alchemists*, p.61.

144 Quoted in Rubenstein R E, *Alchemists*, p.62.

145 Rubenstein R E, *Alchemists*.

146 Hoffman B, *Inside Terrorism*, p.43.

147 Wilkinson P, *Terrorism Versus Democracy*, p.20.

148 Della Porta D, 'Left-Wing Terrorism', in Crenshaw M, *Context*, p.106.

149 Hoffman B, *Inside Terrorism*, p.92.

150 Juergensmeyer M, 'Terror Mandated by God', in *Terrorism and Political Violence*, vol.9, no.2 (Summer 1997) pp.16–23.

151 Wilkinson P, *Terrorism Versus Democracy*, p.35.

152 See, Berman P, *Terror and Liberalism*.

153 Esposito J L, *The Islamic Threat Myth or Reality?* Oxford: Oxford University Press, 3rd ed., 1999, p.31.

154 Rapoport D, 'Sacred Terror: The Contemporary Example from Islam', in Reich W, *Origins*, p.107.

155 Kramer M, 'Hizballah', in Reich W, *Origins*, p.133.

156 Islamic Extremism can be defined as a movement dedicated to the establishment of an Islamic state, under the implementation and sole authority of the Shari'a.

157 See, Esposito, *Islamic Threat*, pp.135–38.

158 Hoffman B, 'Low-Intensity Conflict: Terrorism and Guerrilla War', in Howard L, *Terrorism*, p.144.

159 Laqueur W, *The New Terrorism*, p.81.

160 Laqueur W, *The New Terrorism*, p.81.

161 Rubenstein R E, *Alchemists*, p.132.

162 Bowyer Bell J, *Dynamics*, p.33.

163 Sprinzak E, 'Delegitimation', in *Terrorism and Political Violence*, p.53.

164 Whittaker D, *The Terrorism Reader*, London: Routledge, 2001, p.9.

165 Quoted in Livingston M H, *International Terror*, p.195.

166 Crenshaw M, 'How Terrorists Think: What Psychology can Contribute to Understanding Terrorism', in Howard L, *Terrorism*, p.72.

167 Crenshaw M, 'The Causes of Terrorism', in Kegley J R, *International Terrorism*, p.120.

168 Lustick I S, 'Terrorism in the Arab-Israeli Conflict: Targets and Audiences', in Crenshaw M, *Context*, p.552.
169 Gerth H, Wright Mills C (eds), *From Max Weber*, London: Routledge & Kegan Paul, 1970, p.295.
170 Stern J, *The Ultimate Terrorists*, Cambridge Mass: Harvard University Press, 1999, p.80.
171 Bandura A, 'Mechanisms of Moral disengagement', in Reich W, *Origins*, p.181.
172 Miller M A, 'Intellectual origins', in Crenshaw M, *Context*, p.59.
173 Begin M, *The Revolt: Story of the Irgun*, Jerusalem: Steimatzky, 1977, p.46 quoted in Hoffman B, *Inside Terrorism*, p.174.
174 Post J M, 'Terrorist psycho-logic: Terrorist behaviour as a product of psychological forces', in Reich W, *Origins*, p.36.
175 Rabbie J M, 'A behavioural interaction model: toward a social-psychological framework for studying terrorism', *Terrorism and Political Violence*, vol.3, no.4, Winter 1991, pp.134–63.
176 Wilkinson P, *Terrorism Versus Democracy*, p.20.
177 Wilkinson P, 'Future of Terrorism', Valedictory Lecture University of St Andrews 29 April 2002.
178 Miller A H, Damask N A, 'The Dual Myths of 'Narco-terrorism': How Myths Drive Policy', in *Terrorism and Political Violence*, vol.8, no.1, Spring 1996, pp.114–31.
179 Miller A H, Damask N A, *Dual Myths*, p.119.
180 Miller A H, Damask N A, *Dual Myths*, p.124.
181 Clutterbuck R, *Terrorism and Guerrilla Warfare*, London: Routledge, 1990, p.89.
182 Conrad J, *The Secret Agent*, London: Penguin, 5th ed, 2000.

Chapter 2 Approaches to Conflict: The Root Causes

1 Rapoport A, *Fights, Games and Debates*, Ann Arbour MI: University of Michigan Press, 1967.
2 Keegan J, *A History of Warfare*, London: Pimlico Press, 1994, p.50.
3 See, The UN Charter, preamble, at www.un.org/aboutun/charter.
4 This is contained in Chapter 7, in relation to threats to the peace, breaches of the peace and acts of aggression. See, The UN Charter, Chapter 7, at www.un.org/aboutun/charter.
5 Richmond O, *Maintaining Order, Making Peace*, Basingstoke, Hants: Palgrave, 2002, p.4.
6 See, Kaldor M, *New and Old Wars*, London: Polity Press, 1999.
7 Contemporary conflict refers to the prevailing pattern of political and violent conflicts in the post-Cold War world. Miall H, Ramsbotham O, and Woodhouse T, *Contemporary Conflict Resolution*, Cambridge: Polity Press, 2000, p.21.
8 Concise Oxford Dictionary, Oxford: Oxford University Press, 2001, p.299.
9 Boulding K, *Stable Peace*, Austin Texas: University of Texas Press, 1910, p.135
10 Galtung J, *Peace by Peaceful Means*, Oslo: Sage Publications, 1996, p.21.
11 Boulding K, *Stable Peace*, p.135.

12 Galtung J, *Peace*, p.22.
13 Boulding K, *Stable Peace*, p.15.
14 Wallensteen P, Sollenberg M, 'After the Cold War: emerging patterns of armed conflict 1989–96', *Journal of Peace Research*, 32(3), p.347.
15 Miall et al, *Conflict Resolution*, p.23.
16 Jabri V, *Discourses on Violence*, Manchester: Manchester University Press, 1996, p.13.
17 See, Clausewitz, C V, *On War*, Princeton: Princeton Press, 1976.
18 Holsti K J, *The State, War and The State of War*, Cambridge: Cambridge University Press, 1996, p.1.
19 Kaldor M, *New and Old Wars*, London: Polity Press, 1999, p.29.
20 Holsti K J, *The State*, p.20.
21 Wallensteen P, Sollenberg M, 'Armed Conflict 1989–99', *Journal of Peace Research* 37(3) p.636.
22 Kaldor M, *New and Old Wars*, p.4.
23 Richmond O, *Maintaining Order*, p.17.
24 Jabri V, *Discourses*, p.1.
25 Richmond O, *Maintaining Order*, p.2.
26 Jongman A, Schmid A, *World Conflict and Human Rights Map*, Leiden: Leiden University, 1998, quoted in Miall et al, *Conflict Resolution*, p.23.
27 Miall et al, *Conflict Resolution*, p.30.
28 Azar E A, *The Management of Protracted Social Conflict, Theory and Cases*, Hampshire: Dartmouth Publishing Company, 1990, p.3.
29 See, Keohane R, *Neorealism and its Critics*, New York: Columbia University Press, 1986, especially the chapter by Gilpin who sees little difference between the Realism of Thucydides and that of today.
30 See, Baylis J and Smith S, *Globalisation*, pp.109–24.
31 Thucydides, *History of the Peloponnesian War*, London: Penguin, 1954, quoted in Baylis J, Smith S, *The Globalisation of World Politics*, Oxford: Oxford University Press, 5th ed., 1999, p.113.
32 Doyle M W, *Ways of War and Peace*, New York: W W Norton, 1997, p.45.
33 Hobbes T, *Leviathan*, Cambridge: Cambridge University Press, 1991, p.152.
34 Waltz K, *Man, the State and War*, New York: Columbia University Press, 1959, p.80.
35 Rousseau J-J, *The State of War*, in Brown C, Nardin T, Rengger N, *International Relations in Political Thought*, Cambridge: Cambridge University Press, 2nd ed., 2003, p.416.
36 Rousseau J-J, *The State of War*, in Brown C, Nardin T and Rengger N, *International Relations in Political Thought*, p.417.
37 Rousseau J-J, *The State of War*, in Brown C, Nardin T and Rengger N, *International Relations in Political Thought*, p.418.
38 Waltz K, *Man, the State and War*, p.39.
39 Fawn R, Larkins A, *International Society after the Cold War*, London: Macmillan, p.193.
40 Rousseau suggested that individuals have to surrender the protection of their rights to the state in return for state monopoly of violence see, Rousseau J-J, *The State of War* in Hoffman S, and Fiddler D, *Rousseau on International Relations*, Oxford: Clarendon Press, 1991.

41 Suganami H, *On the Causes of War*, Clarendon: Oxford, 1996, p.21.
42 Buzan B, 'Timeless wisdom of Realism', in Smith et al, *International Theory*, p.61.
43 Wallensteen P and Sollenberg M, *Armed Conflict*, p.638.
44 Suganami H, *On the Causes of War*, p.32.
45 Richmond O, *Maintaining Order*, p.5.
46 Keohane R, *Neorealism*, p.11.
47 Morgenthau H, *Politics Among Nations*, New York: Knopf, 1948, p.11.
48 Morgenthau H, *Politics Among Nations*, p.10.
49 This is quoted in a critique of Morgenthau by Waltz; see Waltz K, *Man, the State and War*, p.39.
50 Morgenthau H, *Politics Among Nations*, p.11.
51 Dunne T, 'Realism', in Baylis J and Smith S, *Globalisation*, p.64.
52 Wright Q, *A Study of War*, Chicago: University of Chicago, 1947, p.254.
53 Vasquez J, *The War Puzzle*, Cambridge: Cambridge University Press, 1993.
54 Baylis J 'International security in the Post-Cold War era', in Baylis J and Smith S, *Globalisation*, p.194.
55 Strange S, 'The Westfailure System', *Review of International Studies*, 25, 1999, p.345.
56 Balance of Power is defined as a state of affairs such that no one power is in a position where it can dominate others. See, Bull H, *Anarchical Society*.
57 Warner R (trans) Thucydides, *History of the Peloponnesian War*, London: Penguin, 1954, p.402.
58 This is termed structural realism see, Waltz K, *The Theory of International Politics*, Reading Mass: Addison-Wesley, 1979.
59 Suganami H, *On the Causes of War*, p.209.
60 See, Rousseau J-J, *The State of War*, in Brown et al, *Political Thought*, p.416.
61 Keohane R, *NeoRealism*, p.199.
62 See, Richmond O, *Maintaining Order*, Ch. 2, pp.41 75.
63 See, Baylis J and Smith S, *Globalisation*, pp.151–3.
64 For Kant's theory of 'perpetual peace' see Kant I, Perpetual Peace in Brown C, Nardin T and Rengger N, *International Relations in Political Thought*, pp.428–55.
65 Held argues that by democratising world institutions conflict can be eradicated see Held D, *Democracy and the Global Order*, Cambridge: Polity Press, 1997.
66 The 'Interventionist' debate questions the legality of entering another states sovereign territory in order to impose a political decision. See, Mayall J, *The New Interventionism 1991–94*, Cambridge: Cambridge University Press, 1996, and Chomsky N, *The New Military Humanism*.
67 The 'new colonialism' debate argues that imposing an alien political system on another state in the name of security or humanitarian principles is a new form of colonialism.
68 Carr E H, *The Twenty Year Crisis 1919–1939*, London: Macmillan, 1946.
69 Ignatieff M, *The Warriors' Honour*, London: Polity Press, 1998, p.51.
70 United Nations General Assembly Resolution 1514, 14th December 1960. Declaration on the granting of independence to colonial countries and peoples. For the complete document see www.un.org/docs/resolution.

71 Baylis J and Smith S, *Globalisation*, p.54.
72 United Nations General Assembly Resolution 1514, 14th December 1960. Declaration on the granting of independence to colonial countries and peoples. www.un.org/docs/resolution.
73 See, www.un.org/charter.
74 www.un.org/charter.
75 Jabri V. *Discourses*, p.3.
76 Simmel call this 'homo homini lupus' ('man is wolf to man') Simmel G, *Conflict*, New York: First Free Press, 1964, p.28.
77 Simmel G, *Conflict*, p.14.
78 Coser L A, *The Functions of Social Conflict*, London: Routledge and Kegan Paul, 1968, p.38.
79 Coser L A, *The Functions of Social Conflict*, p.42.
80 Vayryen R, *New Directions in Conflict Theory*, London: Sage Publications, 1991, p.4.
81 Angell R C, 'The Sociology of Human Conflict', in McNeil E B, *The Nature of Human Conflict*, New Jersey: Prenticehall Press, 1965, pp.93–4.
82 Angell R C, 'The Sociology of Human Conflict', in McNeil E B, *The Nature of Human Conflict*, p.96.
83 Hobbes argued that society is a form of social order that is imposed on others by threat and coercion in Burton J, *Deviance Terrorism and War*, Oxford: Martin Robertson, 1979, p.47.
84 Weber suggested that society is maintained by the existence of a set of shared values that are powerful enough to influence acceptance of inequality and social injustice. Burton J, *Deviance*, p.47.
85 Burton J, *Deviance*, p.48.
86 Deutsch M, 'Subjective Features of Conflict Resolution', in Vayryen R, *New Directions*, p.27.
87 Dollard J, *Frustration and Aggression*, London: Butler and Tanner, 1944.
88 Dollard J, *Frustration and Aggression*, p.15.
89 Yates A J, *Frustration and Conflict*, New York: Methuen & Co, 1962, p.66.
90 Gurr T R, *Why Men Rebel*, Princeton NJ: Princeton University Press, 1970.
91 Maslow suggested five basic needs: Physiological, Safety, Belongingness and Love, Esteem and Self-Actualisation in Maslow A H, *Motivation and Personality*, New York: Longman, 1970, p.15.
92 Burton suggested nine human needs, Consistency in Response, Stimulation, Security, Recognition, Distributive Justice, Rationality, Meaning, Control and Role Defence. See, Burton J, *Deviance*, p.73. Also see, Burton J (ed.), *Conflict: Human Needs Theory*, London: Macmillan.
93 Hoffman M, 'Third Party Mediation and Conflict-Resolution in the Post-Cold War World', in Baylis J and Rengger N, *Dilemmas of World Politics*, London: Clarendon, 1992, p.274.
94 See, Hoffman M, *Third Party Mediation*, pp.273–75, and Richmond O P, 'A Genealogy of Peacekeeping: The Creation and Re-creation of Order', *Alternatives*, 26, 2001, pp.324–25.
95 Richmond O P, 'Genealogy of Peacekeeping', p.325.
96 Azar E A, *The Management of Protracted Social Conflict Theory and Cases*, Hampshire: Dartmouth Publishing Company, 1990.

97 Azar E A, *The Management of Protracted Social Conflict Theory and Cases*, Hampshire: Dartmouth Publishing Company, 1990, pp.7–11.

98 See, Miall et al, *Contemporary Conflict Resolution*, pp.77–91.

99 This relates to the agency debate, the concept of human agency relates to how people may or may not be able to influence their social environment. See, Bleiker R, *Popular Dissent, Human Agency and Global Politics*, Cambridge: Cambridge University Press, 2000, pp.23–50.

100 Marx K, Engles F, *Manifesto of the Communist Party*, Oxford: Oxford University Press, 1992.

101 See, Wallerstein E, *The Modern World System 1*, San Diego: Academic Press, 1974.

102 Wallerstein E, *The Modern World System 1*, p.347.

103 Wendt A 'Collective Identity and the International State', *American Political Science Review*, vol.88, no.2, June 1994, p.384.

104 Galtung's conflict triangle is comprised of three sides, Contradiction, Attitude and Behaviour. Galtung J, *Peace by Peaceful Means*, Oslo: Sage Publications, 1996, p.71.

105 Mitchell sees coercion as threats and acts of violence, reward as imposed offers/benefits and settlement as concessions or compromise, in Mitchell C R, *The Structure of International Conflict*, London: Macmillan Press, 1981, pp.120–1.

106 Mitchell C R, *Structure*, p.18.

107 Giddens A, *Central Problems in Social Theory*, London: Macmillan, 1979, quoted in Jabri V, *Discourses*, p.3.

108 Giddens A, *Central Problems*, in Jabri V, *Discourses*, p.3.

109 Jabri V, *Discourses*, p.4.

110 Jabri V, *Discourses*, p.3.

111 Banks M, *Conflict*, p.41.

112 Fanon F, *The Wretched of the Earth*, London: Penguin, 2001, p.41.

113 Galtung J, *Peaceful Means*, p.71.

114 Galtung J, *Peaceful Means*, p.19.

115 Bercovitch J, *Social Conflicts and Third Parties*, Boulder Colorado: Westview Press, 1996, p.6.

116 Boulding lists the structural causes of conflict as Historical, Military, Political and Ideological. See, Boulding K, *Stable Peace*, Austin Texas: University of Texas Press, 1910.

117 Positive goals are the tangible, such as state formation or resources. Negative goals are avoidance of a situation. See, Mitchell C R, *Structure*, pp.18–20.

118 H Cairns, *Plato, The Collected Dialogues*, Princeton: Princeton University Press, 1961.

119 Rousseau J-J, *The State of War*, in Hoffman S and Fiddler D, *Rousseau on International Relations*, Oxford: Clarendon Press, 1991.

120 Marx K, Engles F, *Manifesto of the Communist Party*, Oxford: Oxford University Press, 1992.

121 See, Mead M and Metraux R, 'Anthropology of Human Conflict', in McNeil E B, *The Nature of Human Conflict*, Englewood Cliffs NJ: Prenticehall, 1965.

122 The framework for cultural analysis is 1. Relative proportions of common behaviour 2. Attitude to strength, weakness and compromise 3. Relations, boundaries; inside and outside/segmentation 4. Relationships to groups and individuals 5. Decision-making groups 6. Types of time perspective. Mead M and Metraux R, 'Anthropology of Human Conflict', in McNeil E B, *The Nature of Human Conflict*, p.116.

123 Mead M and Metraux R, 'Anthropology of Human Conflict', in McNeil E B, *The Nature of Human Conflict*, p.121.

124 Nordstrom C, Robben A (ed.) *Fieldwork under Fire*, Berkeley California: University of California, 1995, p.3.

125 Mead M, '*Warfare is only an invention not a biological necessity*', in Bramson L, Goethals G (ed.) *War*, New York: Basic Books, pp.269–27, quoted in Nordstrom C and Robben A, *Fieldwork*, p.3.

126 Fanon F, *The Wretched of the Earth*, p.48.

127 Bourdieu P, *Outline of a Theory of Practice*, Cambridge: Cambridge University Press, 1977, in Woodhouse T and Ramsbotham O, *Peacekeeping*, p.195.

128 Howell S, Willis R, *Societies at Peace*, London: Routledge Press, 1989, p.14.

129 I suggest the normative understanding of conflict relates to the definition I have adopted for this study, which is actual or potential violent conflicts which range from domestic conflict situations that threaten to become militarised beyond the capacity of domestic civil police to control, through to full-scale interstate war. Miall et al, *Conflict Resolution*, p.23.

130 Fanon F, *The Wretched of the Earth*, p.250.

131 Jabri V, *Discourses*, p.22.

132 Jabri V, *Discourses*, p.22.

133 See, www.un.org/udhr.

134 Lederach J P, *Building Peace*, Washington: US Institute of Peace, 1997, p.23.

135 Kalsor M, *New and Old Wars*, p.58.

136 Maslow A H, *Motivation and Personality*, p.15.

137 Seul J R, 'Ours is the Way of God': Religion, Identity and Intergroup Conflict', *Journal of Peace Research*, vol.36, no.5, 1999, p.554.

138 Smith A D, *The Ethnic Revival*, Cambridge: Cambridge University Press, 1981, pp.65–7.

139 Eriksen T H, *Ethnicity and Nationalism Anthropological Perspectives*, London: Pluto Press, 1993, p.12.

140 Ho-Won Jeong, *The New Agenda For Peace Research*, Aldershot: Ashgate Publishers, 1999, p.56.

141 Enloe C H, *Ethnic Conflict and Political Development*, Boston: Little Brown Publishers, 1973, p.15.

142 Ignatieff M, *The Warriors' Honour*, p.7

143 Eriksen T H, *Ethnicity*, p.90.

144 Fanon F, *The Wretched of the Earth*, p.29.

145 Separatism, the desire to establish self-rule as an ethnic community and Irredentism, the desire for a community divided among different states to seek reunification. Smith A D, *The Ethnic Revival*, p.15.

146 Ellingsen T, 'Colourful Community or Ethnic Witches' Brew', *Journal of Conflict Resolution*, vol.44, no.2, April 2002, p.231.

147 Richmond O P. 'Ethnic Security in the International System: No Man's Land?', *Journal of International Relations and Development*, March 2000, p.24.

148 Posen B, 'The Security Dilemma and Ethnic Conflict', *Survival*, 35(1), 1993, pp.27–47.

149 Richmond O P, 'Ethnic Security', p.30.

150 Connor W, 'A Nation is a Nation is a State is an Ethnic group is a...', in Hutchinson J and Smith A D, *Nationalism*, Oxford: Oxford University Press, 1994, p.45.

151 Smith A D, *The Ethnic Revival*, p.18.

152 Smith A D, *The Ethnic Revival*, p.19.

153 Giddens A, 'The Nation as a Power-Container', in Hutchinson J and Smith A D, *Nationalism*, p.34.

154 Withey S, Katz D, 'The Social Psychology of Human Conflict', in McNeil E B, *The* Nature of *Human Conflict*, p.69.

155 Weber M,'The Nation', in Hutchinson J and Smith A D, *Nationalism*, p.25.

156 Ellingsen T, 'Colourful Community or Ethnic Witches' Brew? p.228.

157 Juergensmeyer M, *The New Cold War?* Berkeley: University of California Press, 1993.

158 Huntington S, *The Clash of Civilisations and The Remaking of World Order*, New York: Touchstone, 1998.

159 Esposito J L, *The Islamic Threat*, Oxford: Oxford University Press, 1999, p.10.

160 Seul J R, 'Ours is the Way of God': Religion, Identity and Intergroup Conflict', *Journal of Peace Research*, vol.36, no.5, 1999.

161 Mitchell C R, *Conflict*, p.18.

162 Jabri V, *Discourses*, p.16.

163 Carment D, James P, 'The International Politics of Ethnic Conflict', *Global Society*, vol.11, no.2, 1997.

164 Woodhouse T, Ramsbotham O, *Peacekeeping and Conflict Resolution*, London: Frank Cass, 2000, p.101.

165 Gurr T R, Harff B, *Ethnic Conflict in World Politics*, Boulder Colorado: Westview Press, 1994, p.88.

166 Coser defines power as the ability to influence the behaviour of others. Coser L A, *The Functions of Social Conflict*, p.137.

167 Foucault M, *Power and Knowledge*, p.122.

168 Fetherston A B, 'Peacekeeping, Conflict Resolution and Peacebuliding', in Woodhouse T and Ramsbotham O, *Peacekeeping*, p.207.

169 Galtung J, *Peaceful Means*, p.71.

170 Miall et al, *Conflict Resolution*, p.14.

171 Mitchell C R, *Structure*, p.28.

172 Lorenz K, *On Aggression*, New York: Bantam Books, 1971, in Ferguson R B, *Warfare, Culture and Environment*, Florida: Academic Press, 1984, p.9.

173 Lorenz K, *On Aggression*, p.9.

174 Simmel G, *Conflict*, p.28.

175 Freud S, 'Why War', in Smoker P, Davies R and Munske B, *A Reader in Peace Studies*, Oxford: Pergamon Press, 1990, p.164.

176 Tidwell A C, *Conflict Resolved?* p.43.

177 Mitchell C R, *Structure*, p.29.

178 Mitchell C R, *Structure*, pp.77–8.
179 Mitchell believes this is the psychological tendency to over-rationalise and perceive that events, circumstances and consequences are all the result of the planned action of the other party. Mitchell C R, *Structure*, p.101.
180 Banks M, *Conflict in World Society*, Brighton: Wheatsheaf, 1984, p.40.
181 Mitchell C R, *Structure*, p.103.
182 Fanon F, *The Wretched of the Earth,* p.67.
183 Mitchell C R, *Structure*, p.106.
184 Vayryen R, *New Directions*, p.29.
185 Lederach attributes the 'perceptions' to the political manipulation of leaders coupled with the need for the security of identity of the individual and sees fear and hatred among the 'emotions'. Lederach J P, *Building Peace*, p.29.
186 Dollard J, *Frustration and Aggression*, p.36.
187 Mitchell C R, *Structure*, p.92.
188 Cox R W, *Approaches to World Order*, p.87.

Chapter 3 Conflict and Terrorism: A Comparative Analysis

1 Miall et al, *Conflict Resolution*, p.23.
2 Zero-sum conflict is self's gain to the other's loss (1+ 0 = 0) See, Miall et al, *Conflict Resolution*, p. 6.
3 Graham J (trans), Von Clausewitz C, *On War*, London: Penguin, 1908, p.23.
4 See, Walker R B J, *Inside/Outside*, Cambridge: Cambridge University Press, 1993.
5 Wilkinson P, *Terrorism Versus Democracy*, p.4.
6 Jabri suggests the existence of a discourse of legitimacy, which establishes a differentiation between criminal and judicial violence, suggesting that those who act within law have rights and those who act outside do not, and are therefore regarded as unlawful combatants. Jabri V, 'The war/ethics nexus: Globalised warfare in late modernity', Lecture, University of St Andrews, 7 October 2002.
7 O'Sullivan N, *Terrorism, Ideology and Revolution*, Brighton Sussex: Wheatsheaf Books, 1986, p.17.
8 Cranna M (ed.), *The True Cost of Conflict*, London: Eartliscan, 1994, p.xvii. quoted in Wilkinson P, *Terrorism Versus Democracy*, p.4.
9 Wilkinson P, *Terrorism Versus Democracy*, p.1.
10 Kaldor M, *New and Old Wars*, p.58.
11 See, Kaldor M, *New and Old Wars*, and Holsti K J, *The State*.
12 Many of those captured in Afghanistan and Iraq were designated terrorists and denied prisoner of war rights. However, on transfer to a United States prison camp in Guantanamo Bay in Cuba, the 'prisoners' were also denied the right to legal representation. This calls into question their position as terrorist 'criminals'. The lack of any approach to explain the status of the prisoners, either as enemy soldiers or terrorist criminals perhaps illustrates the current difficulties in explaining contemporary conflict and terrorism.
13 See, Laqueur W, *The New Terrorism*, and Hoffman B, *Inside Terrorism*.

14 Rubenstein R E, *Alchemists*, p.113.
15 Israel regularly condemns Palestinian attacks as terrorism; Hamas also say that Israel uses 'terrorist actions against civilians'. Ismail Abu Shanab, Hamas Political Leader, Gaza, 24.03.2003, Interview transcripts, p.29.
16 Khalid Al-Batsh, Islamic Jihad Leader, Gaza City, 23.03.2004, Interview.
17 Kalyid Aghol, PFLP Leader, Gaza City, 22.03.2004, Interview.
18 Buzan B, 'Who May We Bomb', in Booth K and Dunne T, *Worlds in Collision*, p.86.
19 Quoted in, Whittaker D J, *Terrorism*, p.66.
20 Bowyer Bell J, *Dynamics*, p.207.
21 Schmid A P and Jongman A J, 'Violent Conflicts and Human Rights Violations in the mid-1990s', *Terrorism and Political Violence*, vol.9, no.4, Winter 1997, p.187.
22 See, Linklater A, *Transformation* and Richmond O, *Maintaining Order*.
23 Thomson D, *Europe Since Napoleon*, London: Penguin, 1966, p.57.
24 Quoted in Hoffman B, *Inside Terrorism*, p.38.
25 Walter E V, *Terror and Resistance*, Oxford: Oxford University Press, 1969, p.340.
26 Jenkins argues that 'terrorism is seen as a means to an end', which is violence for gaining state power, opposition to this is state violence, the deeper causes or roots are not examined. Jenkins B M, in Kegley J R, *International Terrorism*, London: Macmillan, 1990, p.102.
27 Orthodox terrorism theory does explain state-sponsored terrorism as international terrorism sponsored by donor states. However only a few countries are actually listed and others are briefly mentioned for 'supporting' terrorist activity. Therefore the actual role of the state in the generation of terrorism is not directly questioned as a root cause. See, Wilkinson P, *Terrorism Versus Democracy*, London: Frank Cass, 2000, p.62.
28 Richmond argues for reform of the international system as it is failing to provide the tools to resolve conflict because it is constructed by state-centric actors in a predominantly state-centric environment. Richmon O P, 'Ethnic Security in the International System', *Journal of International Relations and Development*, March 2000, p.41.
29 Orthodox terrorism theory suggests that the intention of the terrorists is to incite or provoke a violent or repressive state response intended to deprive the government of legitimacy and radicalise the masses. See, Rubenstein R E, *Alchemists of Revolution* p.161. Wilkinson argues that State responses to terrorism should be kept within the criminal justice model to maintain the rule of law. Wilkinson P, *Terrorism Versus Democracy*, p.125.
30 Wilkinson argues that policies of counter and anti-terrorism should obey Liberal Democratic rights and freedoms otherwise they are self-defeating and undermine the system they are being employed to protect. Wilkinson P, *Terrorism Versus Democracy*, p.117.
31 *The Economist*, 23 August 2003.
32 *The Economist* 13 September and 6 December 2003. Wilkinson argues that the introduction of emergency powers should be accompanied by a number of safeguards to ensure the maintenance of civil liberties. Wilkinson P, *Terrorism Versus Democracy*, p.117.

33 Conrad J, *The Secret Agent*, Penguin, 6th ed., 2000, p.95.
34 States using orthodox terrorism theory and the positivist approach see terrorism as always originating from another state and consequentially fail to understand terrorism from non-state actors.
35 Manwaring M G, *Grey Area Phenomena: Confronting the New World Disorder*, Boulder Colorado: Westview Press, 1993.
36 Hoffman B, *Inside Terrorism*, p.28.
37 Bowyer Bell J, *Dynamics*, p.14.
38 Wilkinson P, *Terrorism Versus Democracy*, p.13.
39 Crenshaw M, quoted in Kegley J R, *International Terrorism*, New York: St. Martins, 1990, p.58.
40 Conflict as a basic forms of human interaction and safety value within society. Coser L A, *The Functions of Social Conflicts*.
41 Conflict as a route to necessary change in society. Vayryen R, *New Directions*.
42 Conflict as a catalyst for the progression of society because it generates political and socio-economic change. Angell R C, 'Human Conflict', in McNeil E B, *The* Nature of *Human Conflict*.
43 Vayryen R, *New Directions*, p.1.
44 Jabri V, *Discourses*, p.4.
45 Vayryen R, *New Directions*, p.4.
46 Burton J, *Deviance*.
47 Burton J, *Deviance*, p.83.
48 Azar constructed a comprehensive multi-level framework for investigating the roots of what he termed Protracted Social Conflict (PSC); one of these levels contained an examination of human needs. Azar E A, *Social Conflict*.
49 See, Azar E A, *Social Conflict*, p.5.
50 See, Gurr T R, *Why Men Rebel*.
51 Gurr T R, *Why Men Rebel*, p.42.
52 Gurr T R, *Why Men Rebel*, p.8.
53 See, Chapter 1.
54 Wilkinson P, *The Liberal State*, p.96.
55 Jabri V, *Discourses*, p.174.
56 Fanon F, *The Wretched of the Earth*, p.48.
57 Jabri V, *Discourses*, p.4.
58 Wilkinson points out that almost without exception leaders of insurgent groups have espoused ideologies of Marxist revolutionism, such as the IRA, ETA, PFLP, DFLP and FLNC. Wilkinson P, *Terrorism Versus Democracy*, p.28.
59 Sorel argued that the function of violence was as a weapon of the proletariat and should be used as the supreme act of resistance. Sorel G, *Reflections on Violence*, New York: Collier-Macmillan, 1969.
60 Fanon argued using the example of Algeria that colonised 'man' is repressed by the coloniser and that only through violence could freedom from oppression be achieved, Fanon F, *The Wretched of the Earth*, p.52.
61 Sartre J P, *Critique de la raison dialectique*, and Introduction to Fanon F, *The Wretched of the Earth*.
62 Camus A, *The Rebel*, London: Penguin, 2nd ed., 2000.
63 Fanon F, *The Wretched of the Earth*, p.27.
64 Wilkinson P, *The Liberal State*, p.76.

65 Crenshaw argues that 'Terrorism as a general phenomenon cannot be adequately explained without situating it in its particular social, political and economic context' Crenshaw M, *Terrorism in Context*, p.I.

66 Fanon F, *The Wretched of the Earth*, p.41.

67 Bowyer, *Dynamics*, p.28.

68 Shabad G and Ramo F, 'Basque Terrorism in Spain', in Crenshaw M (ed.), *Terrorism in Context*, Pennsylvania: Pennsylvania State University Press, p.415.

69 See, Mead M and Metraux R, 'Anthropology of Human Conflict', in McNeil E B, *The* Nature of *Human Conflict*. Also see Chapter 2.

70 See, Galtung J, *Peace*, and Chapter 2.

71 Walker R B J, *Inside/Outside*, p.5.

72 Mitchell C R, *Structure*, p.35.

73 Galtung J, *Peace*, p.72.

74 Della Porta D, *International Social Movement Research*, Greenwich Connecticut: JAI, 1992, p.4.

75 Wardlaw suggests that social reality is situationally dependant and related to a subjective understanding. Wardlaw G, *Political Terrorism*, p.5.

76 Bowyer Bell argues that the terrorists creates a subjective truth established around a faith in the attainment of the goal or dream, this faith is a reality for group members but is difficult for outsiders to understand. Bowyer Bell J, *Dynamics*.

77 See, Rubenstein R E, *Alchemists*, p.108. Laqueur W, *The New Terrorism*, p.105. Krueger A B, Maleckova J, 'Does poverty cause terrorism?' The economics and the education of sucicide bombers', *The New Republic*, 24, 2002.

78 Azar E A, *Protracted Social Conflict*, p.16.

79 A survey found that major armed conflict was more likely in countries low down on the UN development programme and UNDP Human development Index. Jongman A, Schmid A, *Contemporary Armed Conflicts*, quoted in Miall et al, *Conflict Resolution*, p.86.

80 Miall et al, *Conflict Resolution*, p.77.

81 Krueger A B and Maleckova J, 'Does poverty cause terrorism?', p.27.

82 Examples of European terrorist groups such as the IRA, ETA, RAF, and RB are not considered by orthodox terrorism theory as the result of economic underdevelopment.

83 Lattimore R (trans), Homer, *The Iliad*, Chicago: University of Chicago Press, 1961, p.276.

84 Jabri V, *Discourses*, p.22.

85 Crenshaw examines the role of the individual especially within the political and socio-economic context. See, Crenshaw M, *Context*.

86 Bowyer Bell J, *Dynamics*, p.6.

87 Violence caused by religious groups is an expression of political power, which is mandated by God. Juergensmeyer M, 'Terror mandated by God', in *Terrorism and Political Violence*, vol.9, no.2, Summer 1997, pp.16–23.

88 Although Ranstorp does argue that religious terrorism is motivated largely by religion (which he sees as specifically the threat to religion and religious identity from secularism) and the practical political considerations of the context-specific environment, he does suggest the existence of social,

political and economic factors that exacerbate the religious crisis from which religious terrorism emerges. Nevertheless the causes of religious terrorism are firmly rooted in religion and politics. Ranstorp M, *Terrorism in the name of Religion.*

89 Jabri highlights this theory by questioning the composition of the unique construction of the individual and suggesting that the nature of individual identity makes it exclusionist and thus conflict can ensue from the friction between inclusion and exclusion in wider social groups. Jabri V, *Discourses*, p.121. See Chapter 2.

90 Social Identity Theory is the link between individual identity and group identity, which is based on achieving a secure and positively valued sense of self. Hence group formation, differentiation, self-categorisation, social judgements and perceptions can all emanate form social identity. Seul J R, 'Ours is the Way of God'.

91 Hans Mol described the chief function of religion as the stabilisation of individual and group identity. Mol H, *Identity and the Sacred: A sketch for a new social-scientific theory of religion*, Oxford: Basil Blackwell, 1976.

92 Statistics of armed conflict from 1985–94 suggest 44.1 per cent were ethnonationalist in nature. Scherrer C P, *Ethinonationalismus in Weltsystem*, Munster: Agenda Verlag, 1997, quoted in Wilkinson P, *Terrorism Versus Democracy*, p.6. Also see, Chapters 1 and 2.

93 Smith A D, *The Ethnic Revival.*

94 Eriksen T H, *Ethnicity and Nationalism*, p.12.

95 Ignatieff argues that no human difference matters until it becomes a privilege, he suggests that individuals under threat look for protection and security in groups comprised of individuals with similar identities who form a single identity based/ethnic group. Ignatieff M, *The Warriors' Honour*, p.51.

96 Foucault M, *Power and Knowledge*, p.122.

97 Wilkinson defines single issue Terrorism as violence committed with the desire to change a specific policy or practice within a target society. Wilkinson P, *Terrorism Versus Democracy*, p.20.

98 Wilkinson calls it 'incorrigible' terrorism, Wilkinson P, 'Future of Terrorism', Valedictory lecture, University of St Andrews, 29 April 2002.

99 Consensual issues are values sought such as territory and resources. Jabri V, *Discourses*, p.16.

100 See, Bowyer Bell J *Dynamics* and Della Porta D, *International Social Movement Research*, Greenwich Connecticut: Jai Press, 1992.

101 Crenshaw suggests that small group dynamics in conditions of isolation generate feelings of self-righteousness, trust, identity and loyalty. Crenshaw M, 'The Causes of Terrorism', in Kegley J R, *International Terrorism*, London: Macmillan, 1990, p.124.

102 Displacement is violence committed by group members for group leaders, members therefore absolved themselves from blame. Diffusion is acts of violence committed by all members by group decision and therefore everyone and no one is responsible. Bandura A, 'The Mechanics of Moral Disengagement', in Reich W, *Origins of Terrorism*, Cambridge: Cambridge University Press, 1992, p.181.

103 Miller M A,' Intellectual Origins of Modern Terrorism In Europe', in Crenshaw M, *Terrorism in Context*, p.55.

104 Post J M, 'Terrorist psycho-logic: Terrorist behaviour as a product of Psychological forces', in Reich W, *Origins*, p.36.
105 Galtung divides conflict attitude into emotive (feeling) cognitive (belief) and conative (will) see Galtung J, *Peace by Peaceful Means*, p.72.
106 Mitchell suggests a number of factors for consideration when examining the cognitive process; these are selective perception, selective recall and group identification. Mitchell C R, *Structure of Conflict*, p.77.
107 McNeil E B, *The* Nature of *Human Conflict*.
108 Mitchell argues that causes and effects of conflict are a search for group identification and a subsequent polarisation of the in-group and out-group. Mitchell C R, *Structure of Conflict*, p.85. Also see McNeil E B, *The Nature* of *Human Conflict*, p.60.
109 Lustick I S, 'Terrorism in the Arab Israeli Conflict: Targets and Audiences', in Crenshaw M, *Terrorism in Context*, p.552.
110 Sartre J P, *Critique de la raison dialectique*, and Introduction to Fanon F, *The Wretched of the Earth*, also see Fanon F, *The Wretched of the Earth*, p.27.

Chapter 4 Discourses on Conflict and Terrorism: The Palestinian-Israeli Case

1 Carr E H, *What is History?* London: Penguin Books, 2nd ed., 1988, p.23.
2 Foucault M, *Power and Knowledge*, p.122.
3 Edward Said suggests that there can be no neutrality or objectivity on the subject of Palestine, Said E W, 'The Burdens of Interpretation and the Question of Palestine', *Journal of Palestinian Studies*, 16 August 1986, p.29.
4 Kimmerling B, *The Invention and Decline of Israeliness*, Berkeley: California University Press, 2001, p.16.
5 Four major works were first mentioned in this wave: Flapan S, *The Birth of Israel*, New York: Pantheon, 1984; Morris B, *The Birth of the Israeli Refugee Problem, 1947–1949*, Cambridge: Cambridge University Press, 1988: Pappe I, *Britain and the Arab-Israeli Conflict*, New York: Macmillan, 1988; Shlaim A, *Collusion Across the Jordan: King Abdullah, The Zionist Movement, and the Partition of Palestine*, Oxford: Clarendon, 1988. See, Pappe I, 'Post-Zionist Critique on Israel and the Palestinians, Part 1: The Academic Debate', *Journal of Palestinian Studies*, vol.26, no.2, Winter 97, p.29.
6 Flapan S, *The Birth of Israel*, p.8.
7 Finkelstein N G, *Image and Reality of the Israeli-Palestinian Conflict*, New York: Verso, 1995.
8 Hazony Y, *The Jewish State, The Struggle for Israel's Soul*, New York: Basic Books, 2001, p.xx.
9 Pappe I, 'Academic Debate', *Journal of Palestinian Studies*, p.30.
10 Tessler M, *A History of the Israeli-Palestinian Conflict*, Indianapolis: Indiana University Press, 1994, p.69.
11 Kimmerling B, *Decline of Israeliness*, p.16.
12 Masalha N, *Imperial Israel and the Palestinians*, London: Pluto Press, 2000, p.4.
13 Flapan S, *The Birth of Israel*, p.12.
14 Tessler M, *Israeli-Palestinian Conflict*, p.1.
15 See, Peters J, *From Time Immemorial*, London: Michael Joseph Ltd, 1985.

16 Muslih M, 'Arab Politics and the Rise of Palestinian Nationalism', *Journal of Palestinian Studies*, Summer 1987, vol.16, no.4, pp.77–91.

17 See, Schulze K E, *The Arab-Israeli Conflict*, New York: Longman, 1999, p.1.

18 Laqueur W, *A History of Zionism*, New York: Holt, Rinehart and Winston, 1972, p.589.

19 See, the Dreyfus Affair, in Kimmerling B, *Decline of Israeliness*, p.21.

20 See, Masalha N, *Imperial Israel and the Palestinians*, London: Pluto Press, 2000.

21 Lewy G, *Religion and Revolution*, Oxford: Oxford University Press, 1974, p.91.

22 Shlaim A, *The Iron Wall Israel and the Arab World*, London: Penguin, 2000, p.2.

23 Tessler M, *Israeli-Palestinian Conflict*, p.63.

24 Finkelstein N G, *Image and Reality*, p.13.

25 Finkelstein N G, *Image and Reality*, p.14.

26 Netanyahu B, *A Place Among The Nations Israel and the World*, New York: Bantam Books, 1993, p.4. Shlaim A, *Iron Wall*, p.310.

27 Peters J, *From Time Immemorial*, 1985.

28 Netanyahu B, *Place Among Nations*, p.25.

29 Flapan S, *Zionism and the Palestinians*, London: Groom Helm, 1979, p.97.

30 Shlaim A, *Iron Wall*, p.12.

31 Finkelstein N G, *Image and Reality*, p.15.

32 Aggestam K, *Reframing and Resolving Conflict*, Lund, Sweden: Lund University Press, 1999, p.57.

33 Said E W, *The Question of Palestine*, London: Routledge and Kegan Paul, 1980, p.148.

34 See, Schultz H L, *The Reconstruction of Palestinian Nationalism*, Manchester: Manchester University Press, 1999, p.3.

35 Muslih M, *Arab Politics and Palestinian Nationalism*, pp.77–8.

36 The Young Turks revolt is also often seen as the beginning of Jewish-Arab conflict. See, Shafir G, *Land, Labour and the Origins of the Israeli-Palestinian Conflict, 1882–1914*, Cambridge: Cambridge University Press, 1989, p.202.

37 Muslih M, *The Origins of Palestinian Nationalism*, New York: Columbia University Press, 1988, p.3.

38 Morris B, *Righteous Victims, A History of The Zionist-Arab Conflict 1881–1999*, London: John Murray, 2000, p.59.

39 Muslih M, *Arab Politics and Palestinian Nationalism*, p.78.

40 See, Tessler M, *Israeli-Palestinian Conflict*, p.146.

41 Morris B, *Righteous Victims*, p.34.

42 Schultz H L, *Reconstruction*, p.4.

43 Sayigh R, *Palestinians: From Peasants to Revolutionaries*, London: Zed Press, 1979, p.40.

44 Muslih M, *Origins*, p.175.

45 Muslih M, *Origins*, p.155.

46 Kimmerling B, Migdal J S, *Palestinians: The Making of a People*, Cambridge Massachusetts: Harvard University Press, 1994, p.56.

47 Kimmerling B and Migdal J S, *Palestinians*, p.27.

48 See, Tessler M, *Israeli-Palestinian Conflict*, p.146.

49 Khalidi R, *British Policy towards Syria and Palestine: 1906–1914*, London: Ithaca Press, 1980. Quoted in Muslih M, *Origins*, p.72.

50 Muslih M, *Origins*, p.224.

51 Schultz H L, *Reconstruction*, p.6.

52 Kimmerling B and Migdal J S, *Palestinians*, p.94.

53 Muslih M, *Origins*, p.211.

54 Kimmerling B and Migdal J S, *Palestinians*, p.96.

55 Schultz H L, *Reconstruction*, p.29.

56 See, Morris B, *Righteous Victims*, p.156.

57 Smith C D, *Palestine and the Arab-Israeli Conflict*, Basingstoke: Macmillan, 2nd ed., 1992, p.100.

58 Quoted in, Shlaim A, *Iron Wall*, p.18.

59 Morris B, *Righteous Victims*, p.186.

60 Pappe I, 'Academic Debate', *Journal of Palestinian Studies*, p.32.

61 For example, the Irgun bombed the King David hotel in Jerusalem in 1946, which was being used as a British military headquarters, ninety-one people were killed. At the end of this year Irgun and the Stern claimed to have killed 373 (300 of whom were civilians). See, Tessler M, *Israeli-Palestinian Conflict*, pp.231–2.

62 Lustick I S, 'Changing Rationales for Political Violence in the Arab-Israeli Conflict', *Journal of Palestinian Studies*, vol.20, no.4, Autumn 1990, p.59.

63 Pappe I, 'Academic Debate', *Journal of Palestinian Studies*, p.31.

64 Sayigh R, *Palestinians*, p.98.

65 See, Kimmerling B and Migdal J S, *Palestinians*, p.128.

66 Kimmerling B and Migdal J S, *Palestinians*, p.129.

67 Sayigh R, *Palestinians*, p.124.

68 Sayigh Y, 'Armed Struggle and State Formation', *Journal of Palestinian Studies*, vol.26, no.4, Summer 97, p.18.

69 Morris B, *Righteous Victims*, p.255.

70 Sayigh Y, 'Armed Struggle and State Formation', p.18.

71 Schulze K, *The Arab-Israeli Conflict*, New York: Longman, 1999, p.16.

72 Said E W, *The Question of Palestine*, p.115. Furthermore, many second generation refugees when asked where they come from, name the region in Israel where there parents/grandparents once lived, some also still carry the key to their houses round their necks...Field Notes.

73 Smith C D, *Palestine*, p.151.

74 Shlaim A, *Iron Wall*, p.183.

75 See, Shlaim A, *Iron Wall*, p.98.

76 Shlaim A, *Iron Wall*, p.82.

77 See, Morris B, *Righteous Victims*, p.281.

78 However, it was not long before Jordan, Syria, Lebanon and Iraq soon began to produce their own Fedayeen.

79 Shlaim A, *Iron Wall*, p.128.

80 Tessler M, *Israeli-Palestinian Conflict*, p.346.

81 Prior to the conflict Egypt requested the withdrawal of the United Nations Emergency Force (UNEF) from Sinai and closed the Straits of Tiran to Israeli shipping. See, Tessler M, *Israeli-Palestinian Conflict*, pp.387–97.

82 Morris B, *Righteous Victims*, p.329.

83 The suggested hostility and intransigence of the Arabs was part of the historical discourse employed by the Israel to show an aggressive Arab world. See, Tessler M, *Israeli-Palestinian Conflict*, p.410.
84 See, www.un.org/document/sc/res/1967.
85 Tessler M, *Israeli-Palestinian Conflict*, p.421.
86 Hourani A, *A History of the Arab Peoples*, London: Faber and Faber, 1991, p.414.
87 Shlaim A, *Iron Wall*, p.241.
88 Morris B, *Righteous Victims*, p.311.
89 Israel did not face a significant threat and started the war with the intention of reducing the pan-Arab power of Nasser and realising territorial desires. See, Finkelstein N G, *Image and Reality*, pp.141–3.
90 Shlaim A, *Iron Wall*, p.241.
91 Dayan stated that the objective was to frustrate the Arab intention to conquer Israel. Quoted in Morris B, *Righteous Victims*, p.313.
92 Morris suggests 200–300,000 fled the West Bank and Gaza, whilst 80–90,000 left Golan, see Morris B, *Righteous Victims*, p.327.
93 Morris B, *Righteous Victims*, p.332.
94 Masalha N, *Imperial Israel*, p.15.
95 See, Herzog C, *Arab-Israeli Wars*, p.189.
96 Masalha N, *Imperial Israel*, p.16.
97 Morris B, *Righteous Victims*, p.333.
98 Said E W, *The Question of Palestine*, p.138.
99 Shlaim A, *Iron Wall*, p.286.
100 Masalha N, *Imperial Israel*, p.23.
101 Morris B, *Righteous Victims*, p.336.
102 After 1967 over 600,000 Palestinians could now regain direct contact with 300,000 in Gaza. Kimmerling B and Migdal J S, *Palestinians*, p.209.
103 Kimmerling B and Migdal J S, *Palestinians*, p.225.
104 Although Jordanian Forces did most of the fighting it became a Palestinian victory in the historical narrative. O'Neill B E *Armed Struggle in Palestine: A Political Military Analysis* Boulder Colorado: Westview Press, 1978, p.47.
105 Lustick I S, 'Changing Rationales', p.74.
106 See, Laqueur W and Rubin B, *Israeli-Arab Reader*, p.366.
107 Shlaim A, *Iron Wall*, p.315.
108 See, O'Neill B E, *Armed Struggle*, p.58.
109 Herzog C, *Arab-Israeli*, p.314.
110 Finkelstein N G, *Image and Reality*, p.150
111 Shlaim A, *Iron Wall*, p.353.
112 Quoted in Shlaim A, *Iron Wall*, p.353.
113 Morris B, *Righteous Victims*, p.456.
114 See, 'Theory of Palestinian centrality', which is the attempt by Arabs to link all the problems of the Middle East to the Palestinian situation. See, Netanyahu B, *Place Among Nations*, p.130.
115 Cobban H, *The PLO, People, Power and Politics*, Cambridge: Cambridge University Press, 1984, p.56.
116 Sayigh Y, 'Armed Struggle', p.26.
117 Sayigh Y, 'Armed Struggle', p.27.

118 See, Lukacs Y, *Israeli-Palestinian documents*, p.332.
119 Netanyahu B, *Place Among Nations*, p.204.
120 Netanyahu B, *International Terrorism: Challenge and Response*, Jerusalem: Jonathan Institute, 1980, p.1.
121 Said E W, *The Question of Palestine*, p.171.
122 Kimmerling B and Migdal J S, *Palestinians*, p.225.
123 Herzog C, *Arab-Israel Wars*, p.327.
124 See, Lukacs Y, *Israeli-Palestinian documents*, p.326.
125 Quoted in Morris B, *Righteous Victims*, p.377.
126 O'Neill B E, *Armed Struggle*, p.110.
127 Cobban lists the principal groups as Fateh (Black September) – nationalist: PFLP and DFLP-Marxist: PFLP-General Command and Sa'qa – Syrian: ALF – Iraqi. Cobban, *PLO*, pp.145–53.
128 Rubin, *Revolution until Victory*, p.32.
129 The Iraqi sponsored Abu Nidal group acted extensively against Fateh.
130 Such as the Japanese Red Army (JRA) and the Red Army Faction (RAF).
131 Shlaim A, *Iron Wall*, p.396.
132 Quoted in Morris B, *Righteous Victims*, p.518.
133 Quoted in Tessler M, *Israeli-Palestinian Conflict*, p.581.
134 Sayigh Y, 'Armed Struggle', p.28.
135 Shlaim A, *Iron Wall*, p.385.
136 Sayigh Y, 'Armed Struggle', p.28.
137 Sayigh Y, 'Armed Struggle', p.29.
138 Morris B, *Righteous Victims*, p.553.
139 Morris B, *Righteous Victims*, p.603.
140 Pressberg G, 'The Uprising: Causes and Consequences', *Journal of Palestinian Studies*, vol.17, no.3, Winter 88, pp.18–19.
141 Shlaim A, *Iron Wall*, p.452
142 Robert Hunter F, *The Palestinian Uprising, a war by other means*, Berkeley California: University of California Press, 2nd ed., 1993, p.92.
143 Kimmerling B and Migdal J S, *Palestinians*, p.268.
144 Pressberg G, 'The Uprising', p.42.
145 Pressberg G, 'The Uprising', p.46.
146 Schultz H L, *Reconstruction*, p.62.
147 Robert Hunter, *Palestinian Uprising*, p.61.
148 Schultz H L, *Reconstruction*, p.67.

Chapter 5 Rethinking the Roots of Terrorism

1 Blake W, *The Selected Poems of William Blake*, Ware: Wordsworth Editions Limited, 1994, p.201.
2 Ilan Libovitch, M K Shinui, Knesset: Jerusalem, 01.04.2003, Interview.
3 Ilan Libovitch. Interview.
4 Ilan Libovitch. Interview.
5 Laqueur W, *The New Terrorism*, p.37.
6 *The Guardian*, Wednesday 24 July 2002, p.12.
7 *The Economist*, 28 September 2002, p.65.
8 *The Guardian Weekly*, 6–12 November 2003, p.3.

9 Hoffman B, 'The Logic of Suicide Bombers', *The Atlantic Monthly*, June 2003, 291(5), p.44.

10 Yulie Tamir, MK Labour-Menad, Knesset: Jerusalem, 01.04.2003, Interview.

11 Wilkinson P, *Terrorism Versus Democracy*, pp.94–5.

12 *The Economist*, 20 September 2003, p.69.

13 An Opinion poll in Haaretz on September 10 showed; 18 per cent said he should be assassinated, 28 per cent said deportation and 27 per cent said intensified isolation, the same poll suggested 70 per cent in favour of assassinating the spiritual leader of Hamas Sheikh Yassin. *The Economist*, 13 September 2003, p.56.

14 Morris B, *Righteous Victims*, p.204.

15 Hoffman B, 'The Logic of Suicide Bombers', p.40.

16 Yulie Tamir. Interview.

17 Ellis M H, 'The Future of Israeli/Palestine: Embracing the Broken Middle', *Journal of Palestinian Studies*, vol.26, no.3, Spring 1997, p.58.

18 Netanyahu B, *Place Among Nations*, p.370.

19 The demographic problem, Interview with Dr Gershon Baskin from IPCRI.

20 Yulie Tamir. Interview.

21 *The Guardian*, 17 May 2003, p.35.

22 *The Economist*, 11 October 2003, p.14.

23 Ismail Abu Shanab, Hamas Political Leader, Gaza, 24.03.2003, Interview.

24 Yulie Tamir. Interview.

25 Kimmerling B, *The Invention and Decline of Israeliness*, Berkeley, California: University of California Press, 2001, p.87.

26 Teveth S, *Moshe Dayan*, London: Weidenfeld & Nicolson, 1972, p.240. Quoted in Kimmerling B, *Invention and Decline*, p.208.

27 Known in Israeli self-defence language as 'targeted killings'.

28 *The Economist*, 24 April 2004, pp.25–7.

29 For example, a one-tonne bomb was dropped by an Israeli F-16 on the home of the Hamas leader Salah Shehade, killing him and fourteen of his own family, mostly children. *The Guardian Weekly*, 11–17 December 2003, p.3.

30 Kimmerling B, *Invention and Decline*, p.2.

31 *The Guardian Weekly*, 7 August 2002, p.14.

32 In August 2003 Israel assassinated the Islamic Jihad commander Muhammad Sidr, this led directly to a bus bombing in Jerusalem by Hamas killing twenty people. A reprisal Israeli assassination of the Hamas leader Ismail abu Shanab led to the universal rejection of the ceasefire and the return to violence by all the Palestinian groups. See, *The Economist*, 23 August 2003, p.45.

33 Camus A, *The Rebel*, London: Penguin, 4th ed., 2000, p.28.

34 Fanon F, *The Wretched of the Earth*, London: Penguin, 5th ed., 2001, p.48.

35 See, Laqueur W and Rubin B, *Arab-Israeli Reader*, p.367.

36 Dr Haider Abdul Shafi, Gaza City: Gaza, 24.03.2003, Interview. (Dr Abdul Shafi was the independent Palestinian negotiator at the Madrid summit in 1992).

37 Kalyid Aghol, PFLP Leader, Gaza City: Gaza, 22.03.2003, Interview.

38 Ismail Abu Shanab, interview.

39 Khalid Al-Batsh, Islamic Jihad Leader, Gaza City: Gaza, 23.03.2003, Interview.

40 Diab Nemer Allouh, Fateh Leader, Gaza City: Gaza, 24.03.2003, Interview.

41 See, Azar E A, *Protracted Social Conflict*, p.5.

42 Palestinian Central Bureau of Statistics 'Impact of Israeli Measures on the Well-being of the Palestinian household, 2001', Ramallah: Central Bureau of Statistics, November 2001, p.78.

43 Fateh, Interview.

44 See, Laqueur W and Rubin B, *Reader*, p.369.

45 Richmond O P, 'Ethnic Security', p.24.

46 Many Palestinians referred to the Mel Gibson film *Braveheart*, to explain their own use of violence against Israel. al-Aqsa Martyrs Brigade, Gaza, 20.03.03, Interview.

47 Hamas, Interview.

48 Robert Hunter, *The Palestinian Uprising*, p.26.

49 Palestinians are prepared to fight and die as dignity will be found in the next life, so if you make life unliveable you force people (who believe) to seek another life.

50 Palestinian Central Bureau of Statistics 'Impact of Israeli Measures on the Well-being of the Palestinian household, 2001', Ramallah: Central Bureau of Statistics, November 2001, p.61.

51 Palestinian Central Bureau of Statistics 'Impact of Israeli Measures on the Well-being of the Palestinian household, 2001', Ramallah: Central Bureau of Statistics, November 2001, p.56.

52 Marx K, Engels F, *The Communist Manifesto*, Oxford: Oxford University Press, 2nd ed., 1998, p.12.

53 Fanon F, *The Wretched of the Earth*, p.29. Similarly an Israeli MK suggested that the violence is historically connected to the region, he suggested the Jews used it in their struggle against the British and now it is the turn of the Palestinians. Shinui, Interview Transcripts, p.43.

54 al Aqsa interview.

55 Yulie Tamir, Interview.

56 Kimmerling B, *Invention and Decline*, p.208.

57 Fighter, Nuseirat refugee camp.

58 Palestinian suicide bombers are rationalised as 'an eye for an eye'.

59 PFLP, Interview .

60 Green L, 'Living in a state of Fear' in Nordstrom C, Robben A, *Fieldwork Under Fire*, Berkeley California: University of California Press, 1995, p.108.

61 Interview, Hamas, p.31.

62 *The Economist*, 23 August 2003, p.45.

63 *The Guardian Weekly*, 11 December 2003.

64 Hamas, Interview Transcripts p.32.

65 al-Aqsa Interview.

66 Shlaim A, *Iron Wall*, p.18.

67 Fateh, Interview.

68 PFLP, Interview.

69 Islamic Jihad, Interview.

70 Islamic Jihad, Interview.

71 World Bank criteria of $2 per person per day. *Labour force survey report, July–Sept 2002*, World Bank, West Bank and Gaza update, August 2002, http://www. Passia.org.

72 Robert Hunter, *Palestinian Uprising*, p.51.

73 UNRWA Emergency Appeal 2003 pamphlet, UNRWA HQ, Gaza, June 2003, p.3.

74 Palestinian Central Bureau of Statistics 'Impact of Israeli Measures on the Well-being of the Palestinian household, 2001', Ramallah: Central Bureau of Statistics, November 2001, p.69.

75 Depravity, hopelessness and frustration, breeding ground for violence was apparent in the all the Palestinian areas I visited.

76 al-Aqsa Interview.

77 Hamas, Interview.

78 Fateh, Interview.

79 Incidentally the Israel Army had killed her brother the year before, *Guardian Weekly*, 22–28 January 2004, p.32.

80 Ziad Abu-Amr, 'Hamas: A Historical and Political Background', *Journal of Palestinian Studies*, vol.23, no.4, Summer 1993, p.14.

81 Palestinian refugees registered with UNRWA as of June 2001, Public Information office, UNRWA HQ, GAZA, August 2001.

82 Shakespeare W, *Julius Caesar*, Act 1, Scene 3, line 100, in Wells S, Taylor G, (eds) *William Shakespeare: The Complete Works*, Oxford: Clarendon Press, 1988, p.605.

83 However the conflict is so politicised that many fighters when asked why they are fighting, quote abstract political concepts such as state, identity and participation but often have little understanding of what these terms actually mean.

84 Abdul Shafi, Interview.

85 There is a fierce theological debate in Islam over the term Jihad, however it is often employed to justify violence against the non-believer. See, Esposito J L, *The Islamic Threat*, Oxford: Oxford University Press, 1999, 3rd ed., pp.30–1.

86 *The Guardian Weekly*, 22–28 January 2004, p.32.

87 Martyrs are promised to meet the Prophet and see the face of Allah. Furthermore their sins will be forgiven and they can intercede with relatives on the day of resurrection and will live amid rivers of wine and honey and be married to 72 black eyed virgins. *The Economist*, January 19 2004, p.18. The families of martyrs also receive financial benefits and prestige in their community.

88 This is known as the 'great cause' or the existence of heaven.

89 al-Aqsa, Interview.

90 Goethe J, *Faust part one*, London: Penguin, 1949, p.56.

91 Fanon F, *The Wretched of the Earth*, p.118.

92 This came from a meeting with local fighters in the Nuseirat refugee camp.

93 Schultz H L, *Reconstruction*, p.1.

94 Lustick I S, 'Changing Rationales for Political Violence in the Arab-Israeli Conflict', *Journal of Palestinian Studies*, vol.20, no.4, August 90, p.65.

95 B'Tselem, *Land Grab Report*, May 2002, http://www.passia.org.

96 *The Economist*, 11 October 2003, p.27.

97 Palestinian Academic Society for the Study of International Affairs, *Water and Environment*, http://www. Passia.org.
98 Palestinian Academic Society for the Study of International Affairs, *Water and Environment*, http://www. Passia.org.
99 Dr Abdul Shafi, Interview.
100 Hamas, Interview.
101 PASSIA, *Land and Settlements*, http://www.passia.org.
102 This is the total number of Palestinians killed in the Occupied territories and in Israel. 1142 Israelis were killed during the same period. http://www.btselem.org.
103 Islamic Jihad, Interview.
104 *The Guardian Weekly*, 22–28 August 2002.
105 *The Guardian*, 22 March 2002, p.14.
106 http://www.btselem.org.
107 http://www.btselem.org.
108 Dr Haider Shafi Interview.
109 *The Sunday Times*, 24 January 2004, p.19.
110 Fateh, Interview.
111 al-Aqsa, Interview.
112 Islamic Jihad, Interview.
113 *The Guardian Weekly*, 22–28 January 2004, p.31.
114 *The Guardian*, 22 March 2002, p.14.
115 *The Guardian*, 22 March 2002, p.14
116 This is not however always the situation as some operators act independently and others in reaction to Israeli incursions and if killed are 'claimed' by one of the Palestinian groups.
117 The majority of armed fighters I questioned voluntarily showed me their firearms at some point during the meeting.
118 A common method of introduction or referral to a Palestinian was 'this is...who is.....'
119 Hamas, Interview.

Conclusion

1 Milton J, *Paradise Lost*, London: Penguin, 1989, p.12.
2 Aum Shrinkyo is a Japanese religious cult which released Sarin nerve gas in the Tokyo subway system. See, Wilkinson P, *Terrorism Versus Democracy*, London: Frank Cass, 2000, pp.50–1.
3 In an interview with Boaz Ganor, director of the International Policy Institute for Counter-Terrorism (ICT) in Herzliya in Israel, he suggested that a twin track approach to terrorism needs to be adopted, one that employs a method of dealing and countering terrorism whilst concurrently attempting to resolve the deep rooted problems. Boaz Ganor, Director International Policy Institute for Counter-Terrorism, Herzliya, 07.04.2003.
4 Miall H, Ramsbotham O and Woodhouse T, *Contemporary Conflict*, p.94.
5 Miall et al, *Conflict Resolution*, p.94.
6 See, problem solving theory, in Cox R W *Approaches to World Order*, p.88.
7 Richmond O P, 'Genealogy of Peacemaking', *Alternatives*, p.342.
8 See, Richmond O, *Maintaining Order*, pp.75–105.

Bibliography

Personal interviews

Informal:

This comprised of casual conversations and unofficial dialogue with representatives of the Israeli State, including the government, military, and police and intelligence services as well as Israeli soldiers, settlers, and civilians. The Palestinians included members and representatives of principle political groups, namely Fateh, PFLP, Islamic Jihad and Hamas, and members of their respective armed wings: Tansim, Abu Ali Mustapha Brigade, al Quds Brigade, al-Qassim and the al-Aqsa martyrs brigade as well as Palestinian fighters, refugees and civilians.

Formal Interviews:

POLITICAL FIGURES AND REPRESENTATIVES

Allouh, Diab Nemer, 24.03.2003, Gaza City, Political Leader, Fateh.
Aghol, Kalyid, 22.03.2003, Gaza City, Political Leader, PFLP.
Al-Batsh, Khalid, 23.03.2003, Gaza, Political Leader, Islamic Jihad.
Libervitch, Ilan, 2,04,2003, Knesset, Jerusalem, MK Shinui.
Abu Shanab, Ismail, 24.03.2003, Gaza, Political Leader, Hamas.
Abdul Shafi, Haider, M.D, 24.03.2003, Gaza City, Former member of the Palestinian legislative and independent Palestinian negotiator at the Madrid summit 1992.
Tamir, Yuli, 1.04.2003, Knesset, Jerusalem, MK Labour.

ACADEMICS

Baskin, Gershon, PhD, 18 March 2003, Jerusalem, Co-Director Israeli/Palestine Centre for Research and Information (IPCRI).
Ghanem, Assad, PhD, 5 April 2003, Jerusalem, Department of Political Science, University of Haifa.
Ganor, Boaz, PhD, 7 April 2003, Herzliya, Director The International Policy Institute For Counter-Terrorism (ICT).
Merari, Ariel, Prof, 9 April 2003, Tel Aviv, Department of Psychology, Tel Aviv University.
Podeh, Elie, PhD, 2 April 2003, Jerusalem, Department of Middle East Studies, Hebrew University, Jerusalem.
Steinberg, Gerald, Prof, 3 April 2003, Jerusalem, Department of Political Studies and director of Programme on Conflict Resolution, Bar Ilan University.

Secondary sources

Aggestam K, *Reframing and Resolving Conflict*, Lund, Sweden: Lund University Press, 1999.

Alexander Y, Latter R, *Terrorism and the Media*, McLean VA: Brassey's, 1990.

Alexander Y, Cline R, *Terrorism as State-Sponsored Covert Warfare*, New York: Hero Books, 1986.

Andoni L, 'Searching for Answers: Gaza's Suicide Bombers', *Journal of Palestinian Studies*, vol.26, no.6. Summer 1997, pp.33–45.

Aruri N H, Carroll J J, 'A New Palestinian Charter', *Journal of Palestinian Studies*, vol.23, no.4, Summer 1994.

Azar E, Burton J, *International Conflict Resolution*, Brighton: Wheatsheaf Publications, 1986.

Azar E A, *The Management of Protracted Social Conflict Theory and Cases*, Hampshire: Dartmouth Publishing Company, 1990.

Banks M, *Conflict in World Society*, Brighton: Wheatsheaf Publications, 1984.

Barth F, *Ethnic Groups and Boundaries*, London: George Allen and Unwin, 1969.

Baylis J and Rengger N, *Dilemmas of World Politics*, London: Clarendon, 1992.

Baylis J and Smith S, *The Globalisation of World Politics*, Oxford: Oxford University Press, 5th ed., 1999.

Bercovitch J, *Social Conflicts and Third Parties*, Boulder: Westview Press, 1995.

Bercovitch J, *Resolving International Conflicts*, London: Lynne Rienner, 1996.

Berman P, *Terror and Liberalism*, London: W W Norton & Co. Ltd, 2003.

Bleiker R, *Popular Dissent, Human Agency and Global Politics*, Cambridge: Cambridge University Press, 2000.

Boulding K, *Stable Peace*, Austin Texas: University of Texas Press, 1910.

Booth K, Dunne T (ed.), *Worlds in Collision; Terrorism and the Future of Global Order*, Basingstoke Hampshire: Palgrave Macmillan, 2002.

Bowyer Bell J, *A Time of Terror*, New York: Basic Books, 1978.

Bowyer Bell J, *The Dynamics of Armed Struggle*, London: Frank Cass, 1998.

Bramson L, Goethis G, *War*, New York: Basic Books, 1968.

Bull H, *The Anarchical Society*, London: Macmillan, 1977.

Burton J, *World Society*, Cambridge: Cambridge University Press, 1972.

Burton J, *Deviance Terrorism and War*, Oxford: Martin Robertson, 1979.

Burton J, *Resolving Deep Rooted Conflict: a Handbook*, Lanham, MD: University Press of America, 1987.

Burton J (ed.), *Conflict: Human Needs Theory*, New York: St Martin's Press, 1990.

Bundy W P, 'A Portentous Year', *Foreign Affairs*, vol.62, no.3, Fall 1982.

Cassese A, *Terrorism Politics and Law; The Achille Lauro Affair*, Cambridge: Polity Press, 1989.

Camus A, *The Rebel*, London: Penguin, 3rd ed., 2000.

Carr E H, *The Twenty-Year Crisis 1919–1939*, London: Macmillan, 1946.

Carr E H, *What is History?* London: Penguin Books, 2nd ed., 1988.

Carment D James P, 'The International Politics of Ethnic Conflict', *Global Society*, vol.11, no.2, 1997.

Chaliand G, *Terrorism from Popular Struggle to Media Spectacle*, London: Saqi Books, 1987.

Clutterbuck R, *Terrorism and Guerrilla warfare*, London: Routledge, 1990.

Cobban H, *The PLO, People, Power and Politics*, Cambridge: Cambridge University Press, 1984.

Cohen S, Arnone H, 'Conflict Resolution as the Alternative to Terrorism', *Journal of Social Issues*, vol.44, no.2, 1988.

Corm G, 'Thoughts on the Roots of the Arab-Israeli Conflict', *Journal of Palestinian Studies*, vol.21, no.3, Spring 1992, pp.71–79.

Coser L A, *The Functions of Social Conflict*, London: Routledge and Kegan Paul, 1968.

Cox R W, *Approaches to World Order*, Cambridge: Cambridge University Press, 1996.

Finkelstein N G, *Image and Reality of the Israeli-Palestinian Conflict*, New York: Verso, 1995.

Della Porta D, *International Social Movement Research*, Greenwich: Connecticut, 1992.

Denscombe M, *The Good Research Guide*, Buckingham: Open University Press, 1998.

Denzin N and Lincoln Y, *Strategies of Qualitative Inquiry*, London: Sage Publications, 1998.

Der Derian J, *Virtuous War*, Boulder Colorado: Westview Press, 2001.

Dollard J, *Frustration and Aggression*, London: Butler and Tanner, 1944.

Dougherty J, Pfaltzgraf R, *Contending Theories of International Relations*, New York: Harper Row, 1971.

Doyle M W, *Ways of War and Peace*, New York: W W Norton, 1997.

Edkins J, *Poststructuralism and International Relations*, London: Lynne Rienner, 1999.

Eriksen T H, *Ethnicity and Nationalism Anthropological Perspectives*, London: Pluto Press, 1993.

Ellingsen T, 'Colourful Community or Ethnic Witches' Brew', *Journal of Conflict Resolution*, vol.44, no.2, April 2002.

Ellis M H, 'The Future of Israeli/Palestine: Embracing the Broken Middle', *Journal of Palestinian Studies*, vol.26, no.3, Spring 1997, pp.56–66.

Enloe C H, *Ethnic Conflict and Political Development*, Boston: Little Brown Publishers, 1973.

Esposito J L, *The Islamic Threat Myth or Reality?*, Oxford: Oxford University Press, (3rd ed.), 1999.

Ezeldin A G, *Terrorism and Political Violence: An Egyptian Perspective*, Chicago: University of Illinois, 1987.

Fanon F, *The Wretched of the Earth*, London: Penguin (5th ed.) 2001.

Ferguson R B, *Warfare, Culture and Environment*, Florida: Academic Press, 1984.

Flamhaft Z, *Israel on the Road to Peace*, Boulder Colorado: Westview Press, 1996.

Flapan S, *Zionism and the Palestinians*, London: Groom Helm, 1979.

Flapan S, *The Birth of Israel*, New York: Pantheon, 1984.

Foucault M, *Power and Knowledge*, New York: Harvester Wheatsheaf, 1980.

Frankfort-Nachmias C, Nachmias D, *Research Methods in the Social Sciences*, London: St Martin's Press, 1996.

Galtung J, *Peace by Peaceful Means*, Oslo: Sage Publications, 1996.

Gambill G C, 'The Balance of Terror: War by other means in the contemporary Middle East', *Journal of Palestinian Studies*, vol.28, no.1, Autumn 1998, p.62.

George A, *Western State Terrorism*, Cambridge: Polity Press, 1991.

George J, *Discourses of Global Politics*, Boulder Colorado: Lynne Rienner, 1994.

Giacaman G, Jorund Lonning D, *After Oslo, new realities, old problems*, London: Pluto Press, 1998.

Gilbert P, *Terrorism Security and Nationality*, London: Routledge, 1994.

Gilbert P, *New Terror New War*, Edinburgh: Edinburgh University Press, 2003.

Gunaratna R, *Inside al-Qaeda: Global Network of Terror*, London: Hurst Press, 2002.

Gurr T, *Why Men Rebel*, Princeton, NJ: Princeton University Press, 1970.

Gurr T R Harff B, *Ethnic conflict in World Politics*, Boulder Colorado: Westview Press, 1994.

Hassan bin Talal, *Palestinian Self-Determination, A Study of the West Bank and Gaza Strip*, London: Quartet Books, 1981.

Hazony Y, *The Jewish State, The Struggle for the Israeli Soul*, New York: Basic Books, 2001.

Held D, *Democracy and the Global Order*, Cambridge: Polity Press, 1997.

Herzog C, *The Arab-Israeli Wars*, London: Arms and Armour Press, 1982.

Hobbes T, *Leviathan*, Cambridge: Cambridge University Press, 1991.

Hoffman B, *Inside Terrorism*, London: Indigo Press, 1999.

Hoffman B, 'The Logic of Suicide Bombers', *The Atlantic Monthly*, June 2003, vol.291, no.5, pp.40–7.

Holsti K J, *The State, War and The State of War*, Cambridge: Cambridge University Press, 1996.

Honderich T, *After the Terror*, Edinburgh: Edinburgh University Press, 2002.

Hourani A, *A History of the Arab Peoples*, London: Faber and Faber, 1991.

Howard L, *Terrorism; Roots, Impact and Responses*, New York: Praeger, 1992.

Howard M, *Restraints on War*, Oxford: Oxford University Press, 1979.

Howell S, Willis R, *Societies at Peace*, London: Routledge Press, 1989.

Hutchinson J Smith A D, *Nationalism*, Oxford: Oxford University Press, 1994.

Huntington S, *The Clash of Civilisations and The Remaking of World Order*, New York: Touchstone, 1998.

Ignatieff M, *The Warrior's Honour*, London: Polity Press, 1998.

Jabri V, *Discourses of Violence*, Manchester: Manchester University Press, 1996.

Jonah J, 'The Middle East Conflict: The Palestinian Dimension', *Global Governance*, Oct–Dec 2002, vol.8, no.5, pp.413–7.

Jeong Ho-Won, *The New Agenda For Peace Research*, Aldershot: Ashgate Publishers, 1999.

Jeong Ho-Won (ed.), *Conflict Resolution: Dynamics, Process and Structure*, London: Ashgate, 1999.

Juergensmeyer M, 'Terror Mandated by God', in *Terrorism and Political Violence*, vol.9, no.2, Summer 1997.

Kaldor M, *New and Old Wars*, London: Polity Press, 1999.

Keane J, *Reflections on Violence*, London: Polity Press, 1996.

Kegley J R, *International Terrorism*, London: Macmillan, 1990.

Kennedy R, 'Is one person's Terrorist another's freedom fighter? Western and Islamic approaches to "Just War" compared', in *Terrorism and Political Violence*, vol.11, no.1, Spring 1999.

Keohane R, *Neorealism and its Critics*, New York: Columbia University Press, 1986.

Khalidi W, 'The Palestinian Problem: An Overview', *Journal of Palestinian Studies*, vol.21, no.3, Autumn 1991.

Kelman H C, 'Building and Sustaining Peace, The Limits of Pragmatism in the Israeli-Palestinian Negotiations', *Journal of Palestinian Studies*, vol.28, no.1, Autumn 1998, pp.36–49.

Kimmerling B, *The Invention and Decline of Israeliness*, Berkeley: University of California Press, 2001.

Kimmerling B, Migdal J S, *Palestinians: The Making of a People*, Cambridge Massachusetts: Harvard University Press, 1994.

Kimmerling B, *The Invention and Decline of Israeliness*, Berkeley: California University Press, 2001.

Kriesberg L, Northrup T, Thorson S, *Intractable Conflicts and their Transformation*, Syracuse: Syracuse University Press, 1989.

Krueger A B, Maleckova J, 'Does Poverty Cause Terrorism? The economics and the education of Suicide bombers', *The New Republic*, June 24, 2002.

Kvale S, *Interviews*, London: Sage Publications, 1996.

Laqueur W, *A History of Zionism*, New York: Holt, Rinehart and Winston, 1972.

Laqueur W, Rubin B (eds) *The Israeli-Arab Reader*, London: Penguin, 4th ed., 1984.

Laqueur W, Yonah A (eds) *The Terrorism Reader*, New York: Meridian, 1987.

Laqueur W, *The Age of Terrorism*, Boston: Little Brown and Co, 1987.

Laquer W, *The New Terrorism*, Oxford: Phoenix Press, 3rd ed, 2001.

Lederach J P, *Building Peace*, Washington: U.S. Institute of Peace, 1997.

Linklater A, Macmillan J, *Boundaries in Question*, London: Pinter, 1995.

Livingston M H, *International Terrorism in the Contemporary World*, Connecticut Greenwood Press, 1978.

Locke J, *Essay Concerning Human Understanding*, London: Wordsworth Publishers, 1998.

Lodge J, *Terrorism: A Challenge to the State*, Oxford: Martin Robertson, 1981.

Lukacs Y (ed.), *The Israeli-Palestinian Conflict a documentary record 1967–1990*, Cambridge: Cambridge University Press, 1992.

Lund M S, *Preventing Violent Conflicts*, Washington: U.S. Institute of Peace, 1994.

Lustick I, *Arabs in the Jewish State, Israeli's control of a National Minority*, Austin Texas: University of Texas Press, 1982.

Lustick I S, 'Changing Rationales for Political Violence in the Arab-Israeli Conflict', *Journal of Palestinian Studies*, vol.20, no.4, Autumn 1990, pp.55–79.

Malik O, *Enough of the Definition of Terrorism*, London: Royal Institute of International Affairs, 2000.

Manwaring M G, *Grey Area Phenomena: Confronting the New World Disorder*, Boulder Colorado: Westview Press, 1993.

Marighela C (trans. Butt J Sheed R), *For the Liberation of Brazil*, Harmondsworth: Penguin, 1971.

Marx K Engles F, *Manifesto of the Communist Party*, Oxford: Oxford University Press, 1992.

Maslow A H, *Motivation and Personality*, New York: Longman, 1970.

McNeil E B, *The Nature of Human Conflict*, New Jersey: Prentice Hall Press, 1965.

Masalha N, *Imperial Israel and the Palestinians*, London: Pluto Press, 2000.

McDowall D, *Palestine and Israel The Uprising and Beyond*, Berkeley: University of Calfornia Press, 1989.

Miall H, Ramsbotham O, Woodhouse T, *Contemporary Conflict Resolution*, Cambridge: Polity Press 2000 (2nd ed.).

Miall H, Ramsbotham O, Woodhouse T, *Contemporary Conflict Resolution*, Cambridge: Polity Press, 2000.

Migdal J. S, *Palestinian Society and Politics*, Princetown: Princetown University Press, 1980.

Mitchell C R, *The Structure of International Conflict*, London: Macmillan Press, 1981.

Miller A H, Damask N A, 'The Dual Myths of "Narco-terrorism": How Myths Drive Policy', in *Terrorism and Political Violence*, vol.8, no.1, Spring 1996.

Mitchell C R, *The Structure of International Conflict*, London: Macmillan Press, 1981.

Montville J V, *Conflict and Peacemaking in Multiethnic Societies*, Massachusetts: Lexington, 1990.

Morgenthau H, *Politics Among Nations*, New York: Knopf, 1978.

Morris B, *The Birth of the Palestinian Refugee Problem, 1947–1949*, Cambridge: Cambridge University Press, 1988.

Morris B, *Righteous Victims, A History of The Zionist-Arab Conflict 1881–1999*, London: John Murray, 2000.

Muslih M Y, 'Arab Politics and the Rise of Palestinian Nationalism', *Journal of Palestinian Studies*, Summer 1987, vol.16, no.4, pp.77–91.

Muslih M Y, *The Origins of Palestinian Nationalism*, New York: Columbia University Press, 1988.

Netanyahu B, *International Terrorism: Challenge and Response*, Jerusalem: Jonathan Institute, 1980.

Netanyahu B, *A Place Among The Nations Israel and the World*, New York: Bantam Books, 1993.

Nordstrom C, Robben A, *Fieldwork Under Fire*, Berkeley California: University of California Press, 1995.

O'Neill B E, *Armed Struggle in Palestine A Political Military Analysis*, Boulder Colorado: Westview Press, 1978.

O'Sullivan N (ed.), *Terrorism Ideology and Revolution*, Brighton Sussex: Wheatsheaf Books, 1986.

Pappe I, 'Post-Zionist Critique on Israel and the Palestinians, Part 1: The Academic Debate', *Journal of Palestinian Studies*, vol.26, no.2, Winter 1997, pp.29–41.

Pappe I, 'Post-Zionist Critique on Israel and the Palestinians, Part 2: The Media', *Journal of Palestinian Studies*, vol.26, no.3, Spring 1997, pp.37–43.

Pappe I, 'Post-Zionist Critique on Israel and the Palestinians, Part 3: Popular Culture', *Journal of Palestinian Studies*, vol.26, no.3, Spring 1997, pp.37–43.

Pappe I, 'Israel at a Crossroads Between Civic Democracy and Jewish Zealotocracy', *Journal of Palestinian Studies*, vol.24, no.2, Spring 2000, pp.33–43.

Peters J, *From Time Immemorial*, London: Michael Joseph Ltd, 1985.

Pinhas I, *The Palestinians Between Terrorism and Statehood*, London: Sussex University Press. 1996.

Posen B, 'The Security Dilemma and Ethnic Conflict', *Survival*, 35 (1), 1993.

Pressberg G, 'The Uprising: Causes and Consequences', *Journal of Palestinian Studies*, vol.17, no.3, Winter 88, pp.18–19.

Rabbie J M, 'A behavioural interaction model: toward a social-psychological framework for studying terrorism', *Terrorism and Political Violence*, vol.3, no.4, Winter 1991.

Rapport A, *The Origins of Violence*, London: Paragon, 1989.

Rappoport D C, Alexander Y, *The Morality of Terrorism*, Oxford: Pergamon Press, 1982.

Reich W, *Origins of Terrorism*, Cambridge: Cambridge University Press, 1992.

Richmond O, 'Devious Objectives and the Disputants' View of International Mediation: A Theoretical Framework', *Journal of Peace Research*, vol.35, no.6, 1998, pp.707–722.

Richmond O P, 'Mediating Ethnic Conflict: A Task or Sisyphus?' *Global Society*, vol.13, no.2, 1999.

Richmond O P, 'Ethnic Security in the International System', *Journal of International Relations and Development*, March 2000, pp.24–46.

Richmond O P, 'A Genealogy of Peacekeeping: The Creation and Re-Creation of Order', *Alternatives*, 26, 2001.

Richmond O, *Maintaining Order, Making Peace*, Basingstoke, Hants: Palgrave, 2002.

Robert Hunter F, *The Palestinian Uprising, a war by other means*, Berkeley California: University of California Press, 2nd ed., 1993.

Robson C, *Real World Research*, Oxford: Blackwell Publishers, 2002.

Roe P, 'The Intrastate Security Dilemma: Ethnic Conflict as a Tragedy?', *Journal of Peace Research*, vol.36, no.2, 1999.

Rubin B, *Revolution Until Victory, Politics and History of the PLO*, Cambridge: Harvard University Press, 1994.

Rubin B, *The Tragedy of the Middle East*, Cambridge: Cambridge University Press, 2002.

Rubenstein R E, *Alchemists of Revolution: Terrorism in the Modern World*, New York: Basic Books Inc, 1987.

Said E, *The Question of Palestine*, London: Routledge and Kegan Paul, 1980.

Said E, 'The Burdens of Interpretation and the Question of Palestine', *Journal of Palestinian Studies*, vol.16, no.3, Autumn 1986, pp.29–37.

Said E, *The Politics of Dispossession, The struggle for Palestinian Self-Determination 1969–1994*, London: Chatto and Windus, 1994.

Sayigh R, *Palestinians: From Peasants to Revolutionaries*, London: Zed Press, 1979.

Sayigh Y, 'Redefining the Basics: Sovereignty and the Security of the Palestinian State', *Journal of Palestinian Studies*, vol.26, no.4, Summer 1995, pp.5–19.

Sayigh Y, 'Armed Struggle and State Formation', *Journal of Palestinian Studies*, vol.26, no.4, Summer 1997, p.18.

Schmid A, Jongman A, *Political Terrorism: A Guide to Actors, Authors, Concepts, Data Bases, Theories and Literature*, Oxford: North Holland, 1988.

Schmid A P, Jongman A J, 'Violent Conflicts and Human Rights Violations in the mid-1990s', *Terrorism and Political Violence*, vol.9, no.4, Winter 1997.

Schulze K, *The Arab-Israeli Conflict*, New York: Longman, 1999.

Schulze K E, *The Arab-Israeli Conflict*, New York: Longman, 1999.

Schultz H L, *The Reconstruction of Palestinian Nationalism*, Manchester: Manchester University Press, 1999.

Segal J, 'Does the State of Palestine Exist?', *Journal of Palestinian Studies*, vol.19, no.4, Autumn 1989, p.14.

Sela A, *The Decline of the Arab-Israeli Conflict*, New York: State University Press of New York, 1998.

Seul J R, 'Ours is the Way of God': Religion, Identity and Intergroup Conflict', *Journal of Peace Research*, vol.36, no.5, 1999.

Shlaim A, *The Iron Wall Israel and the Arab World*, London: Penguin, 2000.

Silke A, 'The Devil you know: continuing problems with research on Terrorism', *Terrorism and Political Violence*, vol.13, no.4 (Winter 2001).

Silke A, (ed.), *Terrorists, Victims and Society: Psychological Perspectives on Terrorism and its Consequences*, London: John Wiley & Sons, 2003.

Simon J P, *The Terrorist Trap*, Indianapolis: Indiana University Press, 1994.

Simmel G, *Conflict*, New York: First Free Press, 1964.

Slater R, Stohl M, *Current Perspectives on International Terrorism*, London: Macmillan, 1988.

Smith A D, *The Ethnic Revival*, Cambridge: Cambridge University Press, 1981.

Smith S, Booth K, Zalewski M, *International Theory: Positivism and Beyond*, Cambridge: Cambridge University Press, 1996.

Smith C D, *Palestine and the Arab-Israeli Conflict*, Basingstoke: Macmillan, 2nd ed., 1992.

Smooha S, *Arabs and Jews in Israel, Volume 1, Conflicting and Shared Attitudes in a Divided Society*, Boulder Colorado: Westview Press, 1989.

Smooha S, *Arabs and Jews in Israel, Volume 2, Change and Continuity in Mutual Intolerance*, Boulder Colorado: Westview Press, 1992.

Sorel G, *Reflections on Violence*, New York: Collier-Macmillan, 1969.

Sprinzak E, 'The process of Delegitimation: Towards linkage theory of Political Terrorism', *Terrorism and Political Violence*.

Stohl M, Lopez G, *The State as Terrorist*, London: Aldwych Press, 1984.

Strange S, 'The Westfailure System', *Review of International Studies*, vol.25, 1999, p.345.

Sterling C, *The Terror Network: The Secret War of International Terrorism*, New York: Holt, Reinhardt and Winston, 1983.

Stern J, *The Ultimate Terrorists*, Cambridge Mass: Harvard University Press, 1999.

Suganami H, *On the Causes of War*, Oxford: Calrendon, 1996.

Tan A, Ramakrishna K (eds) *The New Terrorism*, Singapore: Eastern University Press, 2002.

Tessler M, *A History of the Israeli-Palestinian Conflict*, Indianapolis: Indiana University Press, 1994.

Tidwell A C, *Conflict Resolved?*, London: Pinter, 1998.

UNRWA Emergency Appeal 2003 pamphlet, UNRWA HQ, Gaza, June 2003

Palestinian Central Bureau of Statistics 'Impact of Israeli Measures on the Well-being of the Palestinian household, 2001', Ramallah: Central Bureau of Statistics, November 2001.

Vasquez J, *The War Puzzle*, Cambridge: Cambridge University Press, 1993.

Vayryen R, *New Directions in Conflict Theory*, London: Sage Publications, 1991.

Walker R B J, *Inside/Outside*, Cambridge: Cambridge University Press, 1993.

Wallensteen P, Sollenberg M, 'After the Cold War: emerging patterns of armed conflict 1989–96', *Journal of Peace Research*, 32(3), p.347.

Wallensteen P, Sollenberg M, 'Armed Conflict 1989–99', *Journal of Peace Research*, 37(3).

Wallerstein E, *The Modern World System 1*, San Diego: Academic Press, 1974.

Waltz K, *Man the State and War*, New York: Columbia University Press, 1959.

Waltz K, *The Theory of International Politics*, Reading Mass: Addison-Wesley, 1979.

Walter E V *Terror and Resistance*, London: Oxford University Press, 1969.

Walzer M, *Just and Unjust Wars*, New York: Basic Books, 1992.

Wardlaw G, *Political Terrorism*, Cambridge: Cambridge University Press (2nd ed.), 1990.

Warner M, Crisp R, *Terrorism Protest and Power*, London: Edward Ellar, 1990.

Webb K, Paulne L, *Conflict*, World Encyclopaedia of Peace, vol.1.

Wendt A, 'Collective Identity and the International State', *American Political Science Review*, vol.88, no.2, June 1994, p.384.

White R W, 'Issues in the Understanding of Political Violence: Understanding the Motives of Participants in Small Group Political Violence', in *Terrorism and Political Violence*, vol.12, no.1, Spring 2000.

Whittaker D J, *Terrorism: Understanding the Global Threat*, London: Longman, 2001.

Whittaker D, *The Terrorism Reader*, London: Routledge, 2001.

Wilkinson P, *Terrorism and the Liberal State*, London: Macmillan, 1977.

Wilkinson P, *Terrorism Versus Democracy*, London: Frank Cass, 2000.

Woodhouse T, Bruce R, Dando M, *Peacekeeping and Peacemaking*, London: Macmillan, 1998.

Woodhouse T, Ramsbotham O, *Peacekeeping and Conflict Resolution*, London: Frank Cass, 2000.

Wright Q, *A Study of War*, Chicago: University of Chicago, 1947.

Yates A J, *Frustration and Conflict*, New York: Methuen & Co, 1962.

Zartman I W, Rasmussen J L, *Peacekeeping in International Conflict*, London: Peace Press, 1999.

Ziad Abu-Amr, 'Hamas: A Historical and Political background', *Journal of Palestinian Studies*, vol.12, no.4, Summer 1993, pp.5–19.

Newspapers

The Guardian Weekly
The Economist
The Jerusalem Post
Haaretz
Al-Ahram Weekly

Internet sources

Palestinian Academic Society for the Study of International Affairs (PASSIA) www.passia.org.

Palestinian Human Rights Organisation (B'Tselem) www.btselem.org United Nations (UN) www.un.org

Index